INDEPENDENCE OF MIND

Independence of Mind

TIMOTHY MACKLEM

OXFORD
UNIVERSITY PRESS

OXFORD

UNIVERSITY PRESS

Great Clarendon Street, Oxford OX2 6DP

Oxford University Press is a department of the University of Oxford.
It furthers the University's objective of excellence in research, scholarship,
and education by publishing worldwide in

Oxford New York

Auckland Cape Town Dar es Salaam Hong Kong Karachi
Kuala Lumpur Madrid Melbourne Mexico City Nairobi
New Delhi Shanghai Taipei Toronto

With offices in

Argentina Austria Brazil Chile Czech Republic France Greece
Guatemala Hungary Italy Japan Poland Portugal Singapore
South Korea Switzerland Thailand Turkey Ukraine Vietnam

Oxford is a registered trade mark of Oxford University Press
in the UK and in certain other countries

Published in the United States
by Oxford University Press Inc., New York

British Library Cataloguing in Publication Data

Data available

Library of Congress Cataloging in Publication Data

Data available

Typeset by Laserwords Private Limited, Chennai, India
Printed in Great Britain
on acid-free paper by
Biddles Ltd, King's Lynn, Norfolk

ISBN 0–19–920803–4   978–0–19–920803–6

1 3 5 7 9 10 8 6 4 2

For Joseph Raz

Preface

The Objective: This book is animated by a desire to explore a familiar and yet in some important ways surprisingly neglected topic, that of the philosophical grounding of certain of our most fundamental political freedoms, namely, those of speech, privacy, conscience, and religion. The thought underlying the project, and expressed in its title, is that each of these freedoms plays its distinctive part, not merely in securing our general freedom to be ourselves, that is, our freedom to act in accordance with our personal convictions (the freedom that most philosophical enquiry has focused upon), but more fundamentally, in securing the conditions under which we can become ourselves. These are the conditions necessary to our becoming the particular kind of people we are, people who are capable of having distinctive personal convictions of their own, the kind of people that political freedom fosters and serves. In short, the fundamental freedoms play a significant, though not exclusive, role in enabling each one of us to develop and secure a more or less distinctive perspective on life and how it should be lived. They provide for the construction as well as the expression of human personality, and recognition of that fact tells us a great deal about their value and their scope.

Not all of our political freedoms have this role to play, of course. Bills of rights, and other like instruments, are not only broad-ranging, so touching a wide variety of concerns, but also local in character and outlook, so responding to the distinctive exigencies and ambitions of the particular societies they serve. That being the case, they contain provisions of many different kinds, not all of them political in character, not all of them having anything to do with freedom. What is more, where bills of rights address the question of political freedom they do so for varying reasons, only some of which have to do with the challenge of thinking, believing and speaking for oneself. Other political freedoms, most obviously those of association and assembly, may serve rather different, perhaps even antithetical values. That, however, is an issue for another day. I simply wish to emphasize here that my focus in this book is on the four freedoms that I take to be central to our development as people of a particular kind, those of speech, privacy, conscience, and religion.

The questions considered in the book are by their nature, it seems to me, of great theoretical interest, but they are also questions with real political and social import. Many years ago now, I took my first steps into the intellectual life of the law by serving as clerk to a judge of the Supreme Court of Canada, Gérard La Forest, in the very year, as it so happened, that the first appeals under the newly entrenched Charter of Rights and Freedoms were heard there. It fell to the Court, in those early decisions, to identify the purposes that were to animate the fundamental political freedoms contained in the Charter and that would consequently define the legal scope of those freedoms, and the political character of Canada as a democratic community. The decisions had of course to be reached on the basis of first principles, without undue reliance on conclusions reached by other communities elsewhere. The ensuing predicament that the Court (and I as one of its assistants) faced in arriving at those decisions is the predicament faced by all those who are forced to consider the nature and scope of the fundamental freedoms of their community as a democratic society. They include not only those who are in the position of articulating those freedoms for the first time (as Canada was twenty years ago), but also those who find themselves forced to re-evaluate the place of the political freedoms in their community in the face of circumstances that are thought to call into question the scope, character, and perhaps even the very existence of those freedoms. That is very much the case in Britain and the United States today, as fundamental freedoms, and the democratic society that they help to define, are attacked from without and questioned from within. Not all of what I have to say is directly relevant to that debate, but it is relevant to the general project of self-examination and enquiry that is constitutive of a successful democratic community and all who are concerned in it, whether as scholars or as citizens.

The Approach: The fundamental freedoms of speech, religion, conscience and privacy are almost always separately guaranteed in the bills of rights and other legal instruments that address and protect them. It is possible to think that this is simply the product of historical circumstance, to think that freedom of religion, for example, has no distinctive value that is not captured by the broader guarantee of freedom of conscience. That is not the conclusion that I have reached. The account that I give of those freedoms in *Independence of Mind* is an account that seeks to show the ways in which each of them secures a distinctive value that is vital to the development and pursuit of a distinctive human personality. The several values secured by these freedoms are interconnected, to be sure, and their realization in any person's life involves a project in which their roles will typically be interdependent. Nevertheless each has something rather different to offer, and what is more, human personality would itself be something different, perhaps something poorer, in the absence of any one of them. The first four chapters of the book explore the specific contributions made to personality by speech, privacy, conscience, and religion, in that order, on the basis that it is roughly the order in which any given personality is developed. The final chapter explores the role played by bills of rights, and their judicial enforcement, in our democratic life, and examines the implications for our social forms and practices of the freedoms they secure. In what follows, I will say something about the content of each of the chapters in turn. As will be clear from my remarks, the book that I have written is not very like any other book on the subject, largely because it delves beneath the politics of civil liberties to their ethics. As I see it, that is part of what it has to offer.

1. Freedom of expression (or freedom of speech as it is sometimes, more narrowly put) is usually regarded as valuable by reason of the security it gives to our ability to represent ourselves to the world as the particular people we are, people with certain politics, people with a certain cultural identity, more generally, people in the possession of certain truths. The underlying assumption is that each of us, or at least each beneficiary of freedom of expression, has something to represent to the world, and that freedom of expression protects, and perhaps encourages, that representation. What this assumption neglects, it seems to me, is the way in which, and the circumstances under which, people come to have anything at all distinctive of their own that they might wish to represent to the world. The thought in response to that neglect, which the chapter entitled 'The Art of Expression' seeks to develop, is that expression is not merely a matter of representing one's thoughts to the world, for the enterprise of expressing oneself is as much about creation as it is about representation. Mediums of expression do not simply convey a person's thoughts to the world; they do a great deal to shape the content of those thoughts. It follows that freedom of expression is not simply the freedom to communicate one's voice to others, but is more fundamentally the freedom to develop a distinctive voice of one's own. Recognition of this fact has significant practical implications, for it moves the arts and other creative forms of expression from the margins of freedom of expression, where they have languished in standard accounts of that freedom, to its core.

2. In many legal settings, particularly that of American constitutional law, privacy refers to the ability of people to conduct personal relations with one another, particularly intimate relations, without interference from the state. That view has been most recently espoused and given philosophical substance by Julie Inness in her book *Privacy, Intimacy and Isolation*. It is a view that presents privacy as necessarily valuable. It is also a view that assumes that people have personalities to share, and relationships to explore, in advance of their occupancy of the private space in which those personalities and relationships are given effect to. It is not the view taken by Virginia Woolf in *A Room of One's Own*, however, and it is not the view that I have taken in the chapter entitled (after the Duke Ellington/Billie Holiday song) '(In My) Solitude'. Privacy, and the isolation from others that it implies, is essential to the development of personality, be it the personality of an individual, which depends on the experience of some degree of individual isolation, as Woolf pointed out, or more broadly and less familiarly, the personality and character of a couple, family, community, or culture. Multicultural societies, for example, and more particularly cosmopolitan cities, ultimately depend for their cultural richness on the existence of monocultural communities elsewhere, the isolation of which, one from the other, permits the development in them of a variety of cultural forms which emigrants then carry abroad, and which, when those emigrants settle together, become the raw material of a multicultural community. So understood, privacy is both a good

and a bad thing, as feminists have emphasized, for isolation, whether of an individual, family, or community, is as apt to be oppressive as it is to be an occasion for creativity.

3. The law, and those philosophers who have concerned themselves with it, has long grappled with the problem of conscientious objection. That grappling has taken place, by and large, over the question of the scope to be allowed to conscientious objection. In considerations of this question a conscience is implicitly understood to be equivalent to the moral convictions of the objector whose conscience it is. Should a conscript be permitted to refuse active military service, and if so, under what conditions? Should a teacher be permitted to refuse to teach what he or she does not believe, about the creation of the world perhaps? However fruitful these considerations of conscientious objection have been, what is missing in them, it seems to me, is an examination of just what a conscience is and how it might be acquired. Is it really no more than our moral convictions? Ordinary experience suggests that conscience has other, rather different roles to play. It often speaks to us in private and in our own voice, reminding us of who we are, what we believe, and what we have committed ourselves to, not only in those matters affecting others, the matters that we think of as our moral life, but also in those matters that affect ourselves alone. What is more, it enhances the significance of some issues and diminishes the significance of others in a way that is personal and idiosyncratic. In 'Conscience and Commitment', the longest chapter in the book and perhaps its centrepiece, I explore a set of puzzles about conscientious objection, drawn from the work of Bernard Williams and Joseph Raz, to arrive at an alternative picture of conscience, as a central element in the development of what I call our *rational personality*, that aspect of our character which makes some portion of the multitude of reasons that apply to us, as to every human being, peculiarly our own. Conscience commits us to some reasons in particular, and so helps us to navigate the uncertain and centrifugal features of the human predicament, as we must, without having to anchor ourselves in the rather less reliable phenomena of motive and attachment. It follows that true freedom of conscience requires that we foster an environment in which people are free to develop within themselves an idealized and aspirational image of themselves as rational beings, reminding themselves of what rationality requires, committing themselves to some portion of what rationality permits, and then conforming to or dissenting from the expectations of others as reason requires in their case.

4. In 'Reason and Religion' I turn from the question of how personality is formed to the related question of the roles played by reason and by faith in its construction. That issue arises most prominently in the setting of freedom of religion, where it has been necessary for the courts to decide just what a religion is. On the one hand, conventional accounts of that freedom (such as those offered by American courts in determining the scope of the First Amendment) take the view that a set of beliefs and practices amounts to a religion when those

beliefs and practices, and the organizations that enshrine them, resemble those of Christianity. On the other hand, psychological accounts of the freedom (such as those offered by American courts in non-constitutional settings) take the view that religion is equivalent to a person's deepest commitments or ultimate concerns. The shortcomings of these explanations are obvious to anyone interested in establishing the value of religion to a secular society, and more fundamentally, in establishing the value that religion can offer to a human life when that life is considered from a perspective that is rational rather than religious, a perspective that is potentially rather than actually committed to religious belief. The first explanation is dogmatic, the second undernourished. My proposal in response is that what is in fact distinctive about religion is its commitment to certain conclusions on the basis of faith rather than reason. Faith is valuable as and when it enables us to make commitments (including religious commitments) in situations where reasons are unavailable, and so cannot be called upon to guide us, yet the commitment in question is potentially valuable. All ventures into the unknowable, all leaps into the dark, depend on faith. Some such leaps involve ordinary commitments, to a new neighbourhood, a new workplace, a new partner. Other leaps are more fundamental, yet are for some people just as unknowable. It is leaps like these, that commit a person to a view as to the nature and purpose of human life, for example, or as to the nature of the good, that religion can facilitate. When religion does this it is entitled to support and protection from a secular society. When it does not do this, it is not entitled to protection, and may even deserve condemnation.

5. The final chapter of the book, 'Entrenching Bills of Rights: Judicial Power and Political Freedom', examines the cost, in terms of democracy and in terms of social forms and practices, of securing these freedoms. Much has been written about the cost of judicially secured freedoms in terms of democracy. Some believe that the price is worth paying; others disagree. As I see it, however, the loss that follows from the securing of fundamental freedoms is less a democratic loss than a loss in terms of social forms and practices. Freedom is characteristically animated by the pursuit of value, but not by the pursuit of stability, with which it is in tension. The more pervasive the presence of freedom in any given society, the more vulnerable the forms and practices of that society become. From certain points of view, that gives no cause for concern. There is no more reason to mourn the loss of a social form or practice than there is to welcome its replacement. Nor is there any reason to believe that short-lived social forms are less valuable than forms of long standing. At some point, however, the fluidity of social forms, a fluidity that freedom fosters, is such that social forms are too short-lived for us to experience them fully, and so learn their true value. The commonly expressed concern at the entrenchment of fundamental freedoms in law is ultimately, I suggest, concern at the corrosive implications of freedom for the social forms upon full understanding of which our access to value depends. Or at least, that is how the concern is best understood.

I would like to thank the following for their contributions towards the five chapters of this book. In particular:

Chapter 1. **The Art of Expression**. Thanks to John Gardner for his perceptive comments on earlier drafts and to Gail Thorson for her sensitive and imaginative editorial amendments. Thanks also to King's College London, where a version of the paper was delivered as my inaugural lecture as Professor of Jurisprudence.

Chapter 2. **(In My) Solitude**. I would again like to thank Gail Thorson and John Gardner for their thoughtful criticisms and suggestions on this paper.

Chapter 3. **Conscience and Commitment**. Thanks, as ever, to John Gardner and Gail Thorson, and to the participants in the Law and Philosophy Program at the University of Texas at Austin, Brian Leiter and Leslie Green, for their presence at a workshop there where the paper was presented, and for their helpful comments.

Chapter 4. **Reason and Religion**. Thanks to Peter Oliver and John Gardner for their role in the development of this paper, and to the Law and Philosophy Program at the University of Texas at Austin and participants in the workshop at which the paper was presented there, including Brian Leiter, Leslie Green, John Gardner, Jennifer Jacobson and Kayla Dreyer. Earlier versions of the paper have appeared as 'Faith as a Secular Value', 45 McGill L J, 1 (2000), and 'Reason and Religion' in Oliver Douglas-Scott (editor) *Faith in Law: Essays in Legal Theory*, Tadros (Hart, 2000) 69.

Chapter 5. **Entrenching Bills of Rights: Judicial Power and Political Freedom**. I would particularly like to thank John Gardner and Peter Oliver for their valuable comments on several drafts. An earlier version of the paper was presented at the Analytic Legal Philosophy Conference in Oxford in May 2003. I am grateful to the participants in the conference for their views, and in particular to Tony Honoré, Joseph Raz, Matthew Kramer, Andrei Marmor, Denise Réaume, and James Nickel, significant aspects of whose suggestions are reflected in the paper as it now stands. A version of the chapter, less the final section, appeared in the Oxford Journal of Legal Studies, 26 OJLS 1 (2006).

Timothy Macklem

Professor of Jurisprudence
King's College London
May 2006

Contents

1

The Art of Expression

For all that has been written about freedom of expression, there is still real uncertainty about the basis of its application to standard forms of artistic expression, such as literature and the visual arts. It is not that anyone doubts the conclusion. On the contrary, all are confident that artistic expression is a central case of the freedom. The difficulty lies in bringing artistic expression within one of the familiar rationales for the freedom, with which such expression sits awkwardly. My goal here is to explore the possibility that there is a distinctive reason for protecting artistic expression, a reason, furthermore, that might help to explain the value of other acts of expression, and so help to buttress the case for their freedom. To do this I need to begin at the beginning, by examining the very nature of expression, and the possible sources of its value.

Expression and its Value

1. Creation and Representation

What exactly happens when we talk? When we laugh, sing, draw, dance, in short, when we express ourselves? Do we capture and then project into the world something that already exists in our mind's eye, or do we, in some measure at least, discover what we have to say in and through the very act of saying it? How far is the expression of our thoughts and feelings shaped by the enterprise of giving form to them in a particular medium, be that medium words, gestures, movements or the special language of some form of art? When we frame the content of our minds in the language of expression does that language serve as a mirror or a catalyst? And what implications might the answer have for freedom of expression?

Suppose that two people decide to spend the evening together. Suppose further that they know one another well, well enough that exchanges between them are fluent and stimulating. Perhaps they are old friends; perhaps they are lovers. They walk through the park to the Underground, drawing one another's attention to elements of the scene: the weight of summer leaves bearing down the branches of the trees, the thickness of the air, the clear sound of children's voices as they chase one another across the grass. Later, in a café, the couple engage in animated conversation, in the course of which they learn more about each other and about what interests them; what they have in common and what distinguishes them. In expressing their thoughts and feelings to one another, through words, gestures, and glances, they both develop their relationship and enlarge their understanding of the world.

For those who are interested in the nature and value of human expression it seems reasonably clear what is happening here and why it matters. Each person expresses, and so *represents* to the other, certain thoughts and feelings, and receives in return certain, related thoughts and feelings from the other person, thoughts and feelings that have been shaped in part by what has just been represented to them. This kind of communicative dynamic can be more or less fruitful, of course, but when it takes place under sympathetic conditions, as it does here, it makes many valuable things possible. On this analysis expression matters because the things it makes possible matter, and since the things representation makes possible in the wider world are very important, including as they do the vindication of personal and cultural identity, the discovery of new truths, and the pursuit of self-government, opportunities for expression are also very important, important enough, perhaps, to make freedom of expression a fundamental right.[1]

But is that the whole story? Does it capture the full significance of the expressive exchange that has taken place in my example? Take a somewhat different set of facts in which, instead of going out together for the evening, the two people follow separate paths. One of them is glad to have some time to himself, to think his own thoughts, to take in the beauty of the evening without the intervention of another, to develop his own character and his own understanding of the world. As he walks he works through a number of issues that have been troubling him, rehearsing his thoughts aloud in the relative privacy of the park. He feels that he is on to something, enough to make him whistle on his way home, although he also knows from experience that promising ideas, even those that have been rehearsed aloud, tend to look rather less promising when they are written down. Just to check, he tries writing them down when he gets home and, as expected, finds it difficult to reproduce the clarity that he thought he had already achieved.[2]

---

[1] I use the qualifier perhaps here because a great deal more would need to be said to establish the connection in this setting between important values and fundamental legal rights: the particular value of expression, so understood; the role played by freedom in securing and/or augmenting that value; the value of a moral right to the exercise of such freedom of expression; the value of a legal right to that freedom (which might or might not depend on the presence of a moral right to it); and the considerations affecting the choice of institutional setting, be it fundamental or non-fundamental, for the entrenchment of that legal right. For exploration of certain aspects of these issues, see the section entitled 'Value, Freedom, and Rights', later in the chapter.

[2] There is an uncertainty here as to the source of the walker's difficulty in making his thoughts concrete. On the one hand, the gap between thought and expression may simply reflect a gap in the fabric of the thought itself, one that went unnoticed in the indefinite and possibly self-indulgent atmosphere of reflections undertaken in the course of a walk in the park. On the other hand, the gap may be evidence of a genuine gulf between thought and expression. The issue is taken up in the next section.

As he writes, he finds that his thoughts go in new directions, some promising, some disappointing. The enterprise of turning even relatively structured thoughts into the words, sentences and paragraphs of a written language seems naturally suggestive. The choice of certain words, phrases and images inevitably triggers new trains of thought that lead in new directions, directions that are at once more concrete and specific than purely mental images, and more complex and literary than the spoken language in which he has already rehearsed them. Even the choice of writing instrument seems to make a difference: he finds that pen and paper are often the best for the most difficult passages; the cramped nature of the technique goes well with the density of the thought.

In the meantime his friend, not unhappy to be alone but less confident perhaps of the rewards of solitude, decides to take a sketch pad into the garden. Humming to herself, she sets out to draw the evening light. Long stems of grass are bent across the gravel, blowing in the breeze, throwing elusive shadows before them. She isn't sure what she has to say, or indeed whether she has anything at all to say, but she knows that the process of composition, of choosing a subject, developing a perspective, and drafting an image, boldly or delicately, in detail or by suggestion, will help her to find out. As it happens, the result is reasonably gratifying. She has learned something about the scene, and about herself. She may keep the sketch or she may not. Making it was what mattered to her, and she has no deep interest in seeing it again, or showing it to another.

In these situations it is much less clear what is happening and why it matters. In part the story seems once again to be a story of representation, although in this case the representation, if that is the right way to understand it, is a representation to oneself rather than to some other person. Assume for the moment that in these situations whistling and humming, writing and drawing, are various ways of representing one's thoughts and feelings to oneself. Is that all they are? Or does expression have a further role to play, a role that is at its most obvious in acts of self-expression like these but that is also present, albeit less prominent, in expressive exchanges between two or more people?

2. Between Thought and Expression

There are three ways to understand the relationship between our thoughts and feelings and the various languages in which they find expression. The first is that the language of expression is always adequate to the task of capturing a thought or feeling because the thoughts and feelings that we experience are always already couched, however nascently, in the language of some expressive medium. It is not simply that our thoughts tend to be influenced by the character of the medium in which they are likely to find expression. It is that our thoughts are and can be no more than reflections of the expressive possibilities of which our imagination is aware and in which it is fluent. Language is not a vessel for ideas; rather, it constitutes their very fabric. We may find it difficult to identify that language and to articulate it properly, whether in words, sounds, images or gestures, but our difficulty in this respect is a technical difficulty not a creative one. On this view of affairs, acts of expression are inherently and exclusively representative, for they consist in presenting to the world, in material terms, what already exists in the mind's eye. This is not to deny the creativity of thought, but it is to distance that creativity from the fact of expression. Our thoughts may draw freely from the world, or even make new worlds, but once they take shape they do so in the language in which they will ultimately find expression.

The second way to understand the relationship between our thoughts and feelings and the various languages of expression is to think of the relationship as one of *perspective*. Thoughts and feelings exist apart from the languages in which they may find expression, and it is the role of such languages to capture, for whatever purpose, some aspect of those thoughts and feelings. Different languages of expression have different aptitudes: some are better at conveying emotions, some are better at conveying abstract ideas. The resources of even a complex language are necessarily finite and specific: they offer rich possibilities for the expression of certain ideas yet relatively constrained possibilities for the expression of others. The thoughts of Aristotle are no more or less profound and complex than those of Bach, but Aristotle could not have said what he had to say in the language of a musical keyboard, nor Bach in the spoken language of ancient Greece. In each case thought is shaped by the horizons of the language in which it is expressed.

The claim here is not that ancient Greek formed the very fabric of Aristotle's thoughts, as on the first view, but rather that Greek was one of a number of languages in which those thoughts were susceptible to expression, as music was not. Every language has its possibilities and its limitations; Aristotle could say some things in Greek that cannot be captured in English, and if he had had English at his disposal he might have been able to say some things that cannot be captured in ancient Greek. Nor should we think of language and its possibilities for the expression of (say) philosophy in purely verbal terms. Any given set of ideas can be successfully expressed in a wide, if not unlimited range of different languages. The languages in which the thoughts of Aristotle are susceptible to expression include not only all the languages into which those thoughts have been successfully translated, but also the example of lives led in fulfilment of the virtues as Aristotle understood them.[3]

On this second view of affairs acts of expression are to be understood as more or less successful attempts to capture some aspect of what a person thinks or feels. On the one hand, those attempts are inherently creative, for they require us to choose a language and then to choose a vocabulary, and a range of imagery

---

[3] The picture here is complicated by the fact that the choice of expression faced by Aristotle is not the same choice faced by his readers and translators, for whom his thoughts exist only as they have been rendered in ancient Greek, in the manner of the first view.

from within that language. On the other hand, those attempts, however striking, inevitably fail to capture the full meaning or the full force of what we have in mind, and they certainly add nothing to it. Their role is one of selective representation; we try to put significant strands of our thought into the most apt language available to us.

The third possible way to understand the relationship between our thoughts and feelings and the various languages of expression might be said to marry and extend the claims of the other two. Thought and language seldom part company, but they have different sources and different capacities.[4] The role of language is to give shape to our thoughts and feelings, thoughts and feelings that would be not only unutterable but in some respects incomprehensible in the absence of language. Without language we would still feel grief, but in the absence of tears, gestures, or words we would not be able to express that grief, even to ourselves, and our inability to express our grief would limit our ability to comprehend it. Conversely, an infant whose only expressive resource is crying can only express grief, and so has a limited capacity to distinguish the various needs, fears and frustrations that he or she must express as grief in the absence of a more apt language in which to express them. And to turn to a more general and more abstract example, an adult struck by a flash of inspiration may say that he or she sees the answer, but in fact will see it only in inchoate terms, so that in order to see it fully, and know its rational contours, will have to put it in language. Otherwise the answer will remain an intuition.

Given the importance of the role it has to play, language has become so familiar to us, in certain of its manifestations at least, and so associated with what it expresses, that thought and language have a tendency to merge in our imagination, inviting us to identify one with the other. Yet although language exists only to express thought and feeling, its capacity for expression always exceeds the demands of existing thought, for the simple reason that language, once in existence, becomes a subject of thought itself. For Bach, the language of a musical keyboard, and more generally of musical theory, was a terrain to explore, not merely a means of recording and transmitting to others a set of musical thoughts which, though necessarily couched in musical language, were not inspired by that language and the resources that it offered. For poets and public orators, language informs the substance of what they have to say, too much so, when we judge their expression merely rhetorical, appropriately so, when we judge that expression inspirational, graceful, or moving. The language employed

---

[4] As the text subsequently indicates, it is possible to have formless thoughts; it is also possible to use language thoughtlessly. Infants who have mastered a few words will often use them to prattle meaninglessly. A few singers do something similar when they use real words as if they were scat. Yet it is important to be careful here. An infant's prattling is meaningful in the sense that it conveys the infant's mood, though it is doubtful that the infant intends this. A singer's voicing of an incoherent lyric, on the other hand, not only conveys mood and musicality but is intended to do so. Exceptional cases aside, the use of language can only ever be partially thoughtless.

by Churchill was not simply an eloquent means of transmitting national resolve in a time of crisis; rather, it was itself a reason for that resolve, for it suggested the rich possibilities for expression of the national culture that was under threat, and in the defence of which resolve was called for. Among the ideas conveyed by Churchill's speeches was the idea that the striking language in which they were couched, language that we now call Churchillian, embodied the very creativity and resourcefulness that the speaker sought to inspire in his listeners.

It follows, according to this third account, that the enterprise of expression is typically, although not invariably, creative at heart. In certain settings a person's expression may amount to no more than the transmission of information. There is normally no creative dimension to the reporting of sports scores, or stock quotations. In most settings, however, expression is more or less creative. This is most obviously the case in those settings that we formally describe as creative, such as the arts, but it is also the case in many everyday forms of behaviour. When we put our thoughts and feelings into words and phrases, and so turn them into spoken or written language, whether for our own benefit or for the benefit of some other, when we sketch our response to a scene before us and so turn that response into line and shading, when we whistle or when we hum, we are necessarily, if modestly, creative. We start to say something, as an attempt to capture some aspect of what we think or feel, and as we say it our speech gains a suggestive momentum of its own, so that what begins as a limited perspective upon a richer thought soon acquires a life that outstrips the bounds of the original thought, inspiring new thoughts that depart from the original in ways that were neither foreseen nor foreseeable in advance.

Not all behaviour is expressive of course, however creative it may be in other respects. There is nothing expressive in the mere filing of information, or in the digging of a ditch, although databases and drains may thereby be created. It is simply a mistake to equate creativity and expressiveness. I suggested in the previous paragraph that expression is typically although not invariably creative. The claim here is to the opposite effect. Many forms of creative behaviour, among them the organization of information and the digging of ditches, are not normally expressive at all, let alone creatively so. Behaviour becomes expressive when it displays thoughts and feelings, whether intentionally or as an effect, whether as an act of creation or as an act of communication.[5] If the filing is done in a bored or an impatient manner, if the ditch is dug sluggishly or resentfully, it is to that extent expressive. Certain forms of behaviour are inescapably expressive, because they inescapably display thought and feeling. These are the paradigmatic instances of expression, of which speech is the most obvious everyday example. Other forms of behaviour, inexpressive in themselves, may be expressive in their

---

[5] I take communication to be a matter of representation, normally by one party to another, although I recognize that it is perfectly possible to use the word more broadly, so as to include the creative aspects of expression.

purpose or their effect. Many acts of protest and civil disobedience fall into this category, for they give expressive purpose to what would otherwise be inexpressive conduct. On the other hand, even conduct that lacks any expressive purpose, such as standard cases of filing or ditch-digging, may be expressive in its effect, if it is undertaken by a person who displays, without intending to do so, an expressive attitude, for example, what is sometimes described as an expressive back.

Which of these views of the relationship between our thoughts and feelings and the languages in which they find expression is the correct one? Given that the third view confirms and extends the claims of the second, the real issue is between those views, which take expression to have both creative and representative aspects, and the first view, which holds expression to be entirely representative in character. It seems to me that broadly speaking there are two reasons to believe that expression is usually creative, and so to reject the first view in favour of its rivals. First, the existence of gaps in our ability to express what we have in mind tells in favour of the second, perspectival account of expression. Secondly, the dynamic, evaluative relationship between language and thought, like the dynamic, evaluative relationship between thought and the material world, tells in favour of the third, creative account of expression.

Expressive Gaps

It is a familiar phenomenon of ordinary life that we frequently experience gaps in our ability to express what we have in mind. There are a number of reasons why this is so. Sometimes the presence of such a gap makes clear to us that our thoughts, like our dreams, have elided a difficulty that we do not know how to confront or resolve, a difficulty that becomes explicit when we try to express ourselves in language and so are compelled to make our thoughts concrete. The gap here is not a gap between thought and expression, but a gap in our thought itself, which the act of expression reveals. In our dreams these gaps tend to be narrative: we enter a nightmare scenario, or escape from it, by means that are never and could never be explained.[6] In our conscious reflections these gaps are usually logical: we know just what the answer is, or just what we are going to say to someone, until an attempt to express our thought reveals a fatal assumption or omission, and so exposes a logical gap. Gaps such as these confirm rather than deny the closeness of the connection between thought and expression.

Sometimes, too, a gap in our ability to express what we have in mind reveals a failure of *capacity* or of *technique*. Most people who set out to sketch a scene or write a poem discover that they lack any capacity for art or poetry. They may be articulate in other respects, but they have no gift for specialist languages such as these. They simply cannot see the world as an artist or a poet sees it, and so have no artistic or poetic vision to express. Thought and expression remain connected

---

[6] Daydreams embody similar narrative gaps; we picture ourselves as leading figures in delightful scenarios that we have managed to enter and occupy by means that are quite beyond explanation.

here: it is the absence of a capacity for thought of a certain kind that leads to the absence of its expression. Other people, who possess the natural ability to sketch or write poetry, may never have developed that ability, and so will discover that they are insufficiently accomplished in art or poetry to express what their native talent would otherwise enable them to visualize. In that case the gap between thought and expression is a technical one. Here too, thought and expression remain connected: the inability to represent thoughts of a certain kind prevents one from thinking them, and so leads to the absence of their expression.

Sometimes, however, a gap in our ability to express what we have in mind does indeed reveal a gap between thought and expression. There are two ways to see this, from the perspective of thought and from the perspective of expression. To approach it from the perspective of thought, people often say that they cannot explain what they mean, in the sense that they cannot put their thoughts into words, but then go on to offer another form of explanation. Perhaps they demonstrate what they have in mind, perhaps they draw it, perhaps they put it in the language of mathematics or of formal logic. Now this might simply show that their original thought was couched in one of those terms, but if so it is not clear why such people should ever have made the mistake of seeking to express their thought in words in the first place. If, as is claimed, the fabric of a thought is fundamentally visual (or practical, mathematical, or formally logical) it could not be expressed in verbal terms without turning it into another thought. If a thought is visual, for example, in the sense of being intelligible only in terms of its visual expression, it would be self-defeating to seek to express that thought in anything other than visual terms. And if a thought can be expressed, with differing degrees of success, verbally or visually, it cannot be true that it is fundamentally either, for it is susceptible to both.[7]

The point can be further illustrated from the perspective of expression. If thought and expression are fused, as is claimed, then if someone asks to have a thought put another way, what they are actually asking for is a different thought, which is not only to demand the betrayal of the original thought, but to do so incoherently, for a new thought could never claim to be simply the old thought put another way, which is just what is being demanded.[8] In fact what the person

---

[7] The explanation might be that words are the standard form of expression, and we sometimes make the mistake of trying to express in that form what is inexpressible there. We do make such mistakes, but the question is what they reveal. If the first view of the relationship between thought and expression is right, the attempt to express in words what is inexpressible there would produce a catastrophic result. It could not yield what it often does yield, namely, an act of expression that is coherent to the listener but falls short of capturing the speaker's intent. Nor could it yield an act of expression that is gap-filled, so far so, perhaps, as to be incoherent to the listener. On the other hand, if the mistake reveals an attempt to express a thought in an inapt language it confirms the second view. See the next note.

[8] If the thought is acknowledged to be roughly the same thought, modified only by the exigencies of its new mode of expression, so as to be in effect a translation of the original, then the first explanation has been conceded to the second, for it has been conceded that thought transcends its expression.

must be asking for is not a different thought, but a different rendering of the same thought.

The existence of gaps of this kind is evidence of the accuracy of the second, *perspectival* explanation of the relationship between our thoughts and feelings and the languages in which they find expression. It is sensible for us to seek to express our thoughts in different ways, and for others to ask us to do so, because the various languages of expression each have distinctive expressive characters, making each adept at capturing certain aspects of a thought, and inept at capturing others. To express a thought in a new way, using a new language of expression, is to attempt to capture a new aspect of that thought, an aspect that may have been suppressed or neglected in the original expression.

The Dynamic of Expression

Yet there is something more than a fresh perspective at work in these examples of attempts to express ourselves in different ways, something that strengthens the claim that expression is creative rather than merely representative in character. As I have already suggested, our perspective on our thoughts, like our perspective on the material world, is itself an object of analysis and evaluation. Just as we have thoughts about our thoughts, so we have thoughts about the expression of our thoughts, thoughts that add directly to the richness of our life and hence become a source of intrinsic value.

Begin with our thoughts about the material world. When we look at the world and appreciate the existence of, for example, a tree, we appreciate many things about that tree: its height, its spread, its colour, the nature of its foliage, the character of its wood, its probable age, and so on. In doing so we do not necessarily fully comprehend the properties of the tree. There may well be dimensions to the tree's existence that we cannot perceive, just as there are dimensions to its existence, such as colour or fitness for cabinetry or construction, that cannot be perceived by those animals that do not share our capacities.

Secondly, when we appreciate a tree we do not appreciate all the properties that we are capable of appreciating in it. Some see trees in terms of their environmental role, some see them as fuel or timber, some see them as objects of beauty, some see them as gods. Development of the capacity to appreciate a tree in one of these dimensions is very often at the expense of the capacity to appreciate it in another dimension, if only for practical reasons. Any appreciation of a tree that prevents us from cutting it down, for example, prevents us from appreciating the beauty or usefulness of its wood.

Finally, and what matters most in the present context, our appreciation often becomes an end in itself. We notice the colour of the tree, the character of its profile, the various features that make it the tree that it is, not merely because these are indicators of the character of the tree and perhaps the state of its health, but because colour, profile, and ultimately the tree itself, are objects of appreciation for their own sake. We notice the quality of the wood, say, not merely because that quality determines the uses to which the wood may be put as timber, but because the grain, texture, durability and even smell of the wood help to make that wood both beautiful and rewarding to work with. Artists paint trees as a way of exploring colour theory, sculptors carve wood as a way of analysing the significance of form, gardeners plant trees as a way of creating an ideal landscape, environmentalists preserve trees as a way of showing reverence for trees themselves, as constituents of the good earth. We do all these things because they are valuable, indeed intrinsically so. Put simply, appreciation is a matter of perceiving value.

When we turn from appreciation of the material world to appreciation of the mental world we cannot help but apply the same intellectual resources, with broadly similar consequences. First, in contemplating our thoughts, whether for the purposes of expression or otherwise, we do not necessarily comprehend those thoughts fully: some aspects of our thoughts are beyond contemplation, other aspects may be recovered only partially and imperfectly through the strategies of psychoanalysis and other methods of psychological intervention. This suggests that it cannot be true that our thoughts are no more than reflections of the expressive possibilities of which our imagination is aware and in which it is fluent, for in many cases their existence is of a kind that renders them inexpressible.

Secondly and what is more to the point, we often develop the ability to appreciate a given aspect of our thoughts at the expense of the ability to appreciate other aspects of that thought. The ability to express oneself successfully in the language of formal logic, for example, does not sit easily with the ability to do so in ordinary English. Similarly, trained singers sacrifice to their training the distinctive expressive possibilities of an untrained voice. This suggests that even expressible thoughts are not always fully expressible, for distinctive capacities to engage in particular forms of expression may be incompatible with one another, even though the thought is expressible through either.

Finally, and once again what matters most in the present context, our appreciation of our thoughts, including our thoughts about expression, often becomes an end in itself. As I have already suggested, we pursue the possibilities of expression for their own sake, in art, poetry, oratory and elsewhere. We do this because it is intrinsically valuable to do so. Indeed, in many cases, particularly in the avantgarde, the overriding purpose of expressive action, to which questions of representation are subordinated, perhaps even subverted, is to explore the expressive possibilities of a particular medium, so that we write free theatre, dance free dance, make conceptual art, and so on, not so much because we have something to say through the medium in question, something that we want to represent to the world by drawing on the medium's resources, but because we want to discover what there might be to say in the distinctive language of the medium that we are exploring. The thought that is represented here is a thought about expression itself.

So far the story tends to confirm the accuracy of the second, perspectival account of expression, and so tends to confirm that in certain settings at least, expression has a creative aspect in the selection and development of a perspective from which to express a given thought. But there is more. Our thoughts about the expression of our thoughts interact with and so have a dynamic impact upon the direction and character of the thoughts being expressed. When in the course of expressing a thought we think about expression as an end in itself, as we are more or less bound to do whenever expression reaches such a level of sophistication as to be capable of being an end in itself, we discover and pursue expressive possibilities that lend new shape and direction to our thought, so that the thought as expressed fuses the possibilities of the original thought and those of its expression. When this happens, as it does in all cases where expression is more than the bare transmission of information, expression becomes a fundamentally creative act. It is this that takes expression beyond a merely representative role, or the partly representative, partly creative role recognized by the perspectival account. The creation of a new expressive thought is just that. Even a philosophical paper, the primary purpose of which must be to transmit certain ideas, never merely represents what is in its author's mind. On the contrary, the process of putting thoughts into written language gives rise to something new, something that has a value that is distinct from the value of the unwritten thought, as well as distinct from the value of the same thought as expressed in another language by the same or another author.[9]

So when we express ourselves, for our own benefit or for the benefit of others, our conduct is primarily creative and only secondarily representative. Some expression, particularly spontaneous expression, need never acquire a representative dimension. When something inspires us to whistle, or to skip up stairs, it need not inspire us to represent anything to anybody, even to ourselves, although on hearing us or seeing us a person (ourselves perhaps) may recognize that we are in a good mood. The same may be true of more considered acts of self-expression, such as dancing, or drawing, or diary-writing, though these often shade into self-awareness, and thereby display an awareness of their representative implications.

Other expression has no creative dimension, either because it consists merely of representing to the world what some other person has created, or because it consists of representing information, such as sports scores or stock quotations, that is the mere tabulation of data, data that arises without the intervention

---

[9] This explanation revives something of what I have described as the first view of the relationship between thought and expression, for if the thought as expressed fuses the possibilities of the original thought and those of its expression, as I have claimed, then the thought as expressed takes shape only in the language in which it is expressed, and so exists only in that form. Had it failed to take that shape the new thought would not merely not have been expressed; it would have been still-born (however many other new thoughts the original thought might be capable of giving rise to), for it is the fact of expression that has brought the new thought into existence as the particular thought that it is. What the first view neglects, however, is the necessary genesis of that new thought in both a prior non-linguistic thought and a prior linguistic thought; and further, the capacity of the new thought, once reflected upon, to give rise to yet more new thoughts by the very process that brought it into being itself. To neglect these things is to neglect the existence of expressive creativity and its possible value.

of any person's thoughts or feelings and whose mode of expression is fixed by convention. One should be careful even here, however, for such purely representative expression is distinctive and unusual. The function of a publisher, for example, who represents to the world what others have created, is seldom if ever exclusively representative, for it is up to the publisher to determine the setting for an author's words, and as many great publishers, typographers and printers have shown, that is a deeply creative enterprise, one that does much to establish the import of what the author has to say. Even the reporting of sports scores or stock quotations is potentially creative, for the mode of expression of such information is never entirely fixed by convention, so that there is always a question of how to couch it, a question that, when answered well, leads us to watch certain broadcasts, or read certain newspapers, for the attractiveness with which they present sporting or financial results.

Most expression, however, has both creative and representative dimensions. So when two people decide to spend the evening in one another's company, and when in the course of that evening they express their thoughts and feelings to one another, their experience is a creative one, not merely because of the intervention of another person, whose thoughts and feelings represent a creative response to the thoughts and feelings that one has expressed to them, but because the very act of expressing one's thoughts and feelings, whether to oneself or to another, is a creative act. Such expression is often valuable, not merely because the things it makes possible are often valuable, things such as the vindication of personal and cultural identity, the discovery of new truths, the pursuit of self-government, or in the present example, the development of a relationship, but because in its ordinary, undramatic, mundane way, such expression is valuable in itself, like art or like poetry, albeit less markedly so. To put it in more formal terms, its value is intrinsic, not merely instrumental.[10] The good of an evening spent in rewarding company is constituted in part by the evanescent good of successful conversation, be that conversation deep or sparkling, and the good of successful

---

[10] Accounts of expression that focus on its representative aspects tend to portray the value of representation in terms of the value that the representation gives rise to. This need not be the case, of course, since there can be value in the representation itself, as Joseph Raz's explanation of the intrinsic value of expression makes clear: *see* 'Free Expression and Personal Identification', in *Ethics in the Public Domain* (1994) 131. It follows that the distinction between the representative and creative aspects of expression does not map on to the distinction between the instrumental and the intrinsic value of expression. Representation can be either instrumentally or intrinsically valuable, as can creation. Nevertheless the creative account of expression tends to focus on questions of intrinsic value, for the instrumental value of creativity in expression is normally dependent on, and always co-exists with, the presence of intrinsic value in that creativity. By contrast, the representative account of expression tends to focus on questions of instrumental value, for the value of representation is dependent on the value of what is represented, which may sometimes be embodied in the act of expression itself, as Raz's account shows, so that the representation becomes constitutive of what is intrinsically valuable, but which is normally distinct from the expression, for which the expression serves as a more or less successful vehicle. This may explain why most accounts of freedom of expression dwell on its representative aspects and its instrumental value, in terms of truth, democracy or self-realization, to take the most familiar examples.

conversation, which is consistent with its evanescence, is in part simply the good of making good conversation, for its own sake.

In conclusion, then, and to move from the mundane to the significant, if freedom of expression serves to protect the value of expression, as it clearly does, it must protect the creative as well as the representative aspects of expression, so that in any assessment of freedom of expression the value of creativity must strengthen or supplement whatever is to be said for freedom of expression in terms of the value of representation.

Three Observations

Three final comments, by way of observation and caveat. First, one explanation for the tendency to think of expression in representative terms is that it is natural to think of expression in terms of speech (which is, after all, its most central instance), and to think of speech in terms of words, whose function is indeed representative. Words, spoken or written, represent concepts, and that is all they do: there is nothing creative in the identification of the correct word for the concept one has in mind, for certain imaginative exceptions aside,[11] the linkage between word and concept is not one for the writer or speaker to forge.[12] Yet quite apart from the fact that not all expression is speech, and that other forms of expression, such as drawing and sculpture, lack a modular vocabulary equivalent to words, speech itself is composed not merely of words, but of sentences, paragraphs, and so on. Each of these is a vehicle for extended thoughts, thoughts whose richness, complexity and relative formlessness leaves open the question of their expression, a question that is answered not only with reference to the thought itself, but to the value of the different possible means of expressing that thought. In this way, the representative function of language, which manifests itself in the choice of words, is subsumed in the creative process of speaking or writing. Furthermore, even with regard to words themselves, it is a feature of speech, particularly in English, that a number of different words can be said to represent roughly the same idea, so that even the expression of thoughts precise and discrete enough to be represented by a word often calls for the exercise of creativity in selecting among synonyms.[13]

---

[11] Such as Lewis Carroll's 'Twas brillig and the slithy toves . . .'.

[12] Two clarifications are necessary here. First, many words are called upon to represent more than one concept, as we know both from the ordinary use of language and from familiar analyses of words like game (a recreation, a form of courage, or an incapacity), bank (river and savings), and perch (fish, temporary resting place, or distance). Secondly, as certain philosophers of language have emphasized, the concepts that words represent may themselves function representatively (in which case the use of the word is representative at two levels) or in a number of other ways, hortatory, laudatory, and more.

[13] The functions and values of a verbal language are far richer than this brief description can acknowledge. The conventional vocabulary, orthography and grammar of spoken and written language is instrumentally valuable by reason of its ability to facilitate communication and understanding for a particular linguistic community. Verbal language is also intrinsically valuable,

Secondly, while it is true that thought is often shaped in advance by the possibilities for its expression, it is rarely if ever so shaped completely. Most thoughts are like partly formed embryos without the built-in guidance of DNA, certain elements of which are recognizable as primitive versions of their final form, and other elements of which exist simply as raw material for development, constrained only by the need for a certain consonance with the structure of what has already been formed.

Finally, if it were true that expression constituted the very fabric of a thought, as is claimed, then expression could only be an end in itself if and to the extent that the thought it embodied was a thought about expression. This would make it impossible for the expression of thoughts (other than thoughts about expression) to be the bearer of any thoughts about expression, and correspondingly, for expression as an end in itself to be the bearer of any thoughts about anything other than expression.[14] The two functions might, of course, be companions in a complex expressive endeavour, but they would have no capacity to inform one another. If true this would give rise to a divide between aesthetic and other meanings, in which aesthetics became a project empty of all substance beyond itself. That is a plausible charge against certain merely decorative artists, one that has often been made against Oscar Wilde and certain of his contemporaries, but is it true of Michelangelo and Vermeer, and their renderings of the sacred and the secular? Did poor Wilde himself only have something to say when he forsook his wit? One's intuition runs in the opposite direction.

Freedom of Expression

There have been many celebrated accounts of the meaning and significance of freedom of expression and as many explanations of its value. As is typically

partly on aesthetic grounds (languages can have distinctive aesthetic appeals, musicality for example), and partly because it is constitutive of certain intrinsically valuable goods and activities (such as poetry, wordplay, Scrabble, crosswords, spelling bees). Finally, language is sometimes the occasion for the creation of certain concepts, by a process of felicitous association, as when it suggests possible connections, and so inspires fresh, non-linguistic ideas, as by-products of its form.

[14] This is not an easy point to capture, and its rendering in the text may be overly compressed. If thoughts exist only as they are expressed there can be no question of how to express most thoughts. The very idea is ruled out by an analysis of expression that regards thoughts as inseparable from the mode of their expression. It follows, then, that the thoughts we commonly have about how to express our thoughts can only be explained as illusions, or as purely aesthetic thoughts, thoughts that are empty of any ideas other than ideas about expression as an end in itself. If that were true, then linguistic and non-linguistic thoughts would have nothing to contribute to one another. This seems implausible from both perspectives. Art usually has something to say about matters other than art, and what it has to say about those matters is deeply entangled with what it has to say about art, so that a work of art becomes a way of saying something about the world which, in and through the very act of saying it, also says something about art itself, not only as a vehicle for the representation of thoughts (whether about matters other than art, or about art, or both), but as a creative medium that is capable of enriching and extending the thoughts it is called upon to represent.

the case with thoughtful scholarship, each of those accounts grasps something important about the freedom, so that when read together, in all their disparity, they form a picture of a complex, multi-faceted phenomenon, a picture that is consistent with the pivotal position of freedom of expression in modern, pluralistic societies. My purpose here is not to challenge that picture but to extend it.

For all their disparity, these accounts of freedom of expression display a common commitment to understanding expression in representative terms.[15] The expression whose freedom they seek to explain and defend is in effect an artefact, something that some people have made and that the same or other people may profit from. The purpose of freedom of expression, however it may be explained, is to secure the display of that artefact, for the sake of the good that such display makes possible. There is no denying that this is a vitally important aspect of freedom of expression. As I suggested at the outset, however, the question remains whether there is anything more to the story. If there is more to expression than the act of representation, as I have contended, is there more to its value, and hence to the justification of its freedom, than representation allows? Or does recognition of the value of representation necessarily capture, directly or indirectly, the value of creation?

Before addressing these questions directly I will have to step back a distance and look more closely at the various connections and disconnections between value, freedom, and rights, and in particular, at the value of freedom. The account that follows is in some ways a digression from the specifics of freedom of expression, but the distinctions it draws will help to clarify the contribution that creativity of expression is capable of making to the value of freedom of expression, whether that freedom is protected as a right or not.

1. Value, Freedom and Rights

There is a common tendency today to simplify the connections between value, freedom and rights. Many believe that if a certain activity is valuable people ought to be free to engage in it. They further believe that if people ought to be free to engage in an activity, that freedom ought to be secured by a right. And further yet, although perhaps less commonly, many believe that if people have a right to a certain freedom that right ought to be fundamentally guaranteed, as part of a

[15] Any account of freedom of expression that justifies that freedom by reference to the valuable role that expression plays in the life of people other than the speaker, or in the life of the speaker through the mediation of other people, necessarily understands expression in representative terms. All accounts of expression of which I am aware regard expression as an interpersonal good, on the model of a conversation, though certain accounts place particular emphasis on the role of one party or the other in that conversation. None contemplates the possibility that expression may be a purely private good, in the sense of being open to pursuit by one person without the direct involvement of others, and that the private, personal good in most cases underwrites the public, interpersonal good, either directly or indirectly.

written constitution or its equivalent. Value is thus thought to entail freedom, and freedom in turn is thought to entail rights. Thoughts like these inspire and underpin much contemporary public debate over the content of individual and social justice, so that claims of value, claims of freedom, and combinations of the two, are now typically couched in the language of rights, and need to be so if they are to be taken seriously.

In optimistic hands the sequence is often reversed, so as to attribute inherent value to the exercise of fundamental rights. Many believe that if there is a fundamental right to engage in an activity, no greater warrant of the value of the activity is needed. This thought has particular currency when applied to the connection between value and freedom. It is often assumed that there is no need to consider whether one ought to do what one is free to do by reason, let us suppose, of a fundamental guarantee. Freedom pre-empts questions of worth, or more precisely, always answers them in the affirmative. Or so it is said.

There is no denying that these common assumptions are in many respects accurate. In liberal societies access to many, perhaps most, values is typically obtained through the exercise of freedom. And in those same societies, where the pursuit of liberty has eroded most traditions, freedom is very often secured by the presence of a fundamental guarantee. So we express ourselves, for example, not through traditional forms, be they oral, such as sagas, or written, such as sonnets, but through the exercise of expressive freedom, the cumulative impact of which over time has been to render nearly every aspect of art, literature and conversation open to formal reconsideration and reinvention. More obviously, perhaps, the particular themes we pursue through the forms we invent are today unconstrained by the conventions that once shaped the content as well as the form of modes of expression. We now say what we want to say in whatever form we please. In effect, formal and substantive innovation have very largely merged. And of course the freedom to say and do these things, in these ways, has come to be embodied, in most societies, in a fundamental legal right.

Yet the connections between value, freedom and rights, though real enough, are all too easy to overstate. Value does not entail freedom, and freedom does not entail rights, moral or legal. In fact the relationships among these phenomena are as marked by disconnection as by connection. There is simply no straightforward chain of dependency by which rights can be derived from freedom can be derived from value. No one of these supposed steps is necessary or sufficient to yield the next.[16] And recognizing this can make a difference to our understanding of certain rights, including the right to freedom of expression.

---

[16] This is perhaps an unduly cryptic way to introduce a rather strong claim, only some aspects of which I will be able to defend in what follows. The disconnections I have in mind here are along the following lines: not all values entail freedom, not all freedom is valuable; not all freedom entails rights, moral or legal; not all rights (moral or legal) are matters of freedom.

Value Without Freedom

We are all familiar with the importance of keeping our options open: it is only by doing so that we can exercise the freedom to choose which option in particular to pursue. Doctrines of positive freedom implicitly acknowledge this idea, for they take special account of the fact that many people are in no position to develop options for themselves, and so are bound to depend for their freedom upon the presence of a social framework that fosters valuable options from among which they may choose from time to time. But whether acknowledged in a doctrine of freedom or not, it is clear that many valuable relationships and endeavours are sustainable only from a condition of freedom. This means several things. Most obviously, to close the door at any point to further choice among one's relationships and endeavours is to imperil one's access to the very values they embody, by making oneself hostage to the success of the choices that one has already made. Freedom thus serves as a form of insurance against options that do not work out. Less obviously perhaps, but more fundamentally, the value of certain relationships and endeavours is dependent upon their having been either freely chosen or freely maintained. To use a familiar example, the value of marriage in the West is by and large accessible only to those who choose their spouses; those who are compelled into marriage by circumstance are able to gain access to the value of marriage if and when they confirm by choice what circumstance once dictated, as the many stories of those who fall in love after the fact are designed to make clear.[17] Other relationships depend for their value on being freely maintained as well as freely adopted. Those couples who live together as partners rather than as spouses often derive part of the value of their relationship from the very fact that it is open to termination at any time. They feel that their attention to one another is rather more lively than it would have been if they had the legal commitment of marriage as security.

And yet the opposite is also true, for the price of keeping one's options open is loss of access to all those relationships and endeavours that are accessible only

[17] The instrumental value of marriage (such as its capacity to provide security and mutual support) can be realized in a number of different ways, and so is almost undoubtedly accessible to most participants in arranged marriages, in whatever culture those marriages may take place. After all, until fairly recently certain indigenous subcultures in the West, the aristocracy in particular, participated in arranged marriages that were at least instrumentally valuable, and there is no obvious reason why non-Western subcultures in the West, and perhaps aristocrats as well, should not be able to do the same today. Indeed one of the claims made by supporters of arranged marriage is that arrangement is a sounder vehicle than choice for the realization of marriage's instrumental value. However, the intrinsic value of marriage in the West today is accessible only through the exercise of choice, and so is inaccessible to those who do not choose their partners, or perhaps even their condition, as the text emphasizes. Other intrinsically valuable forms of marriage have no recognition or support in the social forms and practices of contemporary Western culture and so are unrealizable there. Couples who subsequently confirm by choice what was once compelled are thereby able to gain access to the intrinsic value of marriage, though of course it is not quite the same value they would have participated in had they chosen their condition from the beginning, for it is informed by the value of acceptance in a way that choice-based marriage is not.

through commitment. I do not have in mind here the obvious problem of the incompatibility that comes of the finitude of life. Plainly one cannot keep all one's options open at all times, for to choose any option at any time is not to choose another option then. One can be industrious and career-minded in one's youth and self-indulgent in one's later years, or vice versa, but to be industrious and career-minded at any stage of life is not to have been self-indulgent then, with all that implies. What I have in mind here is foreclosure of a different kind. To keep one's options open is to deny oneself access to all those options in life that yield their value only to the committed. Suppose that one decides to remain in a certain community as long as things work out there, so keeping open the option of moving elsewhere. In doing so one necessarily forgoes one's access to all those aspects of community life that are available only to the committed, most obviously those aspects that yield their value only at a point when the uncommitted cannot be sure of still being part of the community. The same is true of friendships and partnerships, and of careers. Those who refuse to commit themselves to any one of these things thereby preserve their freedom at the price of access to the kinds of relationships and careers, or aspects of relationships and careers, that depend upon full investment. This is not a problem of half-heartedness, for it is perfectly possible to be full-blooded for as long as it lasts. It is a product of the fact that commitment, or lack of commitment, changes the nature of a relationship, and so may well change the identity of the value that one gains access to through the relationship.

I have spoken so far in terms of self-regulation, but the point also has application in settings where the restriction of one's options is imposed by circumstance, or by the will of others. Those who take part in arranged marriages, for example, often speak of the value that is to be found in the process of coming to terms with a relationship that one is more or less bound to live with. Such claims of value are deeply unfashionable today and quite possibly spurious, but they do not involve a logical contradiction. On the contrary, something like them seems to be recognizably true of other less profoundly personal enforced commitments, such as commitments to the community where one was born and raised, or to the job that one was bound to do because one's family expected it, or because need dictated it.

To show that an activity is valuable, therefore, is not to show that people ought to be free to engage in it, for freedom may be at odds with its value. But there is more, for if it is true that the value of a relationship or endeavour need not depend on the freedom to choose it, it is also true that the value of the freedom to choose a relationship or endeavour need not depend on the value of what is chosen.

The Value of Freedom

It is sometimes suggested, plausibly enough, that a liberty interest is a person's interest in the ability to do something other than whatever he or she is doing at the moment, where the idea of an interest is taken to be the idea of something that is both valuable and fit for the person in question. This explanation strikes me as sound but incomplete, for as it stands it fails to distinguish liberty interests from ordinary interests. We have ordinary interests in pursuing whatever valuable options suit us, and so at any given time have an ordinary interest in doing something other than whatever we are doing at that moment, as long as it is valuable and suits us. We have an ordinary interest, for example, in living with people other than our spouse or partner, or having friends other than our friends, provided of course that relationships with such people would both be valuable and suit us. It takes rather more to show that we have a liberty interest in being able to do these things. Freedom is not the corollary of value pluralism.[18]

It seems to me that there are two possible ways to understand the significance of freedom. One might regard freedom as a morally arbitrary feature of certain social practices. On this view freedom matters in certain cultures because circumstance happens to have made freedom an integral feature of many, perhaps most social practices in those cultures, so that access to the values that those social practices yield, or are capable of yielding, depends upon freedom. Yet this seems not to be true. Freedom is not simply the conventional clothing in which valuable practices happen to be garbed in certain cultures, in the way that a handshake or a kiss on the cheek is the conventional form of gesture that a greeting happens to take there. The fact that one chooses one's spouse itself contributes to the value of one's marriage, in a way that morally arbitrary features of that institution, such as the colour of the clothing that one is expected to wear to a wedding, or the particular finger on which one is expected to wear a wedding ring, do not.[19]

The other possible way to understand the significance of freedom, then, is to understand freedom as a value, albeit a value of a special, though not unique kind, one that is both conditional and satiable. The value of freedom is conditional in two ways. It is conditional first upon its service to value itself, in the creation of new values and new vehicles for old values, through the exercise of powers of creativity and modes of creation, themselves partly constituted by freedom. It follows that, indirectly at least, freedom is a value for values, which is what makes it look something like a master value, and explains something of its appeal. The value of freedom is conditional, secondly, upon its service to human well-being (which is itself dependent upon the realization of value in some person's life) in the exercise of choice among existing goods, many of which are constituted, in part at least, by freedom. Freedom entails choice, choice shapes character, and character helps to shape the role of incommensurable values in the service of

18 William Galston takes the opposite view: see *Liberal Pluralism* (2002), especially c 5.
19 I am assuming here, for the sake of argument, that there are such things as features of the world that are free of either value or disvalue. In fact, I doubt this. Handshakes and kisses on the cheek, for example, are both good ways of greeting people, and convention in a particular culture simply establishes which of them is to be recognized as expected practice there.

human well-being, for it establishes which values are in our interest and which are not, in the face of the manifold values we otherwise have reason to pursue.[20]

Most aspects of the explanation of freedom's contribution to the goodness of a life have been well traversed. Freedom serves well-being instrumentally, both by enabling us to decide for ourselves what is valuable in what lies before us more accurately than others might and, more plausibly perhaps, by enabling us to decide what suits us, so permitting us to identify our interests for ourselves. Freedom serves well-being intrinsically, by enabling us to be part authors of our own lives, both in choosing among eligible but incommensurable options, and in redefining the parameters of what suits us in and through such choices. The value of freedom is thus conditional upon its service to value, directly or indirectly. But freedom is not only conditional but satiable, partly because well-being is satiable, and partly because the unbridled pursuit of freedom is ultimately destructive of the social forms upon which our access to value depends, and so is destructive of freedom's own role in the service of value.[21]

What matters in the present setting, however, is the capacity of freedom to serve well-being even in the exercise of bad choices, for it is this that accounts for the disconnection between the value of freedom and the value of the relationships and endeavours that freedom enables us to choose. The most dramatic instance of this is the freedom to choose how to die, which may be either instrumentally or intrinsically valuable. Those who chose to jump to their deaths from the upper storeys of the World Trade Centre, rather than be burned to death in the building itself, exercised their freedom to choose which of two appalling options suited them better. Similar choices are made by those who commit suicide in the face of a terminal illness, whether with assistance or without. The freedom to make such choices is instrumentally valuable not only because it may secure access to a marginally less bad option, but because it may secure access to the bad option that happens to suit the chooser. This latter possibility is frequently developed to the point that the freedom to make such a choice becomes intrinsically valuable,

---

[20] I am assuming here that valuable options differ in kind as well as degree, so that freedom has a special role to play in directing the pursuit of one option rather than another when the two are incommensurable. Yet freedom would play something of the same role even on a monistic picture of value, for freedom would then be a condition of our access to any option other than the one we are pursuing at the moment, and so would be a condition of our ability to maximize the presence of value in our life by undertaking new and more rewarding relationships and endeavours.

[21] See the final chapter of this book, 'Entrenching Bills of Rights: Judicial Power and Political Freedom' and in particular the section entitled 'The Corrosion of Social Forms'. In speaking of the value of freedom as I have here, I do not mean to suggest that freedom is a quality that may be applied to the pursuit of certain valuable relationships and endeavours, such as marriage or a career. Freedom is constitutive of those relationships and endeavours, an indissoluble part of their meaning and value, and so has a somewhat different character and different implications in the different settings in which it manifests itself. Yet the impossibility of severing freedom from the social forms and practices in which it is embedded does not mean that freedom is not analytically severable there, so as to permit us to discern common features in the various forms and practices that are constituted by freedom in contemporary liberal societies. Otherwise it would not be possible to speak sensibly of freedom in general terms.

by becoming constitutive of the value of the life of the chooser as an autonomous being. As both literature and history remind us, people have often chosen to die in a way that brings the story of their life to a relatively satisfying conclusion. I myself had a great-uncle who, when dying of bowel cancer, chose to spend his summer as he always had, in the company of friends at his island cottage. An extra friend had to be invited to replace him at the bridge table; a bed had to be put in the next room so that my uncle could hear the conversation. Doing these things, and others like them, enabled my uncle to end his life in character. It expressed dignity, courage, a certain romanticism, and a belief in keeping the side up by fulfilling one's role as long and as well as one could. These are valuable qualities, although not without their downside, qualities that could not be displayed in a hospital in town, and the ability to express them through a choice between bad options was constitutive, in some small part at least, of the success of George Kirkpatrick's life.

I should emphasize that in speaking of the value of bad choices I am speaking of the possible value to be discovered in choosing one bad thing rather than another.[22] There is no value in choosing the bad over the good, apart from the lessons that may be learned, by oneself or others, from the making of such a mistake, though there may be value in being confronted by bad choices as well as good ones. Nor is there value, or any contribution to well-being, in the bare predicament of finding oneself confronted with an array of exclusively bad options, such as different ways to die. Yet it seems to be the case that if one does find oneself in such a predicament the freedom to choose among bad options can be exercised in a way that contributes to the success of one's life. The significance of this is that in certain settings the value of freedom may itself be warrant for the capacity to choose a bad option, without recourse to the idea of a right to that freedom.

This in turn raises the possibility that there is greater scope for the value of freedom than I have allowed so far. Not all options that we have to choose among are in existence at the moment of our choosing. When we have to choose whether or not to create something, for example, our decision to do so is necessarily sustained by the value of what we may create and by the value of creating it, both of which are speculative. Yet these two are also in tension. The more assured the value of the creation the less value there is likely to be in the process of bringing it about. On the other hand, the more speculative the value of the creation the more value there is likely to be in the process of bringing it about. It follows that there may be value in the exercise of the freedom to pursue a creative option the outcome of which is very likely to be bad, because the goodness of the creativity

---

[22] In referring to bad choices I mean to include the worthless as well as the wrongful. In fact, in the creative setting exploratory choices are much more likely to yield worthless outcomes than wrongful ones. Where an outcome is likely to be wrongful it is very unlikely to be warranted by the value of the creativity involved in bringing that outcome about. Indeed the belief on the part of some artists that a wrongful outcome can be so warranted, perhaps even readily warranted, is a dangerous form of aestheticism, as history reminds us.

involved in bringing that outcome about is constitutive of the value of the choice. The value of experience here is unlike the value of the lessons that may be learned in choosing bad options over good ones, referred to in the paragraph above. The value here is the value of creativity, while the value there is in the order of the value of a lesson learned in the perfecting of a craft or skill. In the one case we do good in doing bad, while in the other case we learn good by doing bad. We have reason to repeat the one experience, but not the other.

Rights, Freedoms, and the Licensing of Error

To the best of my knowledge, none of the countless theorists who have considered freedom of expression has seriously made the common contemporary mistake of overstating the connections between value, freedom and rights. But there is a reason for this, beyond the straightforward matter of professional ability. The focus of theoretical inquiry in these cases has been on the *right* to freedom of expression, what might warrant it, and what scope it might have. To approach the problem in that way is to develop conclusions in a manner that partially obscures the distinctive contributions played by value, freedom and rights in sustaining the case for a particular view of the right to freedom of expression. There is nothing wrong with this on the whole, because there is nothing wrong with making an argument that speaks to the right to freedom of expression as a whole by appealing to reasons that are drawn from the various elements that make up the right. Nevertheless, it raises the concern that any resulting obscurity about the particular contributions of each of those separate elements to the right as a whole may conceal certain features of expression and the distinctive support they can offer to the case for its value and its freedom.

The first possible level of obscurity is in the source of the value that a right to freedom of expression may be thought to yield. On the one hand, that value may flow from the very freedom to express oneself as one sees fit, and the contribution that such a freedom may make to personal autonomy, or to some other human good. In short, what is at issue may be the value of freedom, or at least of freedom in this setting. On the other hand, the value of freedom of expression may flow from the acts of expression that the exercise of such a freedom makes possible, in which case the value would be the value of expression itself. If that is so, then the source of that value might lie in either the representative or the creative aspect of expression (or both), and the contribution of that value to the goodness of human life might be either intrinsic or instrumental. In fact, the ultimate value of the right to freedom of expression might well be composed of all these things at once, and that, as I have acknowledged, is reason enough for a theorist to consider them together, as a whole. Yet even so, it remains the case that the value of the right as a whole does not always absorb and subsume the values it is composed of, and so may sometimes be sustained by the distinctive contributions of its several elements, a distinctiveness that may affect the shape and import of the right in particular settings, such as that of artistic expression.

Yet this analysis of the implications of obscurity tends to grant too much, for it treats the theoretical consideration of the right to freedom of expression as more open-ended and flexible than it is normally capable of being. Justifications of the *right* to a freedom embrace the right to exercise that freedom in ways that are worthless or even wrongful. That being the case, the justification of a right to freedom of expression cannot be founded on the inherent value of the expression that exercise of the freedom may give rise to, because that value may well be absent. It must be founded either on the value of the freedom itself, or on the net value of the expression that exercise of the freedom gives rise to once proper allowance has been made for the bad that may flow from that exercise as well as the good. In fact, to describe this as an alternative is still somewhat misleading, for given that rights to a freedom necessarily secure the consequences of that freedom any justification of a *right* to freedom of expression is bound to take account of the consequences of that right, good and bad. This may explain why justifications of freedom of expression are so often focused on the net consequences for the good of that freedom rather than on the value of the freedom itself, for the justification of bad consequences is most naturally looked for in good consequences, often to the neglect of other sources of value. In practice, therefore, the value of freedom itself is not so much obscured as displaced in assessments of the value of the right to freedom of expression.

The second possible level of obscurity is in the source of the warrant for the freedom to express oneself as one should not. Rights frequently protect what would otherwise be wrongful, indeed so far so, that it is tempting to think that this function is part of the very structure of a right. Moral rights, for example, entitle us to do what would otherwise be morally wrong, so that the moral right to express ourselves freely entitles us to say what we should not say. Legal rights entitle us to do what would otherwise be legally wrong, so that a legal right to express ourselves freely entitles us to demonstrate in ways that would otherwise be illegal. Nor are these consequences confined to rights to freedom, moral or legal. There may be a moral right to make use of another's property when one is in dire straits, to break into a cottage, for example, in order to obtain shelter from a winter storm; there are legal rights of way, which authorize what would otherwise be trespass, and conversely, legal rights of ownership, which authorize exclusion from what would otherwise be common land. Yet not all rights, moral or legal, protect in this way what would otherwise be wrongs, because many such rights are pure entitlements or claim-rights. A right to call upon the support of others, whether in the form of a pension, or unemployment assurance, or social assistance, is not in any sense a right to do what would otherwise be wrong. So if a right protects wrongful conduct, as rights often do, it is not straightforwardly by implication of its status as a right. Something more must be shown.

Nor do all freedoms embrace wrongs, because some, perhaps a great many freedoms are implicitly or explicitly conditional on being exercised for worthy ends. Publicly funded higher education systems, for example, typically give students the freedom to choose which university to go to. The assumption underlying the grant of that freedom is that all universities in the system are worth attending; if they were not worth attending they would not be accredited as part of the system and students would not be free to attend them at public expense. Many of our other freedoms, or at least many aspects of those freedoms, are similarly regulated so as to ensure that they are exercised for worthy ends. Our choice of restaurants, or entertainment facilities, or consumer goods, is regulated by health and safety standards. Many deplore this, in whole or in part, and regard it as an unacceptable restraint on freedom, but their objection is moral, not conceptual.

It follows that the right to freedom of expression, which unquestionably offers protection to worthless forms of expression, may do so by virtue of its status as a right, as a freedom, or both. Justifications of the right to freedom of expression tend to obscure which aspect of the right is doing this work, indeed may actually suggest that the work is being done by the right itself. Yet it is perfectly possible that certain aspects of expression are capable of warranting the freedom to pursue them, for good or ill, without recourse to the idea of a right.

2. Creative Freedom

We can agree, and as a starting point, that expression may be valuable, and its freedom justified, because of the contribution that it makes to the maintenance of a flourishing democracy, or to our grasp of what is true and what is false, or to the vindication of personal and cultural identity.[23] The question is, what that agreement implies.

Such accounts of freedom of expression are entirely persuasive when the expression in issue is principally, perhaps exclusively, representative in character. They become less persuasive, however, when the representative analysis is extended to aspects of expression that are not only representative but profoundly

---

[23] I have neglected the familiar justification of freedom of expression in terms of personal autonomy out of a concern that it risks being question-begging, given that the issue here is whether freedom of expression should be a fundamental feature of personal autonomy, and why. The question would not be begged, of course, if the reference to personal autonomy were to be spelled out, but the spelling would require, among other things, some explanation of what makes freedom of expression valuable. If the claim is that freedom of expression is intrinsically valuable because it is constitutive of the good of personal autonomy, then what must be shown is that freedom of expression augments or at least secures the value of that autonomy. To show that one would need to show the intrinsic value of freedom of expression as well as its autonomous character. Put another way, if autonomy is constituted by various freedoms one can only show the value of autonomy by showing the value of those freedoms. One cannot explain the value of those freedoms by pointing to the value of the autonomy they constitute. The value of the sum (autonomy) may be greater than and/or distinct from the value of its parts (various freedoms), but if so it is only because the relationship among the parts is such as to make the value of each of them greater in combination than it would be on its own. To show that, one would need to show the value of freedom of expression (for example) and more.

creative, such as the arts. There is no doubt that novels, for example, contribute to our understanding of the world, as well as to the vindication of personal and cultural identity, though there might be more difficulty in showing that they contribute to the maintenance of a flourishing democracy, in most cases at least. Yet the status of fiction as a form of art derives from the fact that novels and short stories are, more than anything else, creative explorations of the aesthetic possibilities that fiction itself suggests. People write novels in order to see what novels can do, explicitly so when, like Woolf or Joyce or Faulkner, they form part of the avant-garde, implicitly so when, like most writers, their creative talents and ambitions are more modest and incremental. People read novels in order to take part in these expeditions of exploration, and when they read imaginatively, as good writing encourages them to do, they take the expeditions, however briefly and supplementarily, in directions all their own. Justifications of freedom of expression and its value that fail to address these features of writing and reading, and so regard the novel in exclusively representative terms, overlook and so neglect much of the value of fiction, and much of the warrant for its freedom.

In what follows I will consider three aspects of the relationship between creativity and freedom of expression. The consideration will be relatively brief, because I do not wish to be more than suggestive at this stage. If creativity in expression is in itself a potential source of value, distinct from the value of whatever is represented in the expression, as I have argued, it would be helpful to know whether that value has any distinctive role to play in the justification of freedom of expression. If it has, the full scope and character of that role can be left for another day.

Creative Value

There are two reasons to believe that there is more to the value of expression, and hence to the justification of its freedom, than representation allows. The first stems from the intrinsic value of creative expression, the second from the constitutive role that freedom plays in the process of creation.

Intrinsic value is, of course, not a function of the creative aspect of expression alone. On the contrary, the representative aspects of expression, like its creative aspects, can be either instrumentally or intrinsically valuable. However, as noted above, representative accounts of expression tend naturally to focus on questions of instrumental value, for the value of representation is largely dependent on the value of what is represented. That value is sometimes embodied in the act of expression, as Raz's explanation makes clear, so that the representation becomes constitutive of what is intrinsically valuable, but is normally distinct from the expression, so that the expression serves as a more or less successful vehicle for it.[24] Correspondingly, a creative account of expression tends naturally to focus on

---

[24] See the discussion in n 10.

questions of intrinsic value, for the instrumental value of creativity in expression is normally dependent on, and always co-exists with, the presence of intrinsic value in that creativity.

Or so it seems to me. Others may doubt the truth of these tendencies. No matter. The more capable representative accounts are of capturing the intrinsic value of expression, and what is more, the full breadth and specific nature of that intrinsic value, the less distinctive the contribution of a creative account of expression will be. That does not make the contribution less real, though it would make it less significant. In what follows I will explore the particular contribution that awareness of the creative aspect of expression can make to our understanding of the intrinsic value of expression. That contribution, it seems to me, though not unique, is indeed significant.

One of the difficulties with instrumental justifications of freedom of expression, at least for those whose intuition is that the status of that freedom is not contingent, is that they leave open the possibility that some instrument other than expression could bring about the states of affairs that they regard as valuable and that they see expression as serving. For that reason the protection that instrumental justifications offer to expression is vulnerable to such a discovery. It is possible, for example, that democracy could survive and flourish in the face of significant limitations of freedom of speech. It is doubtful that artistic or even scientific expression is crucial to democracy. Could British democracy in any sense be said to depend on a refusal to regard the work of Lucian Freud as obscene, or the researches of Stephen Hawking as blasphemous? Nor is it clear that democracy depends on complete freedom of even political speech, for in certain circumstances restrictions on political speech may actually advance democracy. In a recent British election the customary political addresses were forbidden at the announcement of the results in certain constituencies, out of concern for what might be said there by members of the British National Party. It is possible that such prohibitions may protect the democratic process, despite their contravention of freedom of expression; perhaps the Weimar Republic would have survived had it been less tolerant of certain exercises of freedom of expression.

What can be said of democracy in this respect can also be said of the other ends served by freedom of expression. To take two of the most prominent of those ends, it is all too easy to doubt the proposition that freedom of expression helps us to discover the truth, or to know it more vividly as Mill put it, for many falsehoods, when freely circulated, are clearly more persuasive to many people than the truth. There is a familiar and depressing record of the power of xenophobia, racism and other similarly demeaning myths to capture the public imagination. Finally, it is often the case that personal and cultural identities are successfully vindicated by conduct that is at best only secondarily and indirectly expressive and so would not fall within the scope of freedom of expression. An Italian chef or a Czech glassmaker; a cyclist or a hiker; an athlete or a scholar: all vindicate their identities without relying upon freedom of expression.

It is possible, of course, that this is not true of everybody. Expression need only be essential to these ends for some people in order to be vindicated as a freedom. Instrumental arguments are not to be faulted just because they do not always apply. Yet true as this is, one is bound to ask whether it can be a complete answer. Surely the concern about instrumental arguments here is that they are arguments of the wrong kind. The possibility of a more effective instrument is troubling, not because we suspect that some people might in fact be neglected by it, though that might well be true, but because we suspect that some aspect of the freedom's value would be overlooked, however well people were attended to by other means.

On the other hand, one of the attractions of accounts of freedom of expression that regard that freedom as intrinsically valuable, of which that based on creativity is one, is that they confirm our instinct that the freedom is fundamental and not contingent, so that the need for it cannot be removed by showing that the ends it serves could be served by other means. Nothing but a novel can supply the goodness of a novel, where that goodness is understood in non-instrumental terms; nothing can stand in for the goodness of a conversation, or for the excellence of art. And as I have emphasized, those forms of goodness inescapably have a creative aspect, such that a fundamental element of their character as goods is that they are creative explorations of the possibilities that the forms suggest. This does not mean, of course, that we are bound to commit ourselves to the creation and consumption of unlimited quantities of fiction, conversation or art. That would be a precious view of existence. The world is full of valuable things and we cannot pursue them all; our lives would almost certainly be the poorer if we did. It does mean, however, that these goods are irreplaceable, and that the creativity they embody, access to which is critical to the success of many people's lives, is of fundamental value.

But the intrinsic value of expression does something more than confirm that freedom of expression is fundamental rather than contingent, for in order to identify intrinsic value it is necessary to ascertain the particular kind of intrinsic value at stake in any given instance of expression. Indeed, it is slightly misleading to speak of the intrinsic value of expression, as I have done so far, as if there were only one, for in fact expression embodies and fulfils a number of intrinsic values. What matters here is that in fulfilling one of those it does not necessarily fulfil the others, so that a complete account of expression's intrinsic value must be a complete account of the intrinsic values that it serves. Put from the opposite perspective, a particular intrinsic value can explain the worth of a given instance of expression only if and to the extent that the instance embodies the intrinsic value in question. Where that value either does not include creativity at all, or assigns it a minor constitutive role, the explanation and support offered by the value to the given instance of expression, for example, to fundamentally creative enterprises such as the making of a sculpture or the writing of a novel, if any at all, is at best incomplete and, perhaps more important, of the wrong kind.

So, for example, political speech can be justified instrumentally by the fact that it furthers democracy, and justified intrinsically by the fact that it is constitutive of our condition as democratic citizens. But the intrinsic value of being a democratic citizen in most cases does little to explain or support the worth of making a sculpture or writing a novel. It is true that some works of art are demotic to the core, and others have demotic elements. But the worth of most works of art is unhappily explained and supported by the intrinsic value of democratic citizenship, in other words, is explained not merely inadequately but in what intuitively feels like the wrong way, a case of wrestling the artefact into the explanation. What can be said of democracy in this respect can also be said of the other intrinsic values generally acknowledged to be served by freedom of expression. If the arts are intrinsically valuable, then the intrinsic value in question must be one rather more apt to their condition, namely, a value based on creativity.

Freedom and Creation

Yet there is more. Not all intrinsically valuable goods depend upon freedom for their existence, although many of them have assumed a freedom-dependent form in modern Western society. The creative aspect of expression, however, and the value that it gives rise to, does depend upon at least some degree of freedom for its existence, for freedom is a basic constituent of creativity. It is not possible to express oneself creatively, in the manner I have described above, in the absence of the freedom to consider and pursue a reasonable range of expressive options, the very range that is secured by freedom of expression. To the extent that one's expressive options are determined in advance, one's pursuit of them, though possibly rewarding by reason of the representative value that they may give rise to, is not creative.

So novelists and other artists, if they are to be truly creative, must enjoy not merely the licence to engage in relatively unrestricted explorations of the form to which they have committed themselves, but a reasonably sympathetic reception from the audience to which their work is directed, sympathetic in the sense of being at least moderately open-minded about experimentation, and so not placing too much emphasis on whether the result is successful. If they do not enjoy such freedom, as many architects and some conceptual artists have not in Britain recently, they will have little opportunity to express themselves creatively, other than through the modest and interstitial development of accepted forms, an option that may well be unavailable to them.[25]

---

[25] I do not mean to deny that the modest and interstitial development of accepted forms may be genuinely creative. On the contrary, it is a mistake to identify creativity with dramatic developments of form, such as took place in Western art and literature in the first half of the twentieth century. Yet the practice of creativity is a social practice, which must be present in a culture in order to be successfully pursued there, so that while the modest and interstitial development of accepted forms might have been genuinely creative in traditional Japan, for example, where such development flourished as a social practice, it cannot be so in contemporary Western society, which identifies creativity with virtually unfettered individual expression.

On the other hand, freedom of expression clearly need not be unlimited in order to secure its creativity. Quite apart from the fact that not all expressive options are compatible with one another and so cannot co-exist, certain constraints upon the options available to us may actually help to shape our thought in fruitful ways, and so save us from much misguided exploration. Put simply, what constrains may also enable. Some such constraints are supplied by the background commitments of our culture, and so constitute an inescapable limitation and resource for creative expression. Other constraints, however, follow from the presence or absence in any given society of certain vital adjuncts to creativity, such as education, experience, and the availability of appropriate facilities and venues for the pursuit of expression. So a society that seeks to secure the creative dimension of expression, in order to secure freedom of expression fully, must teach people to write and to draw in ways that are suggestive rather than stipulative; must provide audiences and performers with spaces and other parameters for production within which it is understood and accepted that performances will be unconventional and ground-breaking; must in general secure a cultural climate that provides all people with the structure and the confidence to express themselves in ways that are unapproved in advance.

The connections between freedom and creativity are real, then, but they are also equivocal and incomplete. They are equivocal because creativity is in fact fuelled by a potent blend of freedom and constraint. Necessity, we say, is the mother of invention, and this is clearly often true, but the adage is misleading in its suggestion that invention can only be begotten of necessity (as is true of children and mothers) for necessity begets invention in its role as a constraint, a role that it shares with a great many other circumstances. The adage is further misleading, however, in its tacit neglect of invention's other parent, freedom. As I have noted, invention is quite impossible in circumstances where everything is necessary, for by its nature invention requires the freedom to imagine and to attempt. Invention becomes possible when necessity demands, and freedom permits, thoughts or actions that go beyond anything that has previously been contemplated by their creator.

The connections between freedom and creativity are incomplete, on the other hand, because freedom is not necessarily creative. It is not just that freedom may be used for worthless or even wrongful ends, for such ends may be creative and even valuable, as I have tried to show. It is that many instances of freedom simply offer no occasion for creativity. The ability to pick one pint of milk rather than another from the shelf of a supermarket is clearly an instance of freedom but just as clearly not an instance of creativity. There is nothing creative in choosing between objects that are equal in every way that might be relevant to one's choice, let alone between objects that are identical for all practical purposes, as are different pints of milk produced by the same dairy on the same day. And where freedom extends to a selection among goods that are incommensurable rather than identical, creativity becomes possible but is still not inevitable. There is nothing necessarily creative in the choice of an apple rather than an orange for one's lunch. Such choices become creative if and when they are, prospectively or retrospectively, made part of the story of a life, where the idea of a story is understood, not simply as a factual record, but as the narrative of a personal encounter with value, the development, recollection, and recounting of which has become a source of value in its own right. People typically aspire to be at least part authors of their own lives, and the metaphor of authorship is an apt one, not only because people often function creatively in making the decisions that govern the shape and direction of their lives, but also because in doing so they are very often conscious of the narrative implications of their decisions, sufficiently so as to take those implications to be elements of great weight in the assessment of their reasons for action. They decide the course of their life at any given moment in much the same way that authors do with respect to fictional lives, so as to develop the character, style, or plot of their particular life story. The point can be put from the opposite perspective: it is one of the truths of fiction that the stories it tells are true to life in their form, albeit false in their facts. But not all lives have stories to tell, sometimes because the people who lived them have had no opportunity to function creatively, and sometimes because those people have never been conscious of their lives as narratives. If and to the extent that either of these things is true, lives are not creative, however free they may otherwise be.

These qualifications suggest that the connections between freedom and creativity are easy to misrepresent or overstate. Nevertheless it remains true, and the qualifications simply confirm, that a full account of freedom of expression must be cast in creative as well as representative terms, for to fail to do so is to neglect much of the value of expression.

Protecting Creativity

It might be thought, however, that accounts of freedom of expression have quite rightly focused upon the representative aspect of expression as the aspect of expression that is most vulnerable to attack. It is difficult to suppress the freedom to engage in a creative endeavour until that endeavour yields a representation. It is only when creativity transcends the mind of the creator and becomes embodied in an artefact that it becomes capable of exercising influence in the world, and so becomes capable of being an object of respect for some and contempt for others. It is at that point that the creative aspect of expression is represented to the world, and it is that representation, rather than the creative endeavour embodied in it, that those with the power to do so are often concerned to suppress. That being the case, it might be thought that in protecting the representative aspect of expression, freedom of expression, protects precisely what needs to be protected. In doing so it protects creativity as well, without needing to say anything about it.

There are a number of reasons to doubt this justification of a purely representative analysis of freedom of expression and its value. The first is that it addresses freedom of expression as a right rather than as a freedom.[26] Freedoms may give rise to rights, and often do so, but we can only know whether they should do so, and in what form they should do so, once we have determined that they are justified as freedoms. It is not possible to justify a freedom by reference to the need for its protection as a right, for such protection can only be legitimately sought for what otherwise deserves to be free.[27] It follows, conversely, that the fact that the creative aspect of expression needs no protection beyond that offered by the protection of the representative aspect of expression, if fact it be, does not establish that such creativity warrants a freedom no greater than that required by the representation. It may well be the case that the right to freedom of expression is more limited than the freedom itself, and that among the things that the right properly neglects are certain creative dimensions of expression. If that is true, then we have reason to be concerned about aspects of freedom of expression that are not protected as a right, including creativity.

Secondly, even were the argument from protection a sound one, it is far from clear that creativity of expression is not in need of a species of protection that is distinct from and perhaps greater than that offered by the protection of representation. One of the most common reasons for the censorship of expression is a distaste for independence of thought, including independence of thought about expression. Very often censorship seeks to enforce conformity not only in what is said but in how it is said. Part of its purpose, in other words, is to stifle aesthetic creativity. Both Nazi Germany and the Soviet Union extended the reach of their ideology to the realm of aesthetics, and condemned as degenerate any expression that failed to conform to official aesthetic doctrine. That doctrine was particularly hostile to innovative forms of expression. Similar views were taken in Britain under the Commonwealth and following the Revolution of 1688. Art for art's sake, rather than for the sake of God, was condemned not simply because it was pleasurable, but because it took something other than God's will to be of intrinsic value. Could independence of thought about expression have been secured under such regimes had they, however implausibly, recognized a right to freedom of expression conceived in representative terms?

Perhaps, but not necessarily so. If and to the extent that the representative case for freedom of expression depends upon instrumental arguments, as it very often does, it offers no protection to forms of expression that cannot be defended in instrumental terms, as is the case with many forms of apparently wilful creativity. Creative attempts to extend the boundaries of a form of expression purely for

[26] Freedom may be, and often is, protected by means other than a right. I have confined my consideration of the implications of protection to the case of rights only because of the familiarity and centrality of rights as a method of protecting freedom in Western cultures. The points made can be applied *mutatis mutandis* to other methods of protection.

[27] I should emphasize that I am speaking here of justifications of freedom of expression as a whole, not of the justification of individual exercises of that freedom, which very often do not deserve to be free, but which it is the purpose of a right to freedom to protect nevertheless.

the sake of that form are only rarely defensible in terms of ends other than themselves.[28] It is notable in this regard that opponents of repressive regimes tend to pursue freedom of expression for the sake of democracy, or truth, or some such earnest good, and, like the despots they oppose, take a dim view of those who seek to defend art for art's sake. These attitudes suggest that such people do not regard the protection of aesthetic creativity as a logical concomitant of the protection of the right to represent certain views in public.

Even if this line of argument is mistaken, however, so that the creative aspect of expression is fully protected in the protection of representation, the claims of creative expression must at least strengthen what can be said for expression in purely representative terms, and so must strengthen the claims of freedom of expression in any setting where the overall value of that freedom is balanced against other values, such as equality, as it often is. This possibility is particularly significant in those legal regimes that give special weight to the protection of instances of expression that are at the core rather than the periphery of the right, in the sense of being central rather than marginal to the values for the sake of which the freedom was guaranteed. Even if instances of creativity fall within the protection offered to representations, they may serve the value of representation only weakly. Recognition of the role played by the value of creativity in justifying freedom of expression would move such instances from the periphery to the core of the right. In particular, artistic speech, which has long been regarded as marginal to prevailing justifications for freedom of expression, might come to occupy a central place in the protection of expression.

---

[28] An historical example of such a defence is the use said to have been made of Abstract Expressionism for propaganda purposes in the Cold War, when the creative inventiveness embodied in that school of painting was celebrated and promoted internationally in order to suggest the boundless possibilities of American freedom in other respects.

2

(In My) Solitude*

In the voice of Billie Holiday, solitude is an agonizing condition, haunted by memory and awareness of loss. To be solitary as she expresses it is to be bereft, deprived of the companionship and support that make life worth living. But is Holiday giving voice to a general truth here, or does her exquisite rendering of Ellington's song reveal, in herself or in her subject, a sensibility that has been distorted by dependency? Is solitude necessarily a wholly negative state of being? Or is there more to the condition than the words of her song, if taken on their own, would allow? Might it not have certain possibilities to offer, including, perhaps, the possibility of the very sensibility that Holiday gives voice to so eloquently, a sensibility that in its power to express loss transforms the circumstance that inspired it and subverts the state of mind that it describes? After all, the song can only be believed if we can imagine the singer in the condition of which she is singing, and we can only do that if we can imagine that someone in such a condition could create such art, not in spite of her experience, for that would require distance, but in and through it. And if some such good is discoverable in the experience of solitude, is it the sort of good that is discoverable in various forms of suffering (as endurance and courage are, and some romantic art is said to be), and thus a good that might reasonably be looked for in solitude as a condition of suffering, or is it a good that is discoverable in the very fabric of solitude itself, the experience of relative isolation, and thus a good that might be pursued without embracing suffering?

Questions like these, it seems to me, are questions about privacy and its value. The experience of privacy, by an individual, by a couple, by a family, by a community, by a tribe, or by a nation, is the experience of solitude (or isolation, as it is sometimes called),[1] and the benefits and burdens that it makes possible are the benefits and burdens of solitude. If we want to know why privacy matters, what it might have to offer and what that might cost, we need to grasp the implications of solitude. Or so it seems to me. Most commentators see privacy as an aspect

---

* The phrase is from 'Solitude', written by Ellington, DeLange and Mills in 1934, as performed by Billie Holiday with Eddie Heywood and Orchestra in 1941.

[1] I take the terms solitude and isolation to be roughly synonymous, though I recognize that solitude is more often applied to the experience of individuals, and that isolation is perhaps more susceptible to negative evaluation.

of liberty, and more precisely, as that aspect of our liberty that enables each one of us to form and pursue intimate relationships with other human beings. In my view intimacy is but one aspect of privacy, and while privacy must keep company with liberty in order to have special value, it is also in tension with it.

Privacy and Intimacy

Julie Inness has made a compact and graceful case for the claim that privacy is a matter of intimacy rather than isolation.[2] Her case is an attractive one, for it reconciles a number of popular and plausible intuitions as to the meaning and value of privacy. As Inness sees it, privacy is inherently valuable because it offers us control over the most intimate aspects of our lives, intimate not because they involve isolation from others, but because they involve loving, caring and liking. Conduct is intimate, in other words, because it expresses these emotions,[3] and only secondarily and consequently because of what it involves or where it takes place. Paradoxical as it may seem, it is perfectly possible to exercise one's privacy in public, because it is perfectly possible to be intimate in public, by kissing or holding hands, for example. It is simply a matter of convention, Inness explains, that certain physical spaces, such as the home, are regarded as the appropriate theatres for the expression of certain forms of intimacy, and so are regarded as private to that extent. Privacy is the word we use to describe control of our intimate relations. Privacy is valuable because control of those relations is a central and distinctive feature of our personal autonomy, distinctive in that it embodies an aspect of autonomy that is inexpressible through purely rational choice.[4] It follows, Inness concludes, that to protect privacy is to show respect for people as creatures who are emotionally as well as rationally autonomous.

It would be difficult to dispute the essence of Inness's account, for intimacy is surely at the heart of most people's experience of privacy. To be private, on any reasonable view, is to establish a degree of seclusion from the world. The question is, what degree? Must the seclusion be absolute? Do people know privacy only in those moments when they are utterly alone? If so, would it not follow that privacy is a condition generally to be regretted? Human experience

---

[2] JC Inness, *Privacy, Intimacy, and Isolation* (1992).

[3] It may be more accurate to describe loving, caring and liking as attitudes or dispositions: cf H Frankfurt, 'On Caring' in *Necessity, Volition and Love* (1999) and M Nussbaum, *Upheavals of Thought* (2001). However, nothing in this chapter turns on the correctness of the description and that being the case, it seems to me both simpler and more courteous to use Inness's own description in considering her work.

[4] Unlike Inness, I believe that emotions are open to rational evaluation, and so are among the reasons we have to respect personal autonomy. I here treat emotion as independent of reason in order to be true to Inness's argument.

seems to contradict such conclusions. Privacy is not the preserve of hermits. For most people, privacy is a matter of restricting the potential range of one's human contacts, so as to form deeper connections with a more limited number of people, people such as spouses, lovers, and children. If one concludes from this, as Inness does, that privacy, and the seclusion it offers, is a shared experience as opposed to an individual one, and further, that privacy is valuable in itself, then one is more or less bound to conclude that privacy is a matter of intimacy, and that intimacy in turn is a matter of such intrinsically valuable and shared activities as loving, caring and liking.

1. The Scope of Privacy: Three Doubts

All this is sensible enough as far as it goes, but that is not very far. The difficulty with Inness's account, it seems to me, stems from its exclusivity. To begin with the most obvious example, it is one thing to say that there is more to privacy than individual solitude, and quite another to offer an explanation of privacy that makes it impossible to be private (or as Inness would put it, to experience privacy) except in company.[5] It is not just that we normally use the idea of privacy more broadly, so as to encompass the experience of individual solitude, though that is important. Rather, it is that one of the things that privacy has to offer us is a refuge from relationships, including relationships of intimacy. When Virginia Woolf emphasized the importance to a woman of a room of her own, she emphasized the need for some degree of refuge even, perhaps particularly, from those we love. Intimate relationships are famously oppressive when they offer few or no resources, and few or no occasions, for the development of individual personality. This is as true of the relationship between children and parents as it is of spousal relationships, be they male, female or heterosexual, although it is most familiar perhaps when intimacy is insisted upon by a man at the expense of a woman's personality.

Less obviously, Inness's account is unpersuasive in its rejection of the possibility that privacy may be valuable for reasons other than intimacy, where intimacy means loving, caring and liking. To put it in Inness's own terms, is there any reason to believe that the meaning and value of privacy are confined to matters of intimacy? Once again, human experience suggests otherwise. The point is ultimately a general one, and will need to be addressed as such, but it can be approached through the examples of shared ideas and activities. One

---

[5] Inness maintains that a distinction must be drawn between privacy and what is private. Privacy is a normative concept, she claims, while private is not. Indeed she goes further. 'In fact, I question whether the adjectival uses of "private" are convertible into the nominal form "privacy"': *Privacy, Intimacy, and Isolation*, 14, n 10. I assume that Inness is seeking here to put some distance between her endorsement of privacy, as she understands it, and an endorsement of the private realm, as feminists understand and object to it. While I do not agree that the distinction can be drawn in the way that she describes, I will try to observe it when speaking of her work.

of the more familiar benefits of privacy is the opportunity it offers for the sharing of confidences. People use privacy to share ideas of various kinds, and correspondingly, to keep those ideas from others, without necessarily becoming intimate with their confidant(e). Both the ideas and the relationship may be political, for example, or scientific, and so may well involve no loving, caring or liking. Indeed, in the view of certain political and scientific organizations, any development of intimacy in the relationships among their members is to be deplored, on the ground that intimacy tends to undermine the integrity of the ideas and commitments that the establishment of the organization as an exclusive (and to that extent confidential) body was supposed to protect. The presence of emotion in such settings is thought to make for bad politics and bad science, and more to the point, to be a misuse of the confidential relationship that the organization embodies.

Nor are confidences the only things that privacy offers people the opportunity to share, or sharing the only relation they may bear to them. On the contrary. People seek privacy in order to pursue activities of many different kinds, not so much as a way of developing or maintaining relationships of intimacy among themselves, though those may sometimes follow, but as a way of avoiding the scrutiny and judgment of others, to whom their activities may be alien, misguided, or even wrong. Such seekers of privacy are sometimes branded as misfits (where their goals are misguided) and criminals (where their goals are wrong), but such branding assumes that the exercise of public scrutiny and judgment is always valuable, and so overlooks the extent to which the pursuit of human creativity, and the diversity of value that it gives rise to, depends upon endeavours that at their outset give every appearance of being foolish or wrong, and may well turn out to be so in fact. Among other things, privacy protects people from the possibility of embarrassment or condemnation for what they do or seek to do. That protection may not always be warranted, but where it is warranted it forms part of the value of privacy. The isolating shield of privacy enables people to develop and exchange ideas, or to foster and share activities, that the presence or even awareness of other people might stifle. For better and for worse, then, privacy is sponsor and guardian to the creative and the subversive.

The claim here can be seen as a development of the idea of the importance of a room of one's own, now applied to shared rather than individual circumstances. Not only is there more to privacy and its value than intimate relationships allow, but there is more to the privacy of intimate relationships, and to their value, than intimacy allows. This in turn suggests a further and final extension of the idea of a room of one's own. I have emphasized so far that in equating privacy with intimacy Inness makes it impossible to experience privacy except in company, and for any purpose other than intimacy. But her focus on intimacy also makes it impossible to experience privacy (for whatever purpose) in any company except that of intimates. Yet there is no obvious reason why the value of a room of one's own should not be realized by any body of people that is capable of functioning as one, in any space that can be described as its own, for whatever purpose and in whatever respect, and whether the body sees itself that way or not. This is clearly not what Woolf had in mind, but the power of her idea, and the ground of its truth, is that it extends to women the benefit of a more general insight as to the creation and realization of value.[6] In this regard Inness grasps more than she herself appears to recognize. Woolf is right to see the value in isolation, in the experience of one person apart from all others, and Inness is wrong to deny that. But Inness in turn is right to see that privacy can be a shared experience, and wrong to restrict that insight to the shared experience embodied in relationships of intimacy. The value of privacy can be realized in many forms of relationship, some of them compact and simple, others extended and complex.

The reason is relatively straightforward. Certain goods, most obviously those that a writer pursues, and so perhaps those that Woolf had uppermost in her mind, depend for their realization, at least in part, on individual endeavour. It is of course possible to write collectively, and often rewarding to do so, but not everything can be written that way, and if it could it would be written differently, and would have a different value. Yet most goods either constitute or rely upon social forms and practices, and so depend for their realization, at least in part, on collective endeavour. Even poetry, for example, one of the purest expressions of individual consciousness and endeavour, is a recognized social form in itself and relies upon structures that are intelligible and accessible to its audience, be they sonnet forms or free verse. Poetry also depends upon a literary culture, in the form of publishers, reviewers, booksellers and readers, for the achievement of its purpose, and full realization of its value.

Woolf's now-famous and familiar perception was that creative endeavour, and the values it sustains, requires privacy. As it happens, when she spoke of those things she had individual creativity in mind, and so spoke specifically of the connections between individual creativity and privacy, between the capacity to think for oneself and possession of a room of one's own. Inness's perception, though this is not the way she would put it herself, is that the truth of Woolf's conclusion is a function, not of individuality, but of value. As she sees it, our respect for privacy is predicated on its value (which Inness believes that individual privacy typically lacks) and its sharing (which individual privacy is by definition incapable of). But if Inness is correct in this analysis she has indeed grasped more than she allows, as I suggested above, for there is then no reason to believe that the value of privacy, and the possibilities for its sharing, are confined to

---

[6] Woolf herself makes clear that the idea of a room of one's own is not to be taken literally, as a reference to a physical space. It is no more than a metaphor for the circumstances of independent thought: '. . . five hundred a year stands for the power to contemplate . . . a lock on the door means the power to think for oneself.': *A Room of One's Own* (1967) 160. It follows that as our understanding of the circumstances of independent thought develops, so as to embrace, for example, the various social dimensions of creativity, so too must our understanding of its requirements, physical and otherwise.

matters of intimacy, as she claims. On the contrary, there is every reason to think that they extend to other values, other endeavours, and other persons. If the value of privacy is embodied in social forms and practices that are sustained by collective endeavour, then it is almost certain to be found in social forms and practices other than those of intimacy, and to be sustained by the endeavours of collectivities other than an intimate relationship.

2. Intimacy and Isolation

As I have already suggested, there is a general concern underlying and underpinning these three doubts about the claim that privacy is a matter of intimacy, and that is that the identification of privacy with control of one's intimate relations is ultimately ambiguous about the meaning of privacy and the source of its value. The reason is that the claim leaves unanswered the question of whether intimacy, understood as loving, caring and liking, requires isolation, and if so, why. Without some connection to isolation the claim is difficult to understand as a claim about privacy at all. On the other hand, once connected to isolation, privacy appears to have implications that extend well beyond matters of intimacy.

One possibility, of course, is that there is simply no connection between privacy and isolation, whatever common parlance may suggest. On the face of it, this is just the view that Inness takes, for she denies that matters of privacy, as she explains them, are the same thing as private matters.[7] The question is whether her denial can be sustained, and if so, in what way. According to Inness, things become matters of privacy when they involve control of our intimate relations, intimate in the sense of engaging the emotions of loving, caring and liking. Put simply, privacy is the name we give, or at least ought to give, to emotional autonomy. That form of autonomy may involve isolation, but it need not do so. We enjoy privacy whenever we are intimate, and we are intimate when we control our emotional relations, wherever that may take place.

There is clearly some truth in this suggestion, and it seems to me that the force of that truth is the source of much of the attractiveness of Inness's account. When Woolf emphasized how important it is to a writer to have a room of her own, she emphasized the vital role that privacy plays in the power to think for oneself. Just what that role is, and what connections there are between privacy and autonomy are questions to be taken up in the next section. What matters here, as Woolf's own image may suggest, is that in itself the appeal to autonomy leaves the basic question of privacy's meaning and value unanswered, the ambiguity unresolved. Put in terms of autonomy (the concern of the next section), we still need to know whether and why the power to think for oneself, or to feel for oneself, on whatever matter, requires isolation, in the form of a room of one's own or otherwise. Put in terms of intimacy (the present concern), we need to know

---

[7] See n 3 for an explanation of this distinction as Inness sees it.

whether and why the development and expression of the particular emotions of loving, caring, and liking require isolation.

Inness has two related suggestions to offer in this regard. On the one hand she maintains that intimacy does not in fact require isolation. It is on this basis that she feels able to disclaim the connection between matters of privacy, as she understands them, in terms of intimacy, and private matters, which involve isolation. In certain settings, Inness appears to be right in this. Public expressions of intimacy are not only intelligible, but extremely common, and the power to engage in them is clearly an important aspect of personal autonomy, as it is easy to see when one thinks of those people whose expressions of intimacy are publicly discouraged or marginalized: young adolescents, gays and lesbians, interracial couples, and the elderly. Expressions of intimacy by people such as these are no less matters of privacy because they take place, or more typically fail to take place, in a public forum.

Inness follows and sustains this claim with a second suggestion, that the connections between privacy, understood to mean control of the intimate relations of loving, caring and liking, and isolation are secondary and consequent. In other words, it is the presence of the emotions of loving, caring and liking, and not the fact of isolation, that makes control of these relations a private matter. And while loving, caring and liking are often present in circumstances of isolation, there is no necessary connection between them and private spaces. It is simply a matter of prevailing convention that certain settings are regarded as appropriate for the expression of these emotions and others are not. Inness concludes that isolation is neither the meaning of privacy nor a necessary consequence of it.

But what, then, is the prevailing convention, which connects the exercise of privacy and certain private spaces, contingent upon? Is it merely arbitrary? How far could it be otherwise? On the one hand it seems implausible that human beings could successfully pursue their intimate relations entirely in public, or that if they could the relations would bear the same meaning and have the same value, and would still be regarded as matters of privacy. But even were such an outcome possible it would not in itself establish the absence of any connection between intimacy and isolation. On the contrary. As the familiar image of people who find themselves alone in a crowd suggests, it is perfectly possible not only to be intimate in public, as Inness rightly recognizes, but also to be isolated there. Sometimes this is a matter of choice, sometimes not. Sometimes a person discovers, to his or her regret, that he or she is at odds with his or her companions, alienated from their emotions, commitments, or activities. At other times people have eyes only for each other, and so are wilfully, blissfully oblivious to their surroundings, and to the expectations and responsibilities that those surroundings give rise to.

Only the second of these situations, of course, involves loving, caring and liking, and so only it would be understood by Inness to involve intimacy, and hence privacy. And in that situation, it might be thought, while people are intimate in public they are not isolated, just because they have one another. Yet it remains a question whether their intimacy, and hence their privacy, flows from the loving, caring and liking they feel for one another, or from the isolation that they have established from their surroundings. Is it their loving that makes them intimate, or their obliviousness? More profoundly, does the expression of loving, caring and liking in such a situation, by its very nature, involve a degree of exclusion, so as to make such people intimate by making them oblivious? Is this what makes their behaviour intelligible as an instance of privacy? Not all loving, caring and liking takes this form, of course, for some kinds of loving are extroverted and inclusive. People are sometimes asked, however idealistically, to love everyone as their brother. But is it the case that what makes a particular instance of loving, caring and liking an expression of intimacy is the degree of isolation from other human beings that it involves? Could one really love everyone as one's brother (or sister), and if one could, would the resulting relationship be one of intimacy?

Most of us are familiar with the experience of finding ourselves, awkwardly and uncomfortably, in the company of lovers who wish to express their love for one another. Some lovers, though not enough of them, are familiar with the etiquette attending the expression of intimacy in the company of a third person who is not a party to that intimacy. Intimacy in the presence of such a person is normally considered to be impolite, or at least insensitive, because it is alienating to someone to whom one owes the duties of a companion (of whatever degree), and it is alienating because it is isolating and excluding. Those who express their intimacy in public in any extended manner, even in a manner that is conventionally regarded as publicly acceptable, thereby make themselves oblivious to the claims of those whose company they are in. They do this because it enables them to focus more closely and attentively on themselves. Of course, if a number of people find themselves excluded in this way, they may be able to form an intimate circle of their own, with an attendant and correlative degree of isolation from the lovers, so that two groups of intimates become mutually excluding without either feeling excluded. If only one person is excluded by the lovers, however, he or she will feel awkward and uncomfortable, because he or she will rightly feel rejected by the isolation of their intimacy and its exclusion of the social responsibilities they owe to him or her.

Not all loving, caring and liking has these consequences, as I have already noted, but that is because not all loving, caring and liking involves intimacy. Love need not be intimate, even when it involves a lover, and some forms of love, such as those felt by friends for one another, might be marred by intimacy. Again the experience is familiar to most. When one attends a leaving reception for a well liked colleague, or takes part in an outing with members of one's extended family, or goes nightclubbing with friends or with a lover, one acts in a manner that expresses and embodies the emotions of loving, caring or liking without necessarily being intimate. Occasions such as these lack the flavour of intimacy, and hence lack the flavour of privacy, precisely because and to the extent that they involve no isolation, either from those who are present but unloved, be they waiters at the leaving reception, other families on similar outings, or other dancers at the nightclub, or from those who are present and loved but not in any focused, exclusive manner (in this setting, at least), be they colleagues, extended family members, friends or lovers.

If these observations are correct then Inness's explanation of privacy as control of the intimate relations of loving, caring and liking raises a false contrast between isolation and intimacy. Intimacy is in truth a function of isolation in some plane, be it physical, psychological, intellectual or emotional. In itself, of course, isolation does not yield intimacy, though it very often raises the question of it, as all those who have experienced the awkwardness of finding themselves confined at close quarters with a stranger, however briefly, will know.[8] It is the combination of relative isolation and feelings of loving, caring and liking that makes a situation one of intimacy. It follows that, despite its denials, Inness's explanation of privacy in terms of intimacy obtains its persuasiveness from the connections, silently observed by both writer and reader (albeit not necessarily in the same way), between intimacy and isolation. Far from being secondary, consequential and arbitrary, as Inness claims, these connections are in fact crucial to the ability to see her account as an account of privacy at all.

3. The Value and Disvalue of Privacy

But if intimacy is constituted, at least in part, by isolation, then it seems probable that other good things may also flow from isolation, as Virginia Woolf claimed with respect to individual creativity and possession of a room of one's own, and as the reach of her argument suggests may be true with respect to other values, other goods, other people, and other forms of isolation. How far this is true is a question that will be taken up later in this chapter. What matters at this stage, because it shapes the scope of further inquiry, is that once it is recognized that privacy is sustained by value, specifically the value of isolation, the question arises whether privacy is necessarily valuable. Inness claims that it is, partly because we generally think of privacy as a condition to be sought rather than avoided,

---

[8] Being confined at close quarters with a stranger raises the question of intimacy if and to the extent that it raises the possibility of a relationship of loving, caring or liking the expression of which depends upon that isolation. Expressed diagrammatically, the realm of intimacy is the field in which the separate fields of isolation and of loving, caring and liking overlap. In practice, the more that other people are present, and the more of them, the less plausible intimacy becomes, simply because of the difficulty in achieving isolation in such circumstances, a difficulty that is frequently overcome by young lovers but that is otherwise an effective bar to intimacy. On the other hand, the less that other people are present, the more plausible intimacy becomes. So the physical proximity of a stranger is more likely to raise the question of intimacy in a lift than on a bus. Of course, the bare implications of physical proximity can be altered by the conduct of the parties, so as to remove the question of intimacy in the lift and raise it on the bus.

and partly because her exploration of the nature of intimacy makes it clear that privacy, at least when understood in terms of intimacy, is intrinsically valuable and not merely instrumentally so. Yet are these claims true? Does analysis not reveal that privacy is a condition that may be used for either good or ill? Surely bad things can flow from it as well as good, as feminists have emphasized, and as too many know to their cost. Does ordinary language not imply as much?

To begin with the question of language, Inness is quite right to notice that we typically speak of privacy in positive terms but too quick, it seems to me, to conclude from this that privacy is necessarily valuable. Not only is it perfectly possible, and reasonably common, to speak of privacy in negative terms, but there are reasons for the prevailing tendency to speak in positive terms other than the necessity of privacy's value. Human beings now live, and may always have lived, in crowded worlds. In the modern age, that crowd is composed of strangers; in aboriginal communities, past and present, it has been composed of kith and kin. Privacy offers relief from such crowding, and for that reason is often spoken of in positive terms. But while crowding may be the norm and isolation the exception, the experience of isolation is common enough to have generated its own, negative idiom, so that we speak of the burden of solitude as readily as we speak of its benefit. Loneliness is a recurring motif in much of our cultural expression, whether the loneliness is experienced by an individual or by a group, and whether it arises through social, physical, intellectual, spiritual, or some other form of isolation. To return to the imagery with which I began, it was the sorrow of loneliness that Billie Holiday sang of, whatever else she may have implied to the contrary through the power of her artistic achievement.

Secondly, while Inness is quite right, it seems to me, to believe that privacy is intrinsically valuable, if for no other reason than that it helps constitute intimacy, and so makes it possible, she is wrong to conclude from this fact that privacy is necessarily valuable. The intrinsic and the necessary are not to be equated here. What is necessarily valuable may indeed be intrinsically so (since it is difficult to imagine something that is necessarily instrumentally valuable) but what is intrinsically valuable is not necessarily so. The reason is that a good may be intrinsically valuable only as and when it is constitutive of another intrinsically valuable good, as privacy is constitutive of intimacy and possibly constitutive of such other intrinsically valuable goods as the individual creativity Virginia Woolf linked to a room of one's own. Strength and cleverness, for example, are intrinsically valuable qualities when they are properly deployed, so as to be constitutive of other intrinsically valuable human goods, but they are not necessarily valuable, as the sorry history of their many abuses makes clear. When constitutive of an intrinsically valuable good privacy is intrinsically valuable, as Inness emphasizes, but it does not follow that privacy is necessarily valuable, for the simple reason that while privacy is sometimes constitutive of an intrinsically valuable good, it is not always so.

If privacy is not necessarily valuable and so has potentially negative implications, because one can always imagine it going awry, an account of privacy
must include an account of those implications and the relation, if any, that they
bear to the value of privacy. It seems clear that the negative implications of
privacy extend not only to the various forms of isolation that Inness seeks to
distance privacy from but also, more disquietingly and more significantly, to the
very forms of intimacy she seeks to commend. As Inness must be fully aware,
feminists have long emphasized the oppressiveness of much that takes place in
the private and intimate realms of family life. Inness plainly hopes to avoid
endorsing that oppressiveness in her endorsement of privacy as intrinsically and
necessarily valuable by basing her account of privacy on the emotions of loving,
caring, and liking, rather than on the inviolability of a private space, such as
the family home. Yet the feminist challenge runs deeper than this hope suggests,
for its concern is not merely with private spaces but, more profoundly, with
the implications of intimacy itself, and hence with the correctness of Inness's
fundamental assumption that the emotional relations of loving, caring and liking
are necessarily valuable, whether because they are intrinsically valuable or otherwise. Might intimacy not be stifling? Does family life not provide bountiful
evidence of its capacity to be so? Private spaces are theatres for paternalism as
well as brutality, and while brutality is incompatible with loving, caring and
liking relationships (special, and quite possibly spurious, cases such as sado-
masochism and tough love aside) paternalism clearly is not. Over-protection of
one's intimates is sometimes insincere and sinister, but it can be just as oppressive
when it is heartfelt and well meaning. And further, moving away from the realm
of intimacy, might recognition of the negative aspects of privacy not be necessary
to the recognition of certain positive aspects that the intimacy account of privacy
neglects? If, like Inness, we are unwilling to acknowledge the value to be found
in individual solitude, because of our awareness of the harm it can cause, and
so refuse to include such solitude in our understanding of privacy, as part of
an attempt to see privacy as necessarily valuable, then we will be unable to see
privacy as Woolf asks us to, as a vital element in the promotion and realization
of individual creativity.

4. Three Concluding Observations

For better and for worse, privacy must mean more than control of one's intimate
relations. Yet though Inness is wrong to deny this she has achieved much in her
exploration of the connections between privacy and intimacy. In the face of a
widespread prevailing tendency to identify privacy and individual solitude she
has shown that privacy has a role to play in social settings, those characterized
by relations of intimacy, and by extension, and despite herself, has shown that
isolation can be experienced in company, for good and for ill. In this respect
her account is incomplete rather than mistaken. Where the account errs, in

my view, is in the exclusivity of its focus on intimacy, at the expense of any acknowledgement of the underlying and sustaining fact of isolation that intimacy implies, and which makes any particular instance of a loving, caring or liking relationship a matter of intimacy.

Inness's second achievement, once again born of her focus on the value of intimacy, is to distinguish privacy from the physical spaces, such as the family home, in which it is typically pursued. According to Inness, the connections between privacy and such spaces are entirely consequent upon the fact that prevailing social convention has identified those spaces as appropriate for the expression of intimacy. Some may believe that we express intimacy in those spaces because they are private, but in fact they are private because and to the extent that we express intimacy there. Or so Inness believes. As I have already indicated, I think it is a mistake to see these connections as conventional rather than informed by the possibility and value of isolation. Nevertheless Inness has performed a great service in undermining the easy identification of privacy with physical spaces such as the home. It is clear from her account that a home may or may not be private depending on what is taking place there. If matters of intimacy are not at stake (unlikely as that may seem) then a privacy claim cannot be maintained. It is just as clear from her account that public spaces may be private on a similar basis, namely, if and to the extent that the value of privacy (which for Inness means the value of intimacy) is being pursued there. When people seek to express feelings of loving, caring and liking for one another in public, in a manner that focuses on themselves to the exclusion of others, they seek privacy in the form of intimacy.

In demonstrating these disconnections between privacy, in the form of intimacy, and private spaces Inness has shown that privacy secures a value, not a physical space, and so has shown, again by extension and despite herself, that if privacy is a matter of isolation, then the value of isolation may well be absent in a private space (if one's existence in that space is dominated by the presence of others, for example) and present in a public space. The reason is that the values of intimacy and isolation exist, and may be pursued, in dimensions other than that of physical space, so that one may be private in public spaces and public in private spaces if one is pursuing privacy in some dimension other than the physical.

The final, perhaps less distinctive but just as important feature of Inness's account is that her attempt to sever privacy and isolation leads her not only to focus on intimacy, and hence to focus on the emotions of loving, caring and liking, but to endorse the idea that privacy implies *control* of such emotions. Privacy, as she sees it, is ultimately a question of autonomy, and its distinctive contribution to our moral life is to secure our emotional autonomy, and in doing so to supplement those other fundamental freedoms that secure what she describes as our rational autonomy. This claim, it will be clear, is a local, focused version of the well known general claim that privacy is a matter of liberty.

Privacy and Liberty

When I was young, the Minister of Justice introduced a bill that, among other things, reformed the criminal law so as to permit homosexual conduct between consenting adults, with the words 'the state has no place in the bedrooms of the nation'.[9] In doing so he tied liberty to privacy (whether understood as intimacy or isolation) in a way that, however rhetorically effective, has long troubled proponents of both values. The particular phrasing may have been Trudeau's, but the linkage was not. When John Stuart Mill insisted that the only ground for restraining the liberty of any person is to prevent harm to others,[10] he suggested to some that people should be free to do whatever they want as long as they do it in private, for what they do in private, whether done alone or in the company of consenting adults, harms only themselves, not others. The logic presumably runs something like this. The consent of those involved in a particular course of conduct, when coupled with the isolation that privacy provides them from those who do not consent, ensures that any harm done is not done to others. Although others are involved in the conduct, their consent makes any harm to them tantamount to self-inflicted. And the others who are *not* involved in the conduct clearly cannot be *directly* harmed by it, for the scope of privacy, which is here understood to mean what cannot be seen, heard, or otherwise sensed, is by definition the scope of what does not *directly* affect (and so harm) others. And where harm is not directly caused liberty may not be restrained, for, according to Mill, the only harm to others for which people can rightly be held accountable is direct harm. Reasoning along these lines makes the realm of liberty coextensive with the realm of privacy. Sexual practices of whatever kind should be free from state regulation just because they take place in the privacy of the bedroom.

Many have objected to this linkage between liberty and privacy on the basis that it does a disservice to liberty. They point out that freedom of sexual expression surely should not be confined to the bedroom, for that is merely the freedom of the closet, and as such is famously inadequate as an account of sexual liberty. Many valuable activities, access to which is a critical element in the well-being of certain people, are constituted by or dependent upon social practices, and many, perhaps most, of those social practices by their nature take place in public. It follows that any sound account of liberty must understand liberty to embrace the freedom to act collectively and in public. So homosexuals,

[9] Pierre Trudeau, 22 December 1967.
[10] JS Mill, 'On Liberty', *Utilitarianism, On Liberty, and Essay on Bentham*, (ed) M Warnock (1962) 135: 'The object of this Essay is to assert one very simple principle. . . . That principle is, that the sole end for which mankind are warranted, individually or collectively, in interfering with the liberty of action of any of their number, is self-protection. That the only purpose for which power can be rightfully exercised over any member of a civilised community, against his will, is to prevent harm to others.'

like heterosexuals, should be free to pursue their sexuality not merely in the bedroom, but in public, and through public institutions, so that they are able to express their relationship in the kinds of gestures that are characteristic of and appropriate to public venues, and to fulfil and secure that relationship through public institutions, from marriage to pensions.[11] At least, that is the form that sexual freedom should take on the assumption, which may or may not be correct, that the distinctive value of those gestures and institutions is, broadly speaking, accessible to homosexuals, given the particular character of their sexuality (with or without a degree of adaptation), and further, is something that at least some homosexuals need access to in order to achieve well-being.[12]

The question that matters here, however, is whether the linkage between liberty and privacy also does a disservice to privacy. Does privacy (whether understood as intimacy or isolation) mean only liberty? Is it just the name we give to our autonomy or to some aspect of it? If there is more to liberty than privacy is there also more to privacy than liberty? Could it be the case that liberty and privacy are separate but interdependent conditions, so that some of the value of liberty depends on privacy and some of the value of privacy depends on liberty? If so, what more might there be to privacy than liberty, and what might be its value? This would be to confirm the linkage between liberty and privacy but put it on a new footing, one that rejects any ready identification of the two conditions and their value, either partial or complete.

1. Beyond Identification

One good way to discover whether there is more to privacy than liberty is to explore the implications of understanding privacy wholly in terms of liberty. If privacy were but a species of liberty we would need to know what it is that characterizes the species. Is it possible to identify a sense of privacy substantial enough to explain the role played by privacy in sustaining liberty, yet not so substantial as to endow privacy with implications that extend beyond liberty? Plainly, the sense of privacy we are looking for must be something more than an arbitrary classification of liberties. At the same time it must be something less than an independent condition with independent value if it is to be but a species of liberty. Is it possible to avoid these alternatives without begging the question? It seems to me that it is not, as an examination of two of the most familiar candidates for such an understanding of privacy makes clear. Each purports to

---

[11] As the example shows, privacy (understood as isolation) is fundamentally (and definitionally) a question of freedom *from* influence, whereas participation in the corresponding public realm is, just as fundamentally and definitionally, a question of the freedom *to* participate in institutions and practices that are essential to one's well-being.

[12] Any linkage that secures the liberty of what takes place in private is also objected to by feminists, on the basis that the private should not be entirely free, given that much of what takes place there causes harm.

describe privacy as a species of liberty, yet does so in a way that ultimately obscures rather than illuminates the very real connections between privacy and liberty.

Many think, however plausibly, that privacy is merely the name we give to that aspect of liberty that affects the individual alone. Clearly this linkage of privacy and individual liberty needs some refinement if it is not to embrace all liberty and so return us to the bare equation of liberty and privacy that was set aside above as a disservice to liberty, and possibly privacy as well. Liberty can only ever be enjoyed by individual people, whether acting singly or in combination, and so can always be legitimately described as individual liberty. If individuality is to characterize a particular species of liberty, and so be distinguished from the individual person, who may enjoy liberty in various different capacities, it must be understood as a capacity itself. Yet once that is done, the reference to individuality either is just that, and so tells us nothing about privacy, or is a reference to an understanding of privacy that it does not explain, so leaving the meaning and value of privacy obscure. What is the connection between individuality and privacy? If privacy is simply a matter of individuality then privacy has no power to explain individual liberty. If, on the other hand, individual liberty is a matter of privacy, then the explanation of individual liberty is attendant upon the explanation of privacy, which must lie elsewhere.

On the face of it, individuality and privacy would seem to be rival ways of interpreting Mill's reference to the self-regarding, in relation to which each person is supposed to be entirely free and accountable only to himself or herself. On one common, if misguided reading of that rivalry, solitude is freedom, for any particular person. But on that reading, privacy means solitude, and it is solitude, therefore, that sustains and demarcates individual liberty. To understand privacy in terms of solitude is to understand privacy as something more than a species of liberty. It is to understand it as an independent condition, and as such, an independent source of value and disvalue. If, however, privacy does not mean solitude, but is only another name for individual liberty, then a reference to either quality is a reference to the other, so that an explanation of privacy in terms of individual liberty either renders privacy merely nominal, or refers privacy to privacy (in some yet-to-be-acknowledged sense) and thereby postpones rather than resolves the question of privacy's contribution to liberty.

The point is more straightforward, and can be made rather more simply, with respect to the linkage of liberty and conduct that takes place in private spaces, the second way in which privacy is commonly linked to liberty. What makes a space private? For those like Inness, who see privacy in terms of intimacy, it is an association, conventional in some cases, perhaps essential in others, with the pursuit of intimacy. Yet this understanding of privacy takes privacy to be a condition and a value distinct from the condition and value of liberty, whether that value is the value of intimacy itself (for Inness, the value of loving, caring and liking) or, as the earlier examination of intimacy suggested, the underlying and sustaining value of isolation. And once privacy is understood as a distinct condition with distinct value, of whatever kind, its implications are likely to extend beyond questions of liberty.

These examples suggest that it is not possible to develop an understanding of privacy that is at once more than arbitrary and less than acceptance of it as an independent condition with independent value. I will outline briefly what I take to be the reason for this before going on to elaborate. Put briefly, the reason is that any non-arbitrary distinction imparts value in its own right (or more precisely, the possibility of value and disvalue), and anything that has value of its own to impart in a particular setting, in this case the setting of liberty, is very likely to impart that value in other settings, and so to have implications that extend beyond liberty. We might, of course, divide liberty on arbitrary lines, and so distinguish Tuesday liberty from Wednesday liberty, but we could learn nothing about liberty in doing so. Yet once we divide liberty on non-arbitrary lines, and so distinguish French liberty from English liberty, we learn something about liberty only because and to the extent that Frenchness and Englishness are values in their own right, each with something distinct to offer liberty, or at least, to put it more precisely, are the names we have assigned to distinct historical developments that have given rise, among other things, to distinct species of liberty, each of which is now characterized by the values and disvalues that the course of its development has made possible. So an understanding of privacy in terms of liberty is only meaningful if and to the extent that privacy is in fact a condition distinct from liberty, for only then can privacy be a genuine species of liberty rather than an arbitrary classification of it. And once privacy is understood as a condition distinct from liberty, the nature and quality of its contribution to liberty, that which marks it out as a genuine species of liberty, can only be grasped by grasping the meaning and value of privacy in its own right, a meaning and value that is very likely to have implications in settings other than that of liberty.

This outline assumes much and leaves much unanswered, in ways that are potentially misleading. There are two convictions underpinning it. The first is that conceptual distinctions are markers of value and disvalue: they are ways of referring to and reasoning about value and disvalue and the bearers of each, ways that often, perhaps typically, are valuable in their own right. The second conviction is that the values (and disvalues) that any concept marks are not confined to those that led to the creation of the concept in the first place: the relationship of any given concept to values (and disvalues) and their bearers is accommodating and open-ended (within the limits the concept can bear). It follows from this that when one concept is used to shade the meaning of another, as privacy is used to shade and so delineate a species of liberty, the shading brings into play all the values and disvalues (and bearers of each) that the shading concept marks and is capable of marking. If and to the extent that the values imported by the shading concept have no imaginable bearing on the concept the meaning of which is supposedly being shaded, the intervention of the shading concept is arbitrary. Arbitrary interventions necessarily imply that the concept that is arbitrary in that setting has value in some other imaginable setting, since the concept necessarily refers, directly or indirectly, to a value or values, all of which must be applicable in some imaginable setting, though none of which, as it happens, have any application in the present setting. The contribution of privacy to the meaning of liberty is not arbitrary in this sense. However non-arbitrary interventions, those that have a genuine bearing on the concept the meaning of which they are said to shade, as privacy has for liberty, are very likely to have the same external implication, for much the same reason. It is possible, but unlikely, for one concept to shade the meaning of another and yet be entirely subordinate to it, so that its distinctiveness is neither imported to its present setting (having been created elsewhere) nor capable of being exported to some other setting. It is usually the case that one can imagine further values, or disvalues, or their bearers, that a concept, however subordinate, might give rise to elsewhere.

This might seem an unnecessarily laboured way of distinguishing privacy and liberty. It might be thought a good deal more straightforward simply to distinguish privacy and liberty as concepts rather than in terms of the values they suggest. Yet it seems to me that in itself a conceptual distinction will not do the work that is needed here. This is not to disparage the drawing of conceptual distinctions. But the significance of such distinctions is, that by reason of their flexibility and lack of commitment to any value in particular, they leave open, to some degree at least, the question of what values the concepts they demarcate might bear. It follows that to draw a conceptual distinction between privacy and liberty would not in itself reveal the value that privacy might bring to liberty, just because the role of conceptual distinctions is to leave that value unspoken (within the limits that the concept of privacy can bear). Put in practical terms, to show that privacy exists where liberty does not, in prison, for example, is to invite either the response that what is thereby demarcated is not in fact privacy but rather something more like confinement (a response that identifies the concept of privacy with the values it is conventionally understood to give rise to), or the response that what is thereby demarcated is an instance of privacy only because and to the extent that imprisonment is in fact capable of yielding freedom (stone walls do not a prison make, Lovelace maintained, because they cannot confine the heart or soul). In short, either the example is an example of freedom or it is not an example of privacy. Both responses are correct as far as they go. Most privacy does generate some sort of freedom. The question is whether that is all it does.

Whatever the respective shortcomings in general of these two approaches to distinguishing concepts, it seems clear that the approaches reinforce one another in the setting of privacy and liberty. One might doubt that the presence of value in one setting implies the possibility of value elsewhere or, if one accepts the implication in some cases, one might doubt that it is borne out in the case of privacy and liberty. On the other hand, one might doubt that the conceptual distinctiveness of privacy yields a corresponding distinctiveness of value. Yet if the presence of value in one setting sometimes implies the possibility of value elsewhere, as clearly it does, then the conceptual distinctiveness of privacy makes it very likely that privacy implies a value or values beyond the realm of freedom in which its distinctiveness and value is conventionally recognized.

What, then, is the meaning and value of privacy, which might or might not be brought to bear on our understanding of liberty? The answer, it seems to me, can be most readily approached by taking a closer look at the candidates for understanding privacy entirely in terms of liberty. What individuality and private space most obviously have in common is the very thing that intimacy ultimately depends upon, namely the experience of isolation in some plane, be it physical, psychological, intellectual or emotional. Individuality describes a kind of isolation; private space secures that isolation. To begin with the clearer connection, we call a space private because, and to the extent that, it is isolated from the scrutiny of other people. The isolation offered by a private space is material and observable, but its value derives not so much from its physical implications (freedom from scrutiny) as from what they are thought to entail, or at least to permit, namely, isolation in other planes. As those who would identify privacy and liberty rightly recognize, and as Woolf emphasized, private space is crucial to the development of individual voice. And individuality is itself a species of isolation, in terms of which people function without regard, or with diminished regard, for their connections to other people.

If that is the meaning of privacy, what might be its value? Part of the answer, clearly, is to be found in the support it offers to freedom. Proponents of privacy are wrong to identify privacy and freedom, but they are right to think that privacy has a vital role to play in fostering and securing personal freedom. That role, and its value, is the product of two interrelated features of our general engagement with value, first, the incompatibility of certain values with one another, and second, the amelioration of interests that is inherent in human exchange and the common ground it fosters and depends upon. Separately and together, these two features make privacy and freedom essential companions to one another.

2. Isolation and Incompatible Values

One must immediately be careful here. Incompatible values do not in and of themselves produce incompatible people. Rather, it is the combination of incompatible values and certain forms of *engagement* with those values that gives rise to incompatible lives, and so makes privacy valuable (or at least potentially so) to the extent of the incompatibility. To begin with a modest example, involving only one dimension of one life, it is good (and so valuable) to strive (at least where the objects of one's striving are worthy of the enterprise) and it is also good to be sybaritic (justifiably so where no neglect of responsibility is involved). The two values are incompatible in the sense that one cannot simultaneously strive and be sybaritic, but it follows from that very description that the incompatibility need only be temporal, and so need only prevent an attempt to engage both at the same time. Put another way, the values themselves are not incompatible, strictly speaking, while engagement with them may, but need not be so. In principle, there is no difficulty whatsoever in combining striving and being sybaritic within a single life. For most people, it is called going on holiday.

Other values are incompatible within the project of a particular life, because the demands of that life project are such as to preclude engagement with both values within its framework. To borrow an example offered by Joseph Raz, it is good to be a nun and good to be a mother, but one cannot be both, for the virtues of the two conditions are at odds with one another. Even if it is possible to do both things in one life, as it may be, by entering a nunnery after motherhood or leaving one to become a mother, it is not possible to do so as part of one life project. To enter or leave a nunnery in such circumstances is to abandon one life project and begin another. It follows that it is in, and indeed only in, their relationship to a particular life project that the two values are incompatible. Yet the special feature of being a nun or being a mother is that these are by their nature life projects. It is not possible to engage with the values on any other basis, and for that reason is not possible to engage with both as part of the project of a single life.[13] A woman who did both things in the course of her life would be very likely, looking back on it, to refer to her past (as nun or as mother) as another life, by which she would mean another life project, as people often do when they look back on former, dramatically different careers, or relationships, or attitudes to life. In this regard, one may contrast the values of striving and being sybaritic, which can be and sometimes are definitive of a life project, in which case their incompatibility means that one value must yield to the other in any and all respects that are definitive of the project. These values can also be no more than incidental features of a life project, and so can be combined in the manner described in the previous paragraph, by pursuing first one, then the other, in ways that fall short of being definitive of one's life.

Still other values, however, are not only incompatible within a single life, but incompatible across lives, so making people incompatible with one another, either comprehensively or in limited respects. Nuns and mothers may get along famously, as may the striving and the sybaritic, despite the incompatibility of the values to which their lives are committed, though just why this is so and how far it is so will need to be explored. But consider first, as a way of approaching the issue, the case of the active and the contemplative. It is clearly possible for a

---

[13] It is important to remember that the values in issue here are the values, for one person, of *being* a nun or *being* a mother. These are life projects by their nature. It is of course entirely possible, as described below, for one person to engage with at least some of the values that flow from another's person's being a nun or a mother, as happens whenever nuns and mothers interact.

person to be both active and contemplative, in the same way that it is possible to be both striving and sybaritic, by alternating periods of activity with periods of contemplation. It is just as clearly possible to be active or contemplative in ways that become definitive of the project of a life, so that either activity or contemplation must yield to the other in all respects definitive of that project. However it is difficult, and often impossible, for one person to be contemplative in the face of another person's activity (though perhaps less difficult for one person to be active in the face of another's contemplation). The possibility of co-existence depends on the nature of each person's engagement with the incompatible values of action and contemplation. If neither person is engaged with those values in a way that is definitive of his or her life project, then both projects, and thus both people, will be compatible with one another. All the two people need do is be active together, or contemplative together, or at least when in one another's company. Alternatively, if one person is engaged with either action or contemplation in a way that is definitive of his or her life project, but the other is not so engaged, then compatibility will depend on the readiness of the latter to be active or contemplative, as the case may be, as long as he or she is in the former's company. But if two people are engaged with incompatible values in ways that are definitive of their respective life projects, their lives become incompatible. Put another way, the successful pursuit of each life project will depend on its isolation from the other in all respects that contribute to its definition as a life project, which may or may not involve the removal of each person from the other's company, temporarily at least.

What this shows is that there is a common thread running through these examples, which in each case links the ability to pursue incompatible values, values with which one may be more or less profoundly engaged, to the possibility of isolation from the pursuit, by oneself or others, of the values with which they are incompatible. It is possible to be both striving and sybaritic just because, and to the extent that, it is possible to isolate periods of striving in one's life from periods in which one is sybaritic. The institution of a holiday offers a formal structure for such isolation. By the same token, it is possible for nuns and mothers to get along famously, despite the incompatibility of the values that define their respective life projects, just because, and to the extent that, their relationships are developed and pursued on bases that either do not include the incompatible values (the two women may share a love of gardening, or of books), or that include only the compatible aspects of those values (they may have, by reason of their very roles as nuns and as mothers, a common commitment to the development of a child's spiritual life), in other words, just because and to the extent that their respective engagements with life-defining incompatible values can be isolated from one another. Something similar is true of lives of action and of contemplation, as described above. In each case successful engagement with a given value depends on its isolation from all those values with which its pursuit is incompatible. The nature and degree of the isolation that is necessary in any given case depends on the nature of the engagement with the incompatible values at stake. Where the necessary isolation is of one person from another we call it privacy.

Important as it is to be precise about it, this is in some ways the most obvious and familiar source of privacy's value. The pursuit of intimacy, for example, clearly requires isolation from all those engagements with value, sometimes on the part of the intimates themselves but more typically on the part of others, that are incompatible with intimacy. It is isolation that secures the freedom to develop and express intimacy in one's own way, the freedom that Inness calls emotional autonomy. Yet familiar as connections such as these are, they have a number of significant implications which, when pursued, suggest rather less familiar but no less valuable connections between privacy and freedom, and what is more and more surprising, also suggest valuable as well as non-valuable connections between privacy and the absence of freedom. One way to see this is to consider what lack of privacy entails.

3. Human Exchange and the Amelioration of Interests

Where engagements with value are incompatible with one another, in the manner described above, the alternative to privacy is accommodation. One engagement is bound to yield to the other to the extent of the incompatibility, unless both yield to a third form of engagement. The deeper the engagement that is yielded the higher the price of yielding it, and the higher the price of yielding it the greater the likelihood that yielding, or the demand for it, will lead to oppression and conflict. These patterns are clearly visible in close relationships, such as marriage, where the proximity of two (or more) life projects creates a high risk of their incompatibility, unlikely as it is that different people, however similar or sympathetic to one another they may be, will develop life projects that either never engage with incompatible values, or that engage with incompatible values only in dimensions of their lives that can be isolated from one another. Typically, incompatibility in marriage means that one spouse yields his or her engagement to the other, all too often, in the case of women, an engagement that is central to the project of her life. This is what makes Virginia Woolf's call for a room of one's own a feminist call as much as it is the call of a creative spirit. Contrary to the rhetoric of many feminists, the ability to isolate oneself from another's engagement with value is crucial to the autonomy of women. Without privacy there is bound to be accommodation, and while in principle men are as subject to the demand for accommodation as women are, in practice the price of accommodation is usually paid by women.

However, this picture of accommodation as a form of sacrifice, while true as far as it goes, is also misleading, for it suggests that privacy has both more and less value than it actually possesses. In fact, the practice of accommodation has positive as well as negative implications for the person who accommodates, as is revealed by the way we speak of it in ordinary language. That being the case, when privacy relieves us of the need to accommodate it offers us less and costs us more than sacrifice suggests. An accommodating person is one who is flexible and so open to the claims, not merely of some other person (such as a husband or wife), but of other values than the ones to which he or she is currently committed. Bad marriages and other bad relationships are bad partly because the accommodation runs in one direction only, but partly and more profoundly, because it expects openness to values of a kind that are inaccessible to the person who accommodates, and so exacts a price not merely in terms of his or her current commitments but in terms of fundamental goals and even interests, a price that is properly understood as a sacrifice and that in bad marriages, as I have noted, is usually paid by women. But in good marriages and relationships accommodation runs fruitfully in both directions, either because the people involved take turns giving way or, more commonly and constructively, because both willingly yield their current commitments in favour of new commitments that are accessible to both of them, that offer fresh possibilities for life together, and so ensure that the separate projects of their lives remain both rewarding and compatible with one another.

It is this process that I described above as the amelioration of interests that is inherent in human exchange and the common ground it fosters and depends upon. In cynical, Wildean eyes it is the process by which husbands and wives come to share lives that suit neither of them. But this is to assume that accommodation is always sacrifice and so to see good marriages (and relationships) merely as those in which the sacrifice is mutual rather than one-sided. Whether or not that is a plausible view of good marriages, it is certainly not a plausible view of good relationships, as ordinary experience confirms. Most of us are reasonably familiar with the consequences for our views of going to a movie, or listening to a new recording, or eating at an unfamiliar restaurant, in company rather than alone. Critical perspectives that are developed in shared experience and then refined through a subsequent exchange of analyses are necessarily adjusted for one another to the extent required for their mutual exchange. Adjustment does not always mean agreement as to conclusions, but it does mean agreement to at least some common ground upon which to disagree as to conclusions. Otherwise the people involved would have nothing to say to one another on the subject of the movie, or the recording, or the restaurant. That is sometimes the case, of course, for exchanges sometimes fail, but when it is the case the people in question have no relationship to the extent of the failure. It is that kind of failure that people revealingly refer to when they say, idiomatically but accurately, that they just can't relate to another person's way of looking at things. More commonly, people can relate to one another's way of looking at things, and so are able to develop at least a partial agreement as to conclusions in a manner that is genuinely constructive, making the exchange between them, and the relationship it helps to constitute, rich and rewarding. As examinations of group dynamics have shown, shared conclusions are often, perhaps typically, richer than those developed by the same people in isolation and then later combined.

But this shows that the earlier picture of privacy as securing the isolation needed for the realization of one's existing character and commitments was drawn too quickly, for it failed to take account of the fact that a person's character and commitments are not simply given, but are artefacts that we develop over time, sometimes through an exchange with others (which isolation prevents), and sometimes through seclusion from them (which isolation defines and secures). To neglect this fact is to accord to privacy both more and less value than it actually possesses, more, because many aspects of our character and commitments are as open to successful development in company as out of it, and so do not depend on privacy for their realization, less, because other aspects of character and commitment, most prominently those we think of as idiosyncratic, depend on privacy not merely for their survival and fulfilment, but for their creation and hence for their very existence.

4. Isolation, Constraint, Creativity, and Diversity

As was the case with the connections between isolation and the freedom to pursue values that are incompatible with those one would meet in company, the connections between isolation and the freedom to develop one's character and commitments in independent and uncompromising directions are in some respects a familiar source of privacy's value. Woolf's metaphor bridges these two kinds of connection between isolation and personal development. A room of one's own is in part a place where one can be oneself, and so give voice to all those aspects of one's creative vision that might well be compromised by the presence of other people (even when they are intimates), but it is also and more profoundly a place where one can develop a creative vision of one's own, free of the shaping influence of others. This is a well recognized condition of the individual creativity that Woolf had in mind. But what is true of individuals and of the formally creative activities that isolation allows them to engage in, such as the writing of a novel, is also true of bodies of people and the ways of life they develop together. Such bodies are isolated from other bodies like themselves by whatever it is that makes them a body distinct from others, and what makes them such a body is either the distinctiveness they have inherited from past isolation, or the distinctiveness they are in the course of creating and developing in their present isolation, or both. The people who make up such bodies, be they members of families, or tribes, or nations, or any other association of human beings that is defined by its distance from some other body like itself, function at two levels of isolation and of company. As individuals they are subject to accommodation in all those aspects of their lives that they share with other members of the body in question; as members of that body they inhabit rooms of their own in all those dimensions of human experience that distinguish the body from others like it. And, to come full circle, what is true of bodies of people is true of the condition of the individuals that compose them, for what we are, even biologically, is but the product of past and future isolation. The constraint of isolation is the source of human difference, for it is the exercise of creativity in isolation that makes it possible for people to reach different conclusions and thereby develop different ways of life, the ways of life that liberal societies draw upon for the diversity that makes freedom valuable there.

To begin with one of the most prominent dimensions of human difference in contemporary Western society, we are so used to thinking of the idea of multiculturalism in terms of diversity that we sometimes fail to distinguish it from cosmopolitanism or to acknowledge its roots in monoculturalism. Where human beings share the circumstances of their existence, as they do in mono-cultures, they develop shared responses to those circumstances, responses that over time may, if sufficiently stable and self-aware, come to constitute a cul-ture. Where such patterns of shared response are isolated from one another the result is cultural difference, to the extent of the isolation. That difference is a feature of human existence as soon as it comes into being, but it only becomes part of human experience when some person travels from one culture to another. If such a traveller is sensitive to what he or she sees and open to its claims, or if the cultural world that he or she visits is similarly sensitive and open to what the traveller is and expresses, then host and visitor alike will experience cultural diversity. The subsequent response of either party to that diversity may be negative and so imperialistic; it may be communitarian and so assimilationist; it may be one of mutual exchange and so cosmopolitan. What matters here is that the very existence of the differences, and the pro-spects for their continuing survival, depend on the presence of isolation and constraint.[14]

Yet something more challenging needs to be said about the connections between isolation and self-development, for otherwise the patterns just described, even if true to life, could be explained as further implications of the freedom that privacy offers from the constraints of company. People who are liberated by isolation from the demands of others, it might be said, are not only free to be what they already are, but free to explore and develop what they already are by taking it in new directions, thereby realizing its full implications. The connections I am trying to trace here, however, are to the opposite effect. Privacy sometimes offers us freedom from the constraints imposed by the company of others, as I have recognized above. At other times, however, as I have also recognized above, it imposes constraints on us by denying us access to the freedoms we would otherwise be able to exercise and develop in the company of others, the freedoms we discover through human exchange and the amelioration of interests that it

---

[14] See the following subsection, 'The Value of Diversity and Access To It,' for a fuller explanation of the distinction between multiculturalism and cosmopolitanism, and for an account of the interlocking contributions that cosmopolitan cultures and monocultures make to the value of privacy.

entails. These constraints of privacy, like the constraints of company, can be for either good or bad.[15]

It seems slightly odd to speak of constraint as a good. Is it not part of the meaning of constraint that it denies people access to what is good for them? And if it follows that one cannot be constrained from the bad, by definition, how could one be constrained to the good? Yet in truth there is nothing deeply odd about the idea, as is clear from the currency of the adage that necessity is the mother of invention. People who are thrown back on their own resources, as a result of their isolation from other people and everything that those others have to offer, are forced to confront their circumstances, and the challenges those circumstances present, not only with whatever resources they have, but with whatever resources they can develop through the exercise of their imagination, strength and will, in short, through the exercise of their creativity. Such people occupy rooms of their own, individually or in combination.

This description associates isolation and its attendant constraints with the distance between one person and another, and with the separation of the physical spaces they occupy, and so associates privacy with the individual and with private spaces, as they are conventionally understood. Yet as the discussion above sought to make clear, there are in fact as many forms of constraint as there are forms of isolation, and isolation may take physical, psychological, intellectual, emotional and other forms. It follows that the nature of the response that constraint demands and enables is a reflection of the dimension in which isolation exists or is secured. Given the diversity of the initial resources, personal and circumstantial, that people are able to call upon in isolation, and the diversity of the responses that it is possible to have to the two kinds of challenges that isolation poses (first, the challenges that otherwise exist in life and that isolation forces one person or body to meet without the support of others, and second, the challenges that arise as a function of isolation itself), the experience of isolation yields diverse actual responses from those who are subject to it, and by extension and constitution, diverse characters and cultures.

The point should not be overstated. Different people, and different bodies of people, frequently come to the same or similar conclusions, sometimes because the challenges they face and the resources they call upon are very fundamental, and so are shared by most human beings, and sometimes because the range of possible responses to the challenges they face is not that great, so that it is not uncommon for different people to reach the same or very similar conclusions. There is great diversity in human experience but there is also great community, not all of which is born of human exchange.[16] Patterns of thought and behaviour

---

[15] I owe this point to Gail Thorson.

[16] What is more, creativity is as apt to take place in community as in isolation, so that it is a mistake to believe that creativity necessarily requires a room of one's own. Furthermore, while the products of creativity in community and in isolation normally differ from one another (given the

are often common to very different peoples, people who have had little or no contact with one another and so are relatively isolated from one another in the relevant respect. This phenomenon, in which people independently arrive at the same conclusion, explains how it has been possible historically for explorers from one part of the world to communicate relatively quickly and successfully, in certain basic ways at least, with the people of other parts of the world, people whose development had in most cases taken place entirely or almost entirely in isolation from contact with the culture of the explorers, just as the development of the explorers' culture had taken place in corresponding isolation from that of the people they encountered.

5. The Value of Diversity and Access To It

One should be careful not to overprize diversity, or too quickly associate it with the bare existence of human difference. To begin with its downside, diversity exacts significant costs both in its origins and in its recognition. If and to the extent that diversity is the product of isolation, the cost of diversity is the cost of isolation, and what isolation costs is access to other people, the resources they have to offer, the community they define, and the freedom they make possible, in whatever dimension isolation has been established. These are real and often profound costs, costs that in principle attend all forms of isolation, whatever people they may be experienced by, but that in practice are most familiar to us in the experience of individual solitude, for in that experience isolation is not offset or disguised by the presence of company (as it is when one body of people is isolated from another, with the consequence that the members of each body are isolated from members of the other body but not from one another).

What is more, as feminists have emphasized, the cost of isolation, even when offset by the benefits of company in this way, in the family for example, is frequently compounded by the abuses that isolation makes possible or even licenses there. Freedom from the public gaze provides a release from accountability to public standards, and while public standards are not always good ones (and so should be open to departure and challenge), and very often are not the only good ones (so that alternatives to them should be permitted), they are sometimes not only good but fundamentally so. It follows that in securing a degree of release from accountability to public standards, by securing the privacy of the family home for example, one secures the isolation necessary to the freedom both to depart from what is bad in public standards, and to pursue alternatives to publicly approved goods, both good things, but at the cost of whatever abuses

---

amelioration of interests characteristic of human exchange), they need not do so. Creativity requires a room of one's own, as Woolf emphasized, only when the creativity in question is the expression and development of individual vision, a vision that might be threatened by the intervention and contribution of another.

that freedom makes possible or even licenses. If the state indeed has no place in the bedrooms of the nation, the isolation of the bedroom from public scrutiny will permit not only sexual practices that are publicly deplored but actually good, as was once the case with homosexual practices, and sexual practices that while not deplored are not publicly endorsed and approved, as many sexual eccentricities still are not, but also sexual practices that involve the abuse of one person by another, usually of a woman by a man, though all too frequently of children by their parents or guardians.

Quite apart from the costs attendant on its origins and recognition, the bare existence of human difference does not in itself give rise to human diversity, for diversity implies both awareness of and access to the differences that constitute it. Many, perhaps most of the differences in the world never meet in the experience of human beings, and so never give rise to the experience of diversity. As long as the isolation of one body of people from another is maintained the differences that the isolation gives rise to are a fact of human existence that does not yet form part of any person's experience. It is only when members of one such body engage members of another body in an exchange such as commercial trade, as has happened in entrepôts around the world throughout human history, that the differences embodied in each party to the exchange come to be united in the experience of human diversity.

As I have indicated above, human exchange depends on the discovery and achievement of common ground upon which to make an exchange, even if it is only the ground of disagreement. The pursuit of such grounds by people who are otherwise isolated from one another is the discovery and negotiation of human differences in the experience of human diversity. There are many ways to establish common ground: one difference may yield to another, or both differences may be yielded in favour of new ground that is accessible to all involved, but at its richest and most hopeful both differences come together in an experience of diversity that we call cosmopolitan, in which two or more ways of life overlap in a common ground without giving way to one another, a ground that not only permits fruitful exchange but also provides an access point to and from the different ways of life that create and sustain it.

It is worth contemplating briefly just how and why such exchanges become fruitful. Not all the multiculturalism with which we are familiar today, and which constitutes our primary engagement with diversity, is cosmopolitan in this sense, because not all multiculturalism embraces diversity. Sometimes what is called multiculturalism is but a special kind of assimilation, in which the distinctive contributions of several cultures are blended to create what is in fact a new monoculture, multicultural only in its origins and in the tenderness it shows to its newest members, who are burdened with the trauma of moving, physically and culturally, from their old, usually monocultural, world to the new. Immigrant societies are necessarily assimilationist to some degree, because they are bound to establish some ground in common in order to establish themselves as societies, and to the extent that they establish such ground they are multicultural without being cosmopolitan. However, immigrant societies differ in the degree of their commitment to assimilation, and some such societies go so far as to reject assimilation altogether, or at least purport to do so. What is called multiculturalism in the latter type of society is the public rejection of any commitment to the development of common ground in favour of public support for the various microcultures on which the society draws, be they immigrant or aboriginal. This multiculturalism is necessarily limited by the need to establish some sort of society in common, however weakly defined, that is at least capable of pursuing the multicultural project. That being so, the multiculturalism professed by such societies is sometimes insincere, no more than a way of disguising the process of assimilation and its cost, and so reconciling people to both.

But whichever is the case, what is important here is that any case of cosmopolitanism, and any case of multiculturalism short of cosmopolitanism in which assimilation is negotiated in a way that respects its contributory elements and those who offer them, depends on the nourishment of contributing monocultures, which in turn depends on their isolation from one another. In short, the cultural diversity that defines many of our great cities and the freedoms that are enjoyed there, depends for its sustenance on the continuing existence, internally or externally, of cultural islands, isolated from one another in all those respects that enable them to differ, and to contribute that difference to cosmopolitan life elsewhere. In principle, of course, those cultural islands might be cosmopolitan themselves, but in fact that is rarely the case, and for good reason. The fact that a cosmopolitan culture is by its nature not only parasitic upon the existence of other cultures and the social forms and practices they give rise to, but also open and fluid in its social structures, limits its ability to define itself in ways that are sufficiently characterful and stable to admit of contribution to another culture. That being the case, the primary sources of contribution to cosmopolitan cultures are insular and non-cosmopolitan themselves. Freedom in one setting depends for its significance on the absence of a like freedom elsewhere.

At the same time, however, dependency runs as strongly in the opposite direction, for the existence of diversity and its value depend on access to that diversity, and that in turn depends on freedom. I noted above that human differences become diversity only when they meet in the experience of human beings, and it follows from this that diversity depends on human exchange and the freedoms that make that exchange possible. It is in this sense that it is correct to say that much of the value of privacy depends on the presence of freedom while being in tension with it. Committed hermits never return from their isolation, and so are never able to know or share the diversity they have laid the foundations for. Those who enjoy human diversity, by contrast, do so through freedom of movement, freedom of association, freedom of expression, and all the barrier-removing aspects of religious freedom and freedom from discrimination, in short, through the exercise of the full panoply of the familiar rights and freedoms of Western culture.

Privacy and Anonymity

Privacy is often linked to anonymity, particularly in light of the significant inroads made by contemporary communications technology into the exercise of both values.[17] Yet it seems to me that privacy and anonymity mean quite different things, although in some cases much the same consequences may be secured by the protection of either. Put briefly, anonymity is something that one enjoys in the public gaze rather than in private, while privacy is not necessarily anonymous. A person walking down Oxford Street, for example, is normally anonymous (that is, unless his or her face is well known, or he or she runs into an acquaintance), but is not private unless and to the extent that he or she establishes some degree of isolation from the crowds of other shoppers on the pavement. A person or a couple in their bedroom, by contrast, are private there but probably not anonymous, since the neighbours are likely to know who they are.

The distinction between privacy and anonymity turns on the way in which each detaches a person from accountability to others for his or her actions. The isolating shield of privacy screens a person's conduct from the gaze of others, and so secures to that person the freedom to act as he or she sees fit in the dimension in which isolation is established. Anonymity, by contrast, detaches a person's conduct from his or her identity as the person he or she is, with a particular name and history, and so secures to that person the freedom to act as he or she sees fit without attribution, or more precisely, with attribution to him or her as an anonymous person (other shoppers may reprove him or her on the spot) but not to him or her in virtue of his or her particular name and history (once off Oxford Street he or she can no longer be visited by others with responsibility for his or her actions). Each form of detachment secures a species of freedom (and sometimes more), but in a different way and with different implications.

1. Anonymity and Freedom

The detachment provided by anonymity enables people to pursue certain forms of freedom that depend on distance from others while remaining in the company of others, that is, without isolating themselves in rooms of their own, of whatever kind. Like privacy, anonymity prevents the public connection of a person's conduct to his or her identity, but it does not do this, as privacy does, by altogether preventing the connection of that person to other people in common

---

[17] See for example, L Austin, 'Privacy and the Question of Technology' (2003) 22 *Law and Philosophy* 119.

endeavours. The two forms of detachment thus break the connection between conduct and identity in opposite ways and with contrasting effects. Where privacy prevents public awareness of conduct (but not of identity), anonymity prevents public awareness of identity (but not of conduct). Just because anonymity permits conduct in the company of the others to whom one is anonymous, it couples the detachment necessary to make that conduct free with a species of belonging, so enabling people to enjoy detachment and belonging at the same time, rather than having to choose one over the other at any particular moment, as must be the case when the only alternative to community is privacy.

The forms of freedom that anonymity secures, through its distinctive brand of detachment, are the forms of freedom characteristic of contemporary urban life, with all their familiar benefits and burdens. When and to the extent that it functions successfully, contemporary urban life is distinctively liberating. In a village, or even a small town or city (one where the constituent communities are akin to villages in their own right), every person knows a great deal, sometimes nearly everything, that every other person does, at a minimum, nearly everything that is not done in isolation. That knowledge, and the possibility of it, is potentially constraining. In a large contemporary city or metropolis, by contrast, such non-isolated activities are not known as the actions of any person in particular, and thus are free just because and to the extent that they can be pursued anonymously. This is not to suggest that it is impossible to be free in a small town, but it is to say that the freedoms one can enjoy there are the freedoms that can be enjoyed, not simply in and through the company of anonymous others, though that is sometimes the case, but rather in mutual recognition of one another's character and place in the community, and of the role that conduct in public plays in defining both. Small towns can be genuinely liberating in this sense, for the strength of community there is as liable to empower as it is to constrain. But small towns are oppressive of ways of life that the community cannot or will not recognize in itself, and that cannot be fully realized in the alternative of isolation from the community (even were that realistic in a small town, where such isolation is often difficult to establish), ways of life that include most obviously minority beliefs and practices that question or challenge the community-defining norm. It is often difficult to be gay in a small town, for example, for to be gay is not simply to engage in certain sexual practices in the privacy of one's bedroom, but to conduct oneself as a gay person in public, and small towns are often, perhaps typically, reluctant to recognize gay life and embrace it as part of their communal identity. The anonymity of urban life, particularly when coupled with its pluralism, makes it possible to conduct oneself as a gay person in public without having to confront the challenge of communal identity, for the embrace of community is simply not forthcoming or indeed available there.

It follows that the freedom that anonymity gives rise to, powerful as it may be, is not quite the same freedom that one enjoys in isolation (though the two may overlap), for the simple reason that the constraint established by the public gaze does not flow entirely from the possibility of being identified with one's actions, and so is not entirely relieved by anonymity. In turn, the freedom that isolation makes possible is not the freedom of anonymity (for isolation may not secure anonymity), but rather the freedom that comes of detaching one's activities from any form of direct accountability to those from whom one is isolated, a detachment that anonymity, which presupposes the presence of others, cannot offer. The distinctive benefit of anonymity, then, as contemplation of contemporary urban life makes clear, is to be found in the support that it is possible to derive from anonymous association with others, and hence in the particular forms of freedom that depend on the presence of such support, such as the freedom to live openly as a more or less fully realized gay person.

The special burden of anonymity, however, when compared to the benefits of isolation and integration respectively, runs in both directions. In comparison to isolation, what is lost in an anonymous life is access to views that one might have developed in isolation, simply because the association with others that anonymity presupposes entails the amelioration of interests that is inherent in human exchange, and so entails the establishment of some ground in common with those with whom one associates. Life as an anonymous gay person, or more precisely, as a person who is free to be gay in the presence of others just because and to the extent that he is anonymous there, is not in fact a fully realized gay life, because the presence of others who are not themselves gay yet must be accommodated to inevitably limits the range of gay expression, and so makes it necessary for gays to have access to some form of isolation, call it a room of one's own, where it is possible for them to express what they cannot express in the public gaze, even anonymously. On the other hand, in comparison to full integration into community life, on the small-town model, what is lost in anonymous life is the public identification of oneself with one's actions, something that is the price of access to the identification of those actions with the actions of others, and thus of access to full participation in the community of which one is otherwise a member, and to the freedoms and other goods that community support makes possible. In this respect too, life as an anonymous gay person is not in fact a fully realized gay life, and for that reason gay people have long pressed for public endorsement of certain aspects of their way of life that cannot be realized in anonymity, isolation, or some combination of the two.

2. Public Scrutiny and the Nature of Its Cost

A number of currents in contemporary Western life are eroding, or threatening to erode, the scope of both privacy and anonymity in our lives. For example, we find ourselves scrutinized by closed-circuit television cameras in a wide range of settings, from the street, to the shopping mall, to the school corridor; we find our transactions electronically monitored and recorded, and the consequent data synthesized for various purposes, commercial and non-commercial, from the cookies on our computers that enable vendors to tailor their websites to match the character of our previous transactions, to the electronic tagging that enables police to monitor the movements of released prisoners who are thought to pose a risk of re-offending (albeit not a risk significant enough to bar release); we find ourselves confronted with demands for information about ourselves as a condition of access to certain goods, so that we have to reveal what we once would not have had to reveal if we want to take a flight, particularly a flight to the United States. In appraising and responding to the challenges posed by these currents it is well to remember that although they may threaten both privacy and anonymity they do not necessarily threaten the one in threatening the other, so that in contemplating the appropriate response to make to them, be it one of welcome, adaptation or resistance, it is necessary to distinguish the two and tailor a response accordingly.

Privacy is diminished by these currents of contemporary life as and when public awareness of what would otherwise have been private conduct is enlarged or disseminated in such a way as to reduce isolation in the dimension in which isolation has been established, and on which privacy depends. Some contemporary surveillance has this effect, some does not. The placement of closed-circuit television cameras on Oxford Street, for example, does not in itself reduce privacy, for any isolation that existed on Oxford Street before the placement of the cameras, such as the tendency of lovers there (as elsewhere) to have eyes only for each other, is no more diminished by the presence of the cameras than by the presence of other people on the pavement, including the police who would be patrolling there were they (or their replacements) not virtually patrolling several streets at once in whatever place such cameras are monitored. Other camera placements as plainly do threaten privacy in themselves, but just because and to the extent that their placement involves the introduction of the public gaze into spaces from which it was formerly precluded.

For its part, anonymity is lost when some current of contemporary life ties data collection to personal identity, either directly or through links to other forms of data collection that are themselves tied to personal identity, whether newly so or historically so. Once again, some data collection and synthesis has this effect, some does not. The placement of closed-circuit television cameras, in whatever setting, does not normally end anonymity, for while it may reduce isolation by enlarging the public gaze, it does nothing to link the conduct of the person whom the camera observes and records to his or her particular name and history. In special cases, however, it may do just that, for example, where the camera is placed in a setting that is itself linked to a person's identity, such as his or her home or office, as it may be in cases where the function of the camera is to monitor the conduct of known people.

Either privacy or anonymity may be lost when information is not only gathered but exchanged. Yet here too one must be careful to establish not only whether it is privacy or anonymity that is at stake, but whether either is at stake, for it may be and often is the case that the collection and synthesis of data that appears to diminish either privacy or anonymity or both, in fact diminishes some other good, a good that in a particular setting may be as important as privacy or anonymity, more so, or less so. If the exchange of data alters the context in which the data is understood and appreciated, one public gaze may become another public gaze.[18] This may or may not be significant. If crowds on Oxford Street are filmed, and the film is shown on television abroad as part of an advertisement for British tourism, or even as part of a news report on demonstrations in London, the shift in context, and the new audience it brings, will do little or nothing to end anonymity, unlikely as it is that any member of the crowd will be identified as a result, and will do little to reduce isolation, since isolation achieved in a crowd is unlikely to be affected by the size of the crowd one is among, or by its character where that character cannot be brought home to one in one's isolation. If, however, hospital records are opened to public health authorities, in an effort to limit the spread of disease, or to health insurance providers as part of the disclosure of risk, privacy is certainly lost, for the confinement of the data to hospital staff, however many they may be, is its isolation from all others who might have an interest, legitimate or otherwise, in the state of one's health. And if one's transactions on the Internet are traced back to a particular computer, whether to create a consumer profile, to detect the commission of crimes, or to monitor the use and abuse of the computer itself, or if one's movements on the street are subject to stop and search procedures, or to filming in order to compile a record of demonstrators, then anonymity is certainly ended, for anonymity consists, in those settings, in the ability to roam the streets or cyberspace without one's wanderings being brought home to one as a person in particular. Finally, if released prisoners are tagged and monitored their privacy and their anonymity are diminished together, for in knowing just where prisoners go, the police will know much, though not all, of what they do, and in knowing exactly who prisoners are when they are in a public place the police will be privy to an identity that would otherwise be anonymous in that setting.

However, many forms of data collection and synthesis threaten neither privacy nor anonymity, objectionable though they may be for other reasons.[19] If the waiter in a restaurant duplicates one's credit card and uses it as an element in what is now known as identity theft, the theft and subsequent fraud do not diminish the victim's privacy or dissolve his or her anonymity. If the bank or other financial institution that issues credit cards then seeks further personal information from the cardholder as a condition of the issuing of a new card, such as an iris scan, there is no loss of anonymity and almost certainly no loss of

---

[18] See, for example, Austin, ibid, at 122, 130, citing H Nissenbaum, 'Protecting Privacy in an Information Age: The Problem of Privacy in Public' (1998) 17 *Law and Philosophy* 559.

[19] As Austin recognizes, above n 17, especially at 133, 144.

privacy, partly because the appearance of one's iris is not something that lends itself to the isolation of privacy, and partly because the scan is encoded in the card and so is not brought within the public gaze. Whether this is true of the issuing of other documentation, such as passports, government health insurance cards, and welfare cards, depends in each case on the nature of the personal information demanded, the way in which it is stored, and the way in which it may be retrieved. If the state issues debit cards that enable recipients of social assistance to draw on their allowances either at cash machines or at a point of sale, and if iris scans are used to ensure that the person drawing on the allowance is the person entitled to it, there may be a loss of both privacy and anonymity if transactions on the card are monitored in such a way as to reveal not only who made them but what they were made for.

A clear illustration of confusion on these points can be found in the well settled distinction drawn in the law of Canada and the United States between administrative inspections and criminal searches of the same premises. Criminal searches require prior authorization in the form of a judicially authorized search warrant because, it is said, they pose a greater threat to privacy. Yet it is difficult to see how this can be so. Certainly more is at stake in the criminal search, but it is not more privacy. If an official of the state has the power to enter a bedroom the loss of privacy entailed by the entry is the same whether or not the search results in the laying of a criminal charge.[20] The reason this is so is that the loss of privacy is the loss of isolation created by the intrusion, and that loss is not affected by the laying of a criminal charge. The real significance of the possibility of a criminal charge, and the reason to insist upon a search warrant where such a possibility exists, is that without a judicially authorized warrant there is a risk that the search will be arbitrary, and thus a violation of the presumption of innocence. A warrant is based on evidence of adequate grounds for the search of the premises in question. Administrative searches raise just the opposite concern, namely, that in the absence of a properly designed regulatory scheme governing the identification of targets, there is a risk that the search will *not* be arbitrary, so that the selection of its target will be biased rather than random, and thus will amount to an abuse of power. There is good reason to be concerned at the loss of privacy entailed by either kind of search, and also good reason to distinguish the two types of searches in terms of their seriousness, but the distinctive seriousness of the criminal search is simply not a function of the extent to which it undermines privacy, for in that respect it does not differ from the administrative inspection.[21]

---

[20] The bedroom of a recipient of social assistance might be searched by an administrative official for evidence there of the presence of a cohabitant, a presence that in some jurisdictions is ground for a reduction in the amount of social assistance. The same search might lead to the laying of a criminal charge if, for example, prohibited drugs were to be discovered in the course of it.

[21] The practical consequence of mapping the distinction between more and less serious invasions of privacy onto the distinction between criminal and administrative searches is that certain criminal

Coda

Running through this analysis of isolation and its relation to intimacy, anonymity, and cultures of freedom and constraint, is the connection between isolation and creativity. It is in isolation that a person (most obviously an individual, but also a couple, family, tribe, or any other body of people that is defined, at least in part, by its detachment from others like itself) is able to develop his or her (or their) existing possibilities, free of the shaping influence of others, and so to be and become recognizably himself or herself (or themselves), and in doing so to give some form of expression to that character, in isolation or out of it. This is the story of privacy and freedom, and part of the story of the significance of a room of one's own. As I have also emphasized, however, privacy is as strongly connected to constraint as it is to freedom. It is in isolation from other people, and the supports they offer and the freedoms they make possible, that a person is forced to confront the constraints of his or her circumstances, as best he or she can, with whatever resources, personal and practical, he or she cannot only call upon but develop, through the exercise of his or her imagination, strength and will, in short, through the exercise of creativity. The challenge involved is not one that every person can meet, which is one good reason for people to avoid isolation and associate with one another instead. Yet most people are at some point called upon to face isolation, willingly or unwillingly, in the short term or the long. Some fail in the face of it, some flourish. Most people, even when they flourish, know the cost of isolation, and for some that cost is deeply and inextricably bound up with what they have achieved and expressed as a consequence of isolation, so that creativity and its products become suffused with the circumstances that gave rise to them, thus reinforcing the picture of creativity as inherently painful and of pain as a hallmark of creativity.

I began with the image of Billie Holiday's articulation of the emotional character of solitude. The story she tells is a story of loss, of a person and all that person had to offer her and she to offer him (or her). In the way that it is told, however, the story is also a story of strength, resilience, and independence of voice, a story of a creative and artistic response to solitude that is suffused not only with the pain of its origins, but with the glory of their transfiguration.

searches will be overrated from the perspective of privacy while certain administrative searches, such as those referred to in the previous note, will be correspondingly underrated. What is more, the protections offered against the presumptively more serious invasions of privacy entailed by criminal searches, protections such as the issuing of a judicial search warrant, are not necessarily the protections that privacy requires. And if they were, they would not necessarily be the protections that the presumption of innocence requires.

3

Conscience and Commitment

Conscience, or at least the possibility of it, is in everything we do. Anything that we believe we have reason to do may, under the correct conditions, become a question of conscience for us. On the face of it, this may seem a surprising, even implausible proposition. After all, certain cases of conscientious objection have become so familiar to us over the years, indeed so notorious, that they have come to seem definitive of the very idea of conscience and its operation. A person, usually a man, is called upon to undertake military service, in the course of which he is expected to be ready to kill enemy combatants. His conscience forbids him to kill other human beings, and so forbids him to undertake military service on those terms. A parent, be it father or mother, is called upon to have his or her child vaccinated as part of a public health regime, or is expected to allow the child to receive a blood transfusion following a serious injury. The parent's conscience forbids such procedures and so forbids their application to the child for whose welfare he or she is responsible. A parent's conscience may similarly forbid the participation of his or her child in public education, or in some aspect of it, such as school prayer, or the wearing of a school uniform (be it a uniform in general or a uniform of a particular kind). From the opposite perspective, a member of one of the professions, be it a doctor or a cleric, a teacher or a lawyer, is called upon to provide his or her services, as part of a public regime, in a way that offends his or her conscience. The doctor may be expected to provide treatment or advice on sexual health that is either more or less permissive than his or her conscience allows. A cleric or municipal official may be expected to marry couples whom conscience will not permit him or her to marry, whether because the couple fall within what was formerly a prohibited degree, or because they are of the same sex, or because their relationship is patently abusive. A teacher may be expected to teach what he or she does not believe, about the creation of the world perhaps. A lawyer may be expected to defend a person whom conscience will not permit him or her to defend, not because of the crime charged, let us suppose, but because of the defence offered to that charge. In some of these cases conscience is married to religious conviction; in nearly all it is political, involving as it does the refusal of a person to do what the political community has called upon him or her to do. In every case it is dramatic and dissentient, principled and autonomous, a matter of following the dictates of one's own reasoning rather than the dictates of others in the discharge of one's moral obligations, and thus a matter of taking a stand against what one has been called upon to do by exempting oneself from its demands. Not me, or at least not in my name, goes the cry.

And yet conscience seems to have other, rather different roles to play, as some equally familiar pictures of it suggest. It often speaks to us in private and in our own voice, reminding us of who we are, what we believe, and what we have committed ourselves to, not only in those matters affecting others, the matters that we think of as our moral life, but also in those matters that affect ourselves alone. It is a conceptual possibility, and a political concern, that the public face of conscience may have obscured its private, inward-looking face, and in so doing, may have misrepresented the underlying nature of conscience, so that the conventional picture we have of conscience, drawn for the most part from its most prominent instances, is not only partial but misleading. In what follows I will pursue this possibility, beginning with an extended exploration of three apparently interconnected issues that have long attended the critical consideration of conscientious action: its relation to civil disobedience, to reason, and to dissent.

Three Puzzles about the Nature of Conscience

1. Conscientious Objection and Civil Disobedience

There is a familiar and long-recognized theoretical distinction between the practice of conscientious objection and that of civil disobedience, although different commentators have over the years given slightly different names to the two practices and drawn slightly different lines between them. On the one hand, the practice generally known as conscientious objection is one in which the objector refuses to comply with an obligation on the ground that it would be wrong for him or her to do so. The objector does not claim that the obligation is illegitimate and that others should not comply with it either. Rather, his or her position is that, in this respect at least, each person is answerable to his or her own conscience. Other men may go to war; other parents may allow their children to be given vaccinations or blood transfusions, to be sent to public school and to engage in prayer there; other doctors may be ready to take a different position on contraception or abortion; other clerics may marry this couple; other lawyers may take this case. Not me. Ronald Dworkin calls this, tellingly, *integrity-based* civil disobedience. His choice of terminology here is a careful one: it tells us what is distinctive about the practice while at the same time linking it (as part of the strategy of his argument) to what is generally regarded as the rather different practice of civil disobedience.

Conventionally understood, a person is civilly disobedient when he or she breaks a law on the ground that the law being objected to (which may be the law being broken or some other) is a bad law, not just for the objector but for everyone. So men and women protest against war because they believe that war itself is wrong, either in general or in this particular case, that no person should be called upon to fight it, and that any person so called upon should refuse to serve. Parents protest against certain treatment of their children (such as vaccinations that are thought to carry unacceptable risks, or the enforcement of religious observance in public education) because they believe that no child should be subjected to it. They withhold their child, not as an exception but as a challenge to the rule. Doctors offer procedures to patients that are forbidden, such as abortions in proscribed circumstances or on proscribed grounds, or refuse to provide procedures that they are expected to provide, such as contraception, or IVF treatment, or abortions in officially sanctioned circumstances and on officially recognized grounds, just because they believe that the procedures in question should be (respectively) either available or unavailable to all who seek them. Clerics refuse to marry certain people because they believe that such people should not be permitted to marry; lawyers refuse to run certain defences because they believe that those defences should not be run at all.

These cases are distinguished from conscientious objection cases by their motive, but other instances of conscientious objection differ in other, possibly more revealing respects. Civil disobedience is a tactic designed to bring about a change in the law. A civil disobedient will refuse to obey a legal requirement that he or she objects to if, and to the extent, that such an act of disobedience is likely to bring about the change in question. This cuts both ways. On the one hand, those who engage in civil disobedience frequently disobey laws other than the law that they object to, sometimes because the law that they object to does not lend itself to being disobeyed. The suffragettes who sought votes for women in the first decades of the last century were in no position to break the law that denied them suffrage (as perhaps an electoral officer might have been) but they could and did break many other laws as a way of drawing attention to their cause. And like many others since, they chose the methods of protest that had the greatest capacity to gain public attention and to express, as vividly as possible, the quality and injustice of their predicament. To chain oneself to the iron railings around the Houses of Parliament is not merely attention-grabbing, for it captures and so symbolizes the idea that citizens without votes are in effect citizens in bondage to their government. And to throw oneself to one's death under the king's horse is an appalling but unforgettably precise way of showing the world that one is being trampled underfoot. Nearly a century later, the dissenters of our time, be they anti-capitalists, environmentalists, animal welfarists, or some other, continue to seek avenues of protest that have similar symbolic power. The site of their protest is but an instrument of the change they seek. It follows, on the other hand and in principle at least, that those who engage in civil disobedience must be entirely ready to comply with the law that they object to if they conclude that to do so is the most effective way of bringing that law into disrepute. After all, it is sometimes possible to make a fool of the law by complying with its requirements, as when a large number of people fulfil their legal obligations simultaneously, thereby deliberately overwhelming a system that is objected to precisely because it is too burdensome.

Neither of these strategies is open to the conscientious objector because neither makes any sense in terms of conscience, at least as I have described it so far. What conscience forbids is one's own implication in the requirements of a particular law or social standard. If one's conscience objects to compliance with a particular law, then conscience is satisfied by non-compliance. Conscience does not then ask for, and would not support, the breach of other laws, laws to which conscience has no objection in themselves, as a means of securing the repeal of the law in question and so preventing its application to other people. That application must be a matter for other consciences. By the same token, it would be not only a false extension of one's own conscience but a contradiction of its spirit and its most basic demand, to comply with a law as a means of undermining it. The site of one's protest is not an instrument of the change one seeks, but rather, integral to it. The opportunity to dissent from the requirements of a law is precisely the change one seeks. There may be special cases, but it seems doubtful. Even where it is possible to make a legal scheme break down and so render a law inapplicable to oneself by complying with it, the enterprise requires that one commit oneself, temporarily at least, to what one's conscience forbids, and moreover, to do so for the sake of a goal, namely repeal of the law, that has repercussions not only for one's own conscience but for the consciences of other people, the operation of which should surely not be pre-empted at the behest and for the sake of one's own conscience.

And yet, granted the conceptual distinctiveness of conscientious objection, it is an obvious question, and one that has troubled many commentators, why conscience does not go rather further than it does, and so compel the objector to become civilly disobedient, by calling for the repeal of the offending law, or the removal of the offending social requirement. If one believes that it is wrong for human beings to kill one another, for example, surely one must believe, not as a further matter but by the same token, that it is wrong for anyone so to kill. What sense does it make for a person to maintain (certain acts of promising not to kill and certain special relationships aside) that it is wrong for him or her to kill, thus warranting acts of conscientious objection to, say, the operation of a military draft, yet not wrong for others to do so, thus warranting acts of civil disobedience against the war? After all, the content of one's conscience must be the product of reflection and consideration as to what one has reason to do and not to do in the conduct of one's relationships with other creatures, human and non-human. What is it, then, that circumscribes the conclusions one arrives at, so that their rational force applies only to oneself and not to others? Broadly speaking, two kinds of answer are possible, one denying, the other defending, the existence of a moral gap between the practice of conscientious objection and that of civil disobedience.

Denials of the Gap

According to some, conscientious objection is simply an aspect or component of the larger practice of civil disobedience. One seeks an exemption from a law just because and to the extent that one believes it is a bad law, and so seeks personal relief from the operation of a military draft, for example, just because one believes that war is wrong, either in general or in this case. In some, perhaps many cases, the requirements of the two practices coincide. Conscientious objection may be the best way of bringing about a change in the law, and so may be the best way of being civilly disobedient. Any person confronted with the draft, it might be said, should seek to bring it to an end only by conscientiously objecting to it. Other forms of protest through disobedience are possible, of course, but pursuit of them would diminish the purity and effectiveness of the challenge. In these cases, conscientious objection is no more than the name we give, somewhat misleadingly, to what is simply a strategy of civil disobedience. Where the two practices diverge, however, there are a number of reasons (leaving aside morally unedifying explanations, such as weakness of will) why the scope of a particular person's protest at the war might be coextensive with the scope of his or her conscience, albeit that other persons in somewhat different circumstances both should and would go further.

Ronald Dworkin suggests that what he calls integrity-based civil disobedience is typically the product of urgency.[1] Nothing more is possible in the circumstances; nothing less will do. The Northerner asked to return the fugitive slave, the schoolchild asked to salute the flag, can at the moment of that request disobey only by objecting. Any other strategy of disobedience would entail compliance. Yet this cannot be a complete answer to the puzzle, and Dworkin does not suggest that it is. Urgency and conscience may warrant objection rather than compliance, but they do not in themselves explain why such objection is enough, that is, why conscience does not then call upon the objector to object further. Without more, the explanation risks being question-begging. Even if, as a conceptual matter, it is correct to describe the practice in question as integrity-based civil disobedience rather than as conscientious objection, and so to present it as a stage in the operation of civil disobedience, one is bound to say something in favour of the moral case for that stage as an independent practice, an issue that Dworkin notes but does not pursue. Without the support of that case the stage is not a morally distinctive category of civil disobedience, as Dworkin takes it to be. Any particular instance of it would simply be a justified or unjustified instance of the operation of the general principle of civil disobedience, where the ground of justification turns on the issue of disobedience rather than the issue of integrity.

An apparently more promising explanation of the gap between conscientious objection and civil disobedience relies upon the reasons we have to attend to the

---

[1] R Dworkin, 'Civil Disobedience and Nuclear Protest', in *A Matter of Principle* (1985) 104, at 108.

costs of disobedience. In some cases, those who object to a law may lack the resources to take their protest beyond personal objection. Yet if what they lack is some quality of character, such as courage, or the ability to persuade others, then their position is no better than that of those who suffer from weakness of will, and so no justification of conscientious objection as an independent practice. To point out that an objector lacks the resources of character necessary to disobedience simply amounts to saying that the objector should be disobedient but finds himself or herself unable to rise to the demands of the occasion. Yet that, in turn, is to say that the conscientious objector deserves blame for merely objecting. It is no defence of the practice of conscientious objection. On the other hand, if what objectors lack is something that they lack through no fault of their own, then it may be that they should not be held personally responsible for being conscientious objectors rather than civil disobedients (although John Gardner would disagree). Yet this is to let conscientious objectors off the moral hook by fastening the practice of conscientious objection securely on to it. Once again, it is nothing more than an acknowledgement of the moral insufficiency of conscientious objection.

In other words, those who would deny the existence of a gap between conscientious objection and civil disobedience must do so in a way that preserves the moral integrity of those who are conscientious objectors, as self-respecting participants in the practice of objection, without going so far as to accept that moral integrity is in itself a sufficient warrant for the objection. It seems doubtful that this balance can be struck. Those who would deny the gap are left in the position of claiming either too much, so stripping conscientious objection of its moral legitimacy, or too little, so acknowledging that conscientious objection is indeed a morally distinctive practice without offering any adequate account of the nature of that distinctiveness.

This may seem close to maintaining that to be morally legitimate the practice of conscientious objection must be genuinely conceptually distinctive. That would clearly be untrue. It is entirely possible for a practice to be conceptually distinctive without being morally legitimate, and morally legitimate without being conceptually distinctive. Yet some degree of moral and conceptual distinctiveness is clearly necessary to the legitimacy of the practice as an independent phenomenon. If the practice of conscientious objection were morally legitimate for reasons that had nothing to do with conscience, the practice would be legitimate only when the requirements of morally legitimate civil disobedience happened to coincide with the practice of objection, without being in any way informed by it.

One last way of explaining the frequent gap between the practice of conscientious objection and that of civil disobedience is by appeal to autonomy of judgment. In respecting conscience we allow people to make up their minds for themselves. If we believe, as we do, that people should be free to make up their minds for themselves, then we should also believe, subject to certain conditions, in their freedom to engage in the practice of conscientious objection. I think there is real promise in this suggestion, and for that reason will return to it in the shape of the second puzzle referred to above, that of the relationship between conscience and reason. At this stage, however, it is enough to note that the appeal to autonomy of judgment does not in itself answer, or even address, the first puzzle, that of the relationship between the practice of conscientious objection and that of civil disobedience. If sound, the argument in favour of autonomy of judgment explains our respect for freedom of conscience, and so explains our respect for the practice of conscientious objection. It does not explain, and does not purport to explain, why objectors, convinced as they are of the merits of their objection, do not extend the force of that objection to people other than themselves. On the contrary, the explanation is entirely compatible with the possibility that conscience may indeed dictate civil disobedience, and so compel the conscientious objector to do more than simply object. Joseph Raz, who defends conscientious objection in terms of autonomy, distinguishes the two practices, not in terms of their rational foundations and what those might imply for the objector, but in terms of the people whom the practices affect, as the kinds of practices they are. Conscientious objection should be respected, he suggests, even if wrong-headed, because of the impact that its suppression would have upon personal autonomy. Civil disobedience, on the other hand, should be respected only if and when it is justified, namely, where its object is good and other paths of protest are unavailable.[2] It would seem to follow that a conscientious objector, who necessarily believes in the soundness of his or her objection, must also believe that the logic of that objection should be extended to other people, and so must believe in pursuing further measures of civil disobedience, unless of course there is no better measure available than conscientious objection.[3]

Defences of the Gap

If there is a reason for conscientious objectors to confine their objection to their own cases, one well known way to account for that reason is through the idea of agent relativity. The label for the idea is one proposed by Derek Parfit,[4] but the idea itself is one that found its most brilliant exposition in the work of Bernard Williams, particularly in his very famous and forceful riposte to the doctrine of utilitarianism in the pithy form of his story of Jim in the jungle.[5]

According to the story, Jim is a botanist whose research happens to have led him to be in the central square of a small South American town at the very

---

[2] See J Raz, *The Authority of Law* (1979), chs 14 (on civil disobedience) and 15 (on conscientious objection).

[3] Raz implies as much in 'A Right to Dissent? II. Conscientious Objection' in *The Authority of Law*, above n 2, 276, at 282.

[4] D Parfit, *Reasons and Persons* (1984) 143. The label was adopted by T Nagel in *The View From Nowhere* (1986) 152.

[5] JJC Smart and B Williams, *Utilitarianism For and Against* (1973) 98–99.

moment that a group of soldiers, led by a captain called Pedro, are about to execute twenty Indians by firing squad. The Indians have committed no crime that Jim or any other decent person would recognize. Rather, they have been randomly selected from the inhabitants of the village, following recent protests against the regime that Pedro and his soldiers serve, and are to be killed, as Williams drily explains it, 'to remind other possible protestors of the advantages of not protesting'. However, in honour of Jim's presence as a guest in the country, Pedro proposes that Jim have the privilege of killing one of the Indians for himself, and further, that the remaining Indians be consequently set free. If Jim does not accept the offer then Pedro will of course proceed as planned. The condemned Indians, unsurprisingly, are very much in favour of the proposal. What should Jim do?

Williams's interest in the story stems from its ability to capture the possible value of Jim's integrity, as a person who does not kill innocent human beings. The story suggests, or at least raises the possibility, that it is a relevant consideration in Jim's reasoning (in a way that utilitarianism would ignore) that according to Pedro's proposal the killing would be done by Jim rather than by Pedro. Williams acknowledges that the consideration is unlikely to be worth nineteen lives. What is important to him is our sense that the consideration is a reason for Jim. If it is a reason, then we can begin to understand the way in which conscience might be a reason for the conscientious objector, reason enough to stop short of civil disobedience in at least some cases, though to be sure not all.

Compelling as the example is, however, and effective as it may be in the case against utilitarianism, one needs to be careful in one's handling of it, given that what is needed to support the practice of conscientious objection is not simply a reason, but a reason of the right kind. Clearly, rather more needs to be said in order to establish that the integrity of one's conscience is a reason for conscientious action (including the action of refusing to kill) than that Jim should decline Pedro's offer. The question before us is what might make conscience a reason for the objector, and further, why, being a reason for the objector, if that is what it is, it is not a reason for others (and correspondingly) the consciences of others are not reasons for the objector. Two things follow from the nature of this question. First, it is not enough to show that Jim should not kill, for his reason not to kill might be a reason of a Kantian kind, which does not rely on the integrity of *his* conscience as such. Secondly, it is not enough, either, to point to the bare fact of integrity if integrity is tantamount to conscience, because the question before us is what conscience means and what makes it valuable. To notice that a given act of conscience is valuable may be all that is needed to meet the utilitarian case, but it is not all that is needed to meet the case posed by civil disobedience. The utilitarian denies that conscience is a reason; the civil disobedient denies that it is a reason of a distinctive kind, distinct, that is, from the reasons to engage in civil disobedience.

One radical response, which it might be helpful to address at the outset as a way of setting up the problem, would be that offered by those who think of morality, or certain aspects of it, as a kind of luxury good, to be welcomed and indulged in circumstances of plenty but to be discarded otherwise and rightly so. According to this view of the world, in situations of extremity, such as the one Jim finds himself in, people are bound to focus only on themselves and on what matters to them. This is not simply a psychological prediction, for few dispute that a person is properly condemned for behaviour that is psychologically predictable. Rather, it is the thought that a course of conduct can be so repugnant to a person that it could not be pursued without yielding something essential to that person's survival. So understood, the conduct becomes something that one should not be called upon to undertake, either because one is not capable of undertaking it (the argument here being that one's psychological limits are a kind of capacity condition on morality), or more promisingly, because one should not be called upon to sacrifice something that is essential to one's survival as a human being, where survival as a human being is understood to embrace not only one's existence, physical and psychological, but one's humanity. This argument, in its latter branch at least, has rather more purchase than it might at first appear to have. Suitably refined, it suggests a moral case for the restraint of moral demands. However, that refinement, it turns out, simply remits the argument to the question of conscience, in two steps. First, to show that something is a condition of value is not to show that it is a value in itself. A valuable life, for example, is conditional on being alive, but it does not follow that to be alive is valuable in itself.[6] Secondly, if and to the extent that survival as a human being embraces not only one's physical and psychological existence but one's humanity, it takes an argument to show that a given moral demand calls for the sacrifice of something essential to one's humanity. That argument is at heart an argument as to the meaning and value of conscience.

Assume, then, that the intuition that Jim has a reason to decline Pedro's offer, because it would make him a killer in Pedro's stead, is a sound one. The question remains whether this reason is an agent-relative reason, in the sense that its reference to Jim is an essential part of its content, or an agent-neutral reason, in the sense that its reference to Jim is a reference to a human agent whose moral significance is a function of reasons that make no reference to him as a person in particular. Does the fact that, according to the terms of Pedro's proposal, it is Jim rather than Pedro who would be doing the killing, matter because it is Jim who is considering the problem, or because Jim's history, character and predicament have a moral significance that bears upon what he should do in this situation, whoever is considering the problem?

The appeal of agent-relative reasons lies in their ability to explain the phenomena of attachment and motivation, both of which are important features of our moral life. Some may feel that better explanations of these phenomena are

---

[6] See J Raz, 'The Value of Staying Alive' in *Value, Respect, and Attachment* (2001) 77–123.

available, be the explanations as ancient as Aristotle's treatment of motivation or as recent as Raz's exploration of the value of attachment.[7] Yet quite apart from the merits of rival explanations, the doubt about agent-relative reasons is that they make too much of the phenomena of attachment and motivation, and in doing so distort the very real role that those phenomena play in moral evaluation. The concern, in other words, is that the function that agent-relative reasons assign to attachment and motivation supplants, and so suppresses, the true nature of the moral significance that we intuitively and accurately recognize in them.

Suppose that Jim simply cannot bring himself to shoot one of the Indians because he is squeamish, frightened, or some combination of those two things. This is not to assume that there is no better explanation of a refusal to shoot; it is simply to give his refusal the widest possible scope, by developing a contrast between its agent-relative and agent-neutral implications. On an agent-neutral reading of his moral predicament (and ignoring what Kant would have to say on the matter) Jim has a clear reason to kill, because to do so would save nineteen lives.[8] In the face of that reason Jim's squeamishness or cowardice is not only a failing, although it certainly is that. It is, first of all, a mark of Jim's overall and admirable commitment to the sanctity of life. A person should be deeply revolted at having to carry out such a project. Secondly, it is a countervailing reason, for if one is very disgusted or very afraid one may well shoot badly and so cause terrible suffering to one's victim. This means that on an agent-neutral reading Jim's attachments and motivations figure both as markers of his engagement with reason, well or badly, and as reasons in their own right. Their shaping of his engagement with reason is, on the one hand, direct but largely unsuccessful (in declining to kill for the wrong reason), and on the other hand, indirect but successful (in thinking of the possible wounding).

On an agent-relative reading of Jim's predicament, however, attachment and motivation threaten not only to occupy the entire space of reason but to displace much of the question of the success or failure of his moral life. For a start, on that reading Jim is, strictly speaking, neither squeamish nor cowardly, other than as a psychological matter. Squeamishness and cowardice, after all, are particular functions of one's success or failure in meeting the demands of reasons that exist apart from oneself, in the sense of making no essential reference to oneself. The distancing that they describe cannot, from Jim's point of view, be both a mark of moral failure (as the agent-neutral reading by and large would have it) and a moral justification (as the agent-relative reading would have it). The concern here is twofold. On the one hand, it is that failings in one's moral life may come to be treated as questions of conscience, in a way that betrays the proper claims not only of one's

---

[7] Aristotle, *Nicomachean Ethics*; J Raz, 'Attachment and Uniqueness' in *Value, Respect and Attachment* above, n 6, 10–40.

[8] As I have already noted, if one is a Kantian neither agent-relativity nor conscience as such can be an issue.

moral life but of one's conscience. On the other hand, the concern is that the moral claims of conscience may come to be treated as no more than matters of motivation, in a way that misrepresents the moral status of both conscience and motive.

Secondly, and by the same token, much of the complexity of the moral predicament in which Jim finds himself, according to the agent-neutral reading of that predicament, is simplified and polarized by the agent-relative reading, so that the disparate values that would otherwise appear to confront Jim are aligned in such a way as to make the divisions between them coincide with the division between Jim and other people. What the former reading would present as a conflict of values the latter reading presents as a conflict between value and self-interest. The concern here is that the extent to which these two dimensions of conflict align with one another has been overstated. It seems to be the case in ordinary experience that the conflicts of value that conscientious reflection regularly encounters are all too often internal conflicts, with little or no connection to the division between oneself and others. This is what gives rise to the presence of angst in our lives. If the agent-relative reading of Jim's predicament is an account of the way in which Jim's conscience is a reason for Jim, one is bound to ask how closely the picture of conscientious reasoning that it offers matches the operation of conscience that we are familiar with. It is vital that a picture of conscience be not only one that can be related to an agent, as consciences surely must be, but one that presents the claims of conscience as reasons that in their capacity as reasons operate in ways that we know to be characteristic of reasons. The agent-relative reading of Jim's predicament quite properly captures the profound role that attachment and motivation play in a person's moral life, but makes that role both simpler and less fraught than most take it to be. As Williams might say, in many cases (though not Jim's perhaps) it makes it too obvious just what we should do and not do.

Thirdly and finally, quite apart from the question of whether the agent-relative reading of Jim's predicament succeeds in capturing the role of conscience as a reason for Jim, there is the question of whether that reading succeeds in capturing the role of Jim's conscience as a reason for others. We know, of course, or at least fully expect, that Pedro will pay no attention to any such reason and that the condemned Indians are unlikely to be much moved by it. What we may legitimately wonder is whether there is any reason for these or other people to pay attention to. Given that the reason is agent-relative, it cannot be a reason for others in the way that it is a reason for the agent, without denying its own character. Were Jim's reasons in this respect reasons for others they would by definition be agent-neutral, not agent-relative. And if Jim's conscience itself, rather than the reasons that inform it, is taken to be a reason for others, it can only be because there is good reason to respect conscience, as an aspect of personal autonomy perhaps. That reason is an agent-neutral reason.

I do not for a moment wish to make light of the claims made on behalf of agent relativity. Able scholars have devoted lives to the issue. And yet, given that it is impossible to discuss conscience without discussing agent relativity, and further, that it is impossible to treat agent relativity fully within the compass of a consideration of conscience, it is necessary to say something brief about the impact that an agent-relative view of the world would have upon the claims that conscience can make upon others. There are three concerns here, the last of which has the most direct bearing on the place of conscience in our collective life. The first concern is that on the agent-relative view of the world the scope of the agent, and of the interests that appertain to him or her, is not informed by morality (in the broad sense) and the reasons that it gives rise to. If it were, the agent-relative would not be a self-referential domain. Rather, it would be ultimately answerable to agent-neutral reasons for its purchase on the agent. The second, consequent concern is that, despite their name, agent-relative reasons are not reasons in the sense that agent-neutral reasons are. They have no capacity to make deep demands on the agent and his or her interests.

The third concern, and the most significant in this setting, is that the existence of agent-relative reasons to respect the claims of conscience precludes the possibility of agent-neutral reasons to do so. It is not a question of conflict between the substance of the two perspectives. Such conflict would only be possible if both perspectives could be contemplated simultaneously, which they cannot be without denying the notion of their relativity. Rather, it is a question of which perspective should prevail in any given case, a question which, to repeat, cannot be answered by reference to the content of the perspectives. If and to the extent that the agent-relative perspective prevails, as it surely must in the case of conscience if anywhere, there is no room for an agent-neutral account of the same matters. An account can only be genuinely agent-neutral if it has a claim upon the agent, something that the priority of the agent-relative precludes wherever that priority obtains. In relation to such matters, agent-neutral reasons are in fact reasons for people other than the agent, reasons that call upon the agent only vacuously.

This has important implications for the place of conscience in our collective life. Given that agent-relative reasons have no claim upon people other than the agent, and that agent-neutral reasons in respect of the same matters have only vacuous claims upon the agent and so are not truly agent-neutral, then if conscience gives rise to agent-relative reasons it has no claim upon anyone but the agent (assuming that it is enough of a reason to have that), for it has neither an agent-relative nor an agent-neutral claim upon others. This is not because conscience is incapable of generating rational claims (as those who would deny the gap with civil disobedience might say). It is because the claims that it generates have no purchase on people other than the agent (except perhaps from within their own agent-relative perspectives). To the extent that this is implausible, there is reason to prefer an agent-neutral reading of conscience and its claims.

The appeal of the agent-relative reading of Jim's predicament, it seems to me, stems not only from the attention it pays to the role of attachment and motivation in our reasoning, in which respect it is appears to be only indifferently successful, but from its ability to capture the capacity of conscience to cut certain of the Gordian knots in our moral life. This is not to suggest that there are easy answers to moral predicaments, with or without the operation of conscience. Part of the objection to the agent-relative reading of Jim's predicament was that it made a moral life seem easier than common experience of it would indicate. Yet experience does more than confirm the complexity of our day-to-day practical reasoning, for it also suggests that conscience may have a kind of authority in our lives, one that we are able to invoke, within certain limitations, as an arbiter and guide, in order to resolve, in ways that are both personal to us and reasons for others, certain intractable conflicts of value. In other words, conscience does make the conduct of our moral life simpler in at least one respect, by giving us a way of negotiating its complexities without distorting their character or diminishing their claims upon us.

The first puzzle, then, growing out of the distinction between the practices of conscientious objection and civil disobedience, is whether there is anything morally distinctive about conscience and its operation. On the one hand, we have a strong sense that acts of conscience are acts of integrity, not only because they are consistent with the character of the actor, but because they are consistent with the requirements of morality, not in terms of their substance but in terms of their conscientious character. Yet on the other hand, it is obscure just what the moral basis for conscientious objection might be. Put in agent-relative terms, what reason do we have to pay attention to and, more important, to respect agent-relative reasons (assuming that there are such reasons)? Put in agent-neutral terms (as I will from now on), what reason do we have to respect acts of conscience as independent phenomena? There is no shortage of argument to show that acts of conscience are consistent with the character of the conscientious actor, but that is not the sort of integrity that needs to be shown here. What we need to know is what role conscience properly plays in human reasoning. Perhaps, as I have suggested, conscience is a helpful device that we call upon from time to time as an aid in practical reasoning, not only in tragic situations, such as that faced by Jim, but in our everyday living. Perhaps, however, conscience is only the name we give to the moral judgment of any particular person, so that it has a special role to play in our collective life (in the question of how far any person's judgment should be respected and accommodated there), and correspondingly, in the engagement of conscientious people with our collective life (and the liberty of thought and action that they are entitled to expect there), but not otherwise.

2. Conscience and Reason

Joseph Raz has offered an account of conscientious objection that treats conscience as the name we give to a person's moral judgments. Conscience is entitled to respect because and to the extent that people's moral judgments are entitled to respect. In liberal societies such as ours, where respect for people includes respect for personal autonomy, moral judgments are entitled to respect regardless of whether they are right or wrong, as long as they are central to the self-image and self-respect of the person making them, subject to certain limits dictated by the need to ensure social co-operation and a similar respect for the judgments of others.[9] Moral judgments, though definitive of conscience, are not the only personal judgments entitled to such respect, because they are not the only judgments that are crucial to a person's self-image and self-respect. As Raz puts it, 'a law preventing dedicated novelists from pursuing their vocation with the freedom essential to it is as bad, and bad for the same reasons, as a law conscripting pacifists to the army'.[10]

There is some reason to wonder whether Raz's argument here is at heart an argument about personal autonomy rather than conscientious objection, given that autonomy not only serves as its foundation but also describes its conclusion. In other words, it is not clear that Raz, at this point in his work, has any fundamental interest in defending the practice of conscientious objection *as such*. On the contrary, it is enough for his purposes to show that the practice should be respected, and in what ways, and to what extent. He has no need to show that it should be respected on grounds that are distinct from the grounds of our respect for civil disobedience, and so has no need to probe the particular meaning and value of conscience. It is enough for him to know that there is a practice that is commonly identified with individual moral judgment, and then to ask whether that practice is entitled to protection, be it for its own sake or for the sake of some larger good. Indeed, Raz makes clear that he sees civil disobedience and revolutionary political action as conflicts between law and conscience, and so makes clear that in his view the significance of the distinction between conscientious objection and civil disobedience is a function, not of any difference in the rational foundations of the two practices, but of the difference in the gravity of their consequences.[11]

The puzzle that Raz's argument distinctively brings to the fore, then, is that of the relationship between conscience and reason. As I have argued in the previous section, to distinguish conscientious objection and civil disobedience without offering adequate ground for the distinction is to say too little in favour of conscience as an independent phenomenon. However, to decline to distinguish the two practices, and so to see conscience as the moral judgment of the dissenter (and thus as a subset of his or her overall rational beliefs) is to risk saying too much. The issue here, and the source of the puzzle, is twofold. First, is it correct to see conscience as a feature of our beliefs and judgments about reason, or is conscience a feature of the rational landscape itself, albeit one that is brought into being by particular people, in the creation of their self-image and self-respect?

---

[9] Raz, 'A Right to Dissent? II. Conscientious Objection' in *The Authority of Law*, above n 2, 277, at 280.
[10] ibid at 281.   [11] ibid at 282.

Secondly, and by extension, is it correct to see conscience as the outcome and expression of individual reasoning (moral or otherwise), and thus to see it as a feature of the relations between people, or does conscience have a prior existence in the role that it plays within individual reasoning? In the next two sections I will address each of these issues in turn.

Conscience and Belief

According to Raz, when we speak of conscience we speak of a set of personal beliefs about what is morally required, beliefs that are protected in a liberal society as part of the protection of autonomy. It does not matter to Raz's argument that these beliefs are moral in character, although he takes that to be the character they possess in conscience as it is generally understood. It does matter, however, that they are beliefs, for it is the centrality of certain beliefs to people's self-image and self-respect, together with the humanist thought that to respect people one must respect what is necessary to their self-respect, that sustains Raz's argument in support of conscientious objection. But is conscience indeed a set of beliefs about one's (moral) reasons, or is it a source as well as an expression of belief? Does it have a role to play in the formation of moral and other beliefs?

Mistaken Beliefs

Two crucial features of belief are relevant here. The first is that beliefs can be wrong, and often are. The military conscript who refuses to serve in a particular conflict because he or she believes the conflict is unjustified may well be mistaken in that belief, either because of ignorance as to the facts or because of rational failure in the handling of them, in other words, because of the vulnerabilities that economists commonly refer to as imperfect information and imperfect rationality. Beliefs are the products of our rational judgment, with or without reflection and deliberation, and as such are vulnerable on two grounds. First, we may lack the information we need to reach a fully justified conclusion, whether because we lack the opportunity to discover it, or because we don't know enough to know what we don't know and why it might matter, and so fail to pursue and acquire the information we need. Secondly, we may lack the capacity to reach a fully justified conclusion, whether because we are for whatever reason morally inexperienced, in the sense that we have failed to undergo the moral habituation needed to arrive at sound judgments without reflection, that is, because we lack virtue as Aristotle saw it, or because we have been irrational in our deliberation, most commonly because we have given undue weight to our attachments and motivations. In either of these ways, the claims of our conscience may be mistaken. It follows that when considering the scope to be given to the practice of conscientious objection, as Raz does, it is vital to take into account the possibility that the objector may be wrong, for the right to conscientiously object, if there is one, holds even when the objector is wrong, and so must be examined on that basis. There can be no doubt that Raz is correct to proceed on this assumption.

And yet, that having been said, errors of conscience, regrettably and distressingly frequent though they may be, are aberrations in the operation of conscience and something of a distraction in its analysis. To see disputes of conscience in terms of truth and falsehood is to take the view that if the parties to the dispute were perfectly informed and perfectly rational they would not be in dispute. Conscience is an issue between them only because one side or the other is mistaken. If the military conscript who refuses to serve in a particular conflict because he or she believes that the conflict is unjustified is mistaken in that belief, then there is ultimately no reason for him or her to disagree with the state, no reason to resist conscription. Conscientious objection may be the proper response for him or her to make in the short term, given his or her mistaken belief, and a corresponding right to that objection may be the proper reaction on the part of the state, given the importance of personal autonomy and the respect for deeply held beliefs that it entails. But in the longer term, reason calls for the parties to agree with one another, and so calls for the objector to know better, and for the state to limit its respect for his or her objection, lest in doing so it respect, and to that extent commit itself to, the objector's error.

Conscience doesn't normally feel like that, however, although any person with a decent sense of intellectual humility will recognize that it sometimes does. Normally one regards one's conscience as misguided if and when it is founded on a mistaken belief, and thinks of the actions that it calls for on that basis as something less than true acts of conscience. It might even be claimed that we are mistaken in thinking of actions as acts of conscience at all when the conscientious beliefs that we take to sustain them are mistaken. This is not to deny that such acts are acts of conscientious objection. It is simply to say that the right of conscientious objection properly protects acts that would be acts of conscience were they based on sound beliefs.

Mistakes can be set aside and yet disputes of conscience do not disappear. People can disagree about the legitimacy of a military conflict when they know all they need to know about the facts of the conflict and when they have reflected on the issue entirely successfully, without overemphasizing the significance of their attachments or motivations, simply because there is as good reason to believe that the conflict is justified as there is to believe that it is unjustified. This is surely typical of the operation of conscience, and of the objections that people make in the name of conscience to what those with authority over them call upon them to do and not to do. Conscientious objection characteristically takes place when both sides to a question of conscience have a justified belief in their actions (and inactions) and what those actions and inactions expect of others. The dispute exists in the realm of belief simply because the commitments that give rise to it are objects of belief, as they are bound to be by reason of their presence in the consciousnesses of the parties to the dispute, but its roots are in the realm of value, and in the tensions and conflicts that disparate values, with their disparate claims upon us, can give rise to.

Belief and Commitment

The second crucial feature of belief is that of commitment. To believe something, whether rightly or wrongly, is to be committed to the content of that belief. This has two aspects. The first is simply a function of our rationality, for to be a rational being is to be committed to reasons. If there is reason to believe something, there is reason to be committed to that belief, for the alternative is irrationality. This is so fundamental that it is all but impossible to contemplate the alternative. If we have reason to believe that it is hot outside we have reason to act in accordance with that belief, by not putting on a hat and coat when we go out (unless we are trying to lose weight that way), by telling those who ask us about the weather that it is hot outside (unless we have reason to deceive them), and so on. Even when we have reason to be perverse, as we sometimes do, it is in fulfilment of our commitment to the belief in what we would pervert.

The other, and just as significant, aspect of our commitment to our beliefs is in part a function of our rationality and in part a function of our character, our goals in life, and other previous commitments within which the belief in question is nested. Reasons are objects of a person's belief when they have a connection of some kind to that person's life. Some reasons, and some aspects of reason, are more or less inescapable, and so are objects of belief for any rational being. Other reasons are more or less optional for us, either because the surfeit of reasons in the world and the finitude of life means that we must dedicate ourselves to some reasons only, or because the multiplicity and variety of the reasons before us means that we have to dedicate ourselves to some reasons rather than to others where there is room for either in our life but not both, given their incompatibility. In regard to reasons of this kind we must be doubly committed in order to be committed to their place in our life. Our very rationality commits us to a belief in them as reasons. However, our character, our goals in life, our histories, and our previous commitments must be called into play if we are to commit ourselves further to a belief in them as reasons for us.

In Raz's account of conscience the first kind of commitment is crucial to the understanding of conscience, for conscience is the name we give to our moral beliefs, and like any other belief we are at least prima facie committed to our moral beliefs by virtue of our rationality alone. However, not all moral beliefs are subject to the protection of conscientious objection, and some beliefs that are entitled to that protection are not moral beliefs. As I have already indicated, Raz makes clear that the dedicated novelist who is prevented from pursuing his or her vocation with the freedom essential to it is entitled to the same protection, and for the same reason, as the conscripted pacifist. Conscience, as he sees it, is a function of our commitment to reason (the commitment that is implicit in any belief), but its *protection*, in the protection of conscientious objection and in the avoidance of legislation to which conscience is likely to be sensitive, is a function of the further commitment that we make to the content of our conscience in the exercise of our personal autonomy, the commitment that makes its claims central to our self-image and to our goals in life.

As far as the understanding of conscience goes, one wonders whether the order of influence has not been reversed here. Is it not the case that what is fundamental to our conscience is our commitment to its claims, whether that commitment is a function of our rationality alone, or of our particular self-image and goals in life as well? The fact that we may be mistaken in our beliefs, and so may be mistaken in what we take our conscience to call for, is of central importance in any consideration of a right to conscientious objection, for all the reasons that Raz gives. Yet in order to be mistaken in a belief one must be committed to that belief. Another way of expressing this is to say that it is in fact the commitment to the belief that may be mistaken. That commitment, in turn, is the product of personal autonomy, in two ways. On the one hand, it reflects our freedom to discover truth for ourselves, and to make mistakes in doing so. On the other hand, it reflects our freedom to make certain truths our truths. Conscience is, at least in part, a product of these two freedoms, and the question of how far we are entitled to exercise these freedoms, and so be true to our conscience, is, at least in part, a question of the scope of conscientious objection, in the ways that Raz maintains.

This aspect of the second puzzle, then, has to do with the relationship between conscience and our beliefs. It is common ground that not all our beliefs are matters of conscience. And while Raz accepts that it is conventional to identify conscience with our moral beliefs, he also maintains that this is neither necessary nor sufficient: beliefs need not be matters of conscience to enjoy the protection offered to conscientious objection, and beliefs that are matters of conscience may not be entitled to that protection. Protection turns on commitment, and commitment turns on the exercise of personal autonomy. It is more than tempting to conclude that what grounds conscientious objection is what grounds conscience itself, and to look for the meaning and value of conscience in the idea of commitment. Yet to know whether that is indeed the case it is necessary to look at the other aspect of the second puzzle, the question of whether conscience is something more than the outcome of our reasoning.

Conscience and the Internal Life of Reason

The conscience that figures in conscientious objection, according to Raz, is the sum of our personal (moral) beliefs on the matter in question. The person who objects to conscription expresses his or her belief that war is wrong, either in general or in this particular case. This may well commit that person to do more than object, as I have already noted and as Raz's argument assumes. What matters at this stage, however, is that, so understood, conscience amounts to the sum total of the conscientious objector's beliefs on the matter in question, be that war or something else. Conscience is no more than that belief, and no less. The only conflict that it can sensibly give rise to is a conflict between the believer, in this case the man or woman who objects to conscription, and other people. The claims of conscience conflict only with the claims of other consciences.

Yet there must be more to conscience than this, to the kinds of objections that it can sustain and to the kinds of conflicts that it can give rise to, for we are all familiar with the phenomenon of struggling with our own conscience in the course of deciding what to do. Time and again we find our conscience nagging at us, in ways large and small, reminding us to do what we would otherwise be tempted to leave undone, or to resist doing what we would otherwise be tempted to do. Some of the most familiar examples, unsurprisingly perhaps, are some of the most trivial. It is late at night, let us suppose, and I want nothing more than to go to bed, but there are dishes unwashed, essays unread. Quite apart from my desire to go to bed, there is good reason to sleep now, do the dishes in the morning, and read the essays after breakfast. I will be refreshed then, and more efficient. Yet my conscience may tell me to finish my day's work before going to bed. Other examples, just as familiar though less frequent in our lives, are far from trivial. The person who objects to his or her conscription into the army; the parent who objects to the vaccination of his or her child; the doctor, cleric, teacher or lawyer who objects to his or her participation in the requirements of a particular public regime, all may be tempted to conform to those requirements, given the personal cost of objection. This is not necessarily a matter of weakness of will, for the cost of objection may be high enough to give adequate reason to conform. There may be greater goods to be served by conformity than by objection. Even if that is so, however, conscience will call upon the objector to resist. Certainly, in cases where we not only see but are inclined to exaggerate the attraction of reasons to be something less admirable than we expect ourselves to be, as the particular kind of person that we have committed ourselves to being, conscience is there to remind us to live up to the demands of our self-image. More significantly, however, conscience may tell us to do the same thing where there is no question of exaggeration.

Conscience as a Source of Reason

It seems to me that examples such as these bring to light four things that are concealed when conscience is thought of entirely in terms of the practice of conscientious objection. The first and most obvious is that conscience has a role to play in the development as well as in the articulation of our practical reasoning. This means that conscience must be something more than our concluded beliefs on a topic, for it has a part to play in generating those beliefs in the first place. Conscience, it would appear, is a rational resource that we are able to call upon when we want to know what we should do, and the conclusions that we reach with its aid are the conclusions that we subsequently present to the world as the products of our conscience. It is true to say, therefore, that the conscience that we express to others represents our concluded beliefs on the matter in question. What is more, it is correct to describe those beliefs as the claims of our conscience.

Yet it is also true that the beliefs in question have the content they do only because they have already been shaped, within the process of our reasoning, by the existing claims of that same conscience.

Put in those terms, this seems close to an equivocation. In order to avoid that implication I should make clear that there are two forms of distancing taking place here. The first is the distance of the conclusions that we reach with the aid of conscience, and that we subsequently describe as the claims of our conscience, from what would otherwise have been our rational conclusions. These are not the beliefs that we would have had without the intervention of our conscience. It is true, of course, that there would be no rational difference between the content of the beliefs that we express to others (and that we describe as the claims of our conscience) and the content of our conscience as we call upon it in the course of our own reasoning, were the considerations disposed of by the workings of our inner conscience entirely irrational. Yet the examples offered above suggest that that is sometimes but not always the case. Sometimes conscience simply reminds us to be rational (indeed, that is one of its most important and most famous functions), but at other times it reminds us of certain reasons in particular, reasons that we have committed ourselves to in some way, and calls upon us to attend to those reasons rather than to others. When it shapes our reasoning in this way conscience operates so as to displace reasons that would otherwise have figured in our conclusions. What is more, in doing this it may revise as well as affirm its own content. The second form of distancing taking place, then, in some cases at least, is that of conscience as we express it from conscience as we call upon it in the course of our reasoning. This is not to suggest that there are two kinds of conscience at work here. There is only one conscience, but it is an artefact that regularly reshapes itself in the forge of its own operation, so that the conclusions it embodies in any given setting may well have evolved from the conclusions it embodied previously, and may in turn evolve themselves when next called upon.

Conscience as Authority

It follows that the second, and perhaps more important, aspect of what is revealed by these examples of the inner working of conscience, is that the role conscience plays within our reasoning seems to be different from the role played by other reasons. Conscience appears to possess a kind of authority over other reasons, so as to be able to overrule their claims. In some cases, it is true, it may tell us to follow one path rather than another when both are eligible. In such cases it merely serves as a supplement to reason. In other cases, however, it may tell us to follow a path that is less eligible than another when assessed in terms of reasons other than the reasons conscience provides. Indeed, it seems to be the case that conscience can call upon us to do something that is fairly clearly less sensible than the alternative. If I am tired and aching for bed it would almost certainly be more sensible for me to turn in now and finish my work in the morning, be the work in question washing dishes, or reading essays, or both. Nevertheless, conscience may call upon me to finish my work before I go to bed, despite the fact that, all things considered, it is fairly silly for me to do this. The point is not that I am bound to do what conscience calls upon me to do. Were that the case there would be no such thing as struggles with one's conscience, other than as struggles between the rational and the irrational. Rather, the point is that conscience can and does make the claim that in order to honour it I should do something that, all things considered and apart from the claims of conscience, there would be good reason not to do. In other words, conscience claims rational authority.

Conscience as a Supplement to the Moral

The third aspect of what is revealed by these examples of the inner working of conscience, is that the claims that conscience makes upon us are not entirely moral (in the sense of describing our obligations to creatures other than ourselves). Most obviously, conscience appears to make claims that we owe only to ourselves. There is nothing incongruous in thinking that conscience may call upon me to do the dishes before going to bed, or to make my bed before going to work, or any other similar domestic obligation, even if it is the case that I live alone. It is true that many such routines are vestigial survivors of obligations that we once owed, as children, to our parents, but it is also true that we owed those obligations to our parents as placeholders for the obligations that our parents expected us to owe to ourselves as adults, and further, that as adults we normally revise the content of our conscience in this regard, both so as to abandon obligations that we were brought up to recognize, and so as to recognize obligations that formed no part of our upbringing and that may indeed embody a rejection of that upbringing, thereby holding ourselves to standards that our parents did not hold either us or themselves to.

By the same token, and more important perhaps, conscience has a content that is not entirely moral in that it calls for us to treat other people in ways that our moral reasons would not call for and might even forbid. It does this in two ways, each of which has a moral and a non-moral branch. In its more attractive aspect, conscience converts what is morally permissible into a personal duty. It may do this either by calling upon us to assume more than our share of what, like every other person, we are morally obliged to do, so as to be more generous, for example, than morality expects us to be, or by calling upon us to follow through on projects and goals that we have personally committed ourselves to (in the absence of any moral obligation to make that commitment), and more important, to do so to a standard of performance that we ourselves have determined to be necessary and so have made more or less distinctive to ourselves.

To elaborate, in its first, moral branch, the attractive aspect of conscience makes the supererogatory a matter of obligation. Morality only requires us to do our fair share of what is good for others (though it gives us reason to do more), but our conscience may expect better of us and often does. Conscience often compels a person to be more generous, more tolerant, more compassionate, or more forgiving than morality requires him or her to be. It does this by personalizing the quality of a reason's claim upon us, so as to make what is optional for others a duty for us. Among other things, then, the commitment that conscience embodies is a commitment to regard the status of certain reasons in a way that is personal to us.

In its second, non-moral branch, this aspect of conscience makes projects and goals that would otherwise be no more than eligible options in life personally essential for us once we have adopted them as our own, and further, makes the standards of success in those projects and goals personal to us in the same way that it makes the supererogatory obligatory. Having committed ourselves to a project or goal we may feel conscience-bound to continue in it, even when the balance of reasons, including the reliance that our commitment may have inspired in others, calls for its abandonment. We feel conscience-bound to continue to do what we have committed ourselves to do just because we have pledged ourselves in that way. More familiarly, perhaps, we often hold ourselves to standards of performance in our projects and undertakings that are higher than either the projects and undertakings themselves, or other people's expectations of performance in them, would call for. Work of a certain standard, we may tell ourselves, might be good enough for other people but it is simply not good enough for us. A person will often say that his or her conscience will not let work of less than a certain calibre go out with his or her name upon it. Here again, the reference to a name is revealing, because it suggests that what is at issue is a question of conscience.

Conscience and the Immoral

In both these ways conscience creates moral obligations where none existed otherwise. We become obliged merely because we have committed ourselves to being so obliged. This, however, makes possible the distortions and corruptions that characterize conscience in its less attractive aspect. In this aspect, conscience performs the same functions on what is morally impermissible, and so gives rise, whenever it prompts action in opposition to the will of a community that is not similarly misguided, to the problem of misguided conscientious objection considered by Raz. Conscience may mislead us either by calling upon us to attend to moral concerns in a way that distorts their relative importance, thus personalizing to wrongful effect the *quality* of a reason's claim upon us, or by calling upon us to attend to the standards laid down by our own conscience when those standards are in fact mistaken, thus personalizing to wrongful effect the *content* of a reason's claim upon us.

So, for example, conscience may call upon us to tell the truth at all times and may thereby compel us to be truthful when it would be better to be untruthful.

Suppose that a friend asks me what I think of the way that he or she has dressed, or what I think of work that he or she has done. It is likely that he or she is seeking reassurance from me, among other things, in the hope and expectation, of course, that the reassurance will be genuine. While it would certainly be wrong, therefore, for me to give false assurances, build false confidence, and so expose my friend to just what he or she sought protection from in seeking my advice, it would also be wrong for me, in some cases at least, to be entirely truthful, for to do so might exact a price in terms of my friend's confidence that the protection of my friend from the possible consequences of a misplaced sense of confidence does not warrant. If the hurt caused by criticism from me now is greater than the risk of hurt caused by a like criticism from others later, then I should not tell my friend the truth. Yet my conscience may call upon me to do just that, for my conscience may insist upon truthfulness from me. And assuming that I act in accordance with my conscience I will have hurt my friend unnecessarily. My moral error here is a straightforward product of the way in which my conscience has raised the commitment to truthfulness to the status of an unqualified duty, and thus is a byproduct of what is one of the central functions of conscience and an important source of its value.

On the other hand, it must be said, personalizing the *content* of a reason's claim upon us raises few concerns when what is at stake is a person's projects and the standards applicable to them. Doing so may make the person in question more single-minded and obsessive than is desirable, given his or her other commitments in life, it may make him or her persist in ventures that would be better abandoned as far as the success of his or her own life is concerned, but it is otherwise unobjectionable. Behaving in these ways is not immoral.

However, this function of conscience does give rise to a related concern that is the fourth and final aspect of what is revealed by these examples of the inner working of conscience. I have noted the ways in which the claims that conscience makes upon us are not entirely moral, but of course the most familiar and famous role of conscience is to remind us of the substance of what morality requires. Conscience does this by crystallizing in its content certain selected moral conclusions that we have either previously reasoned through for ourselves or adopted from other people on whom we have reason to rely, whether through their example or by their instruction. In performing this function, conscience saves us from having to reason our way to the conclusions it embodies on every occasion to which they are relevant. In this respect it might be said that the role of conscience is something akin to a self-conscious and deliberative version of the embodiment of reason that takes place in the shape of personal virtue. Yet it follows that in the same way that a person's character is as liable to embody vice as it is to embody virtue, the content of that person's conscience, vulnerable as it is to the fragility of both his or her own reasoning and the reasoning of others upon whom he or she may have relied, is as liable to entrench what is morally forbidden as it is to entrench what is morally required.

What is more troubling, perhaps, once entrenched in the content of a person's conscience, mistakes are relatively immune to correction, for the authority of conscience, which after all is the source of its value, is such as to protect its content against much of the force of ordinary reasons. As I have emphasized, we do what our conscience requires of us even when, all things considered and apart from the claims of conscience itself, there is good reason to do otherwise. This relative immunity of conscience to the revision of the conclusions it embodies in the light of competing reasons is further enhanced by the fact that what is at stake in the integrity of a person's conscience, and thus what conscience exists to preserve, is not only the substance of the reasons that conscience entrenches but the contribution that such entrenchment makes to the self-image and self-respect of the person in question. Conscience makes it sensible for a person to claim exemption from a reason that is applicable to others simply on the basis that it is not a reason for him or her, as the person that he or she has committed himself or herself to being, and that the actions it calls for are not to be taken in his or her name.

So conscience will not only tell a person, for example, that war is wrong, whether in general or in this particular case, and that conscription should accordingly be resisted, but as important, will add the rider that arguments to the contrary are not to be attended to, or at least are to be given short shrift, other than as a matter of courtesy or tact. To do otherwise, and take seriously arguments that deny the claims of one's conscience, is in itself a violation of what conscience requires, for it makes the content of one's conscience nothing more than ordinary reasons for belief and action, and in so doing renders vulnerable the personal integrity that conscience serves to establish and protect. It is this feature of conscience that is at once the source of its strength and its danger. In suppressing the claims of certain reasons for belief and action conscience disables our concern for all those people whose lives are shaped by those reasons. The claims that those people may make against us are the very claims that our conscience exists to deny. How far this matters depends on both the content of our particular conscience and on the presence or absence of other agents who are able to answer the claims in question. If, as in Jim's case, what is at stake is nineteen lives, and no other person is present to answer to the moral claim that those lives represent, then the danger posed by conscience is quite literally lethal. If, all things considered and apart from the claims of his conscience, it is wrong for Jim not to kill, as may be the case, then his omission will have been the cause of nineteen wrongful deaths, and his ability to recognize that fact, by assessing the ordinary reasons that apply to the situation before him, will have been disabled by the operation of his conscience. To move away from the hypothetical, we are all too familiar today with very real examples of consciences that have called for the killing of innocent human beings, many of them here in London as I write these words. In cases like these the content of conscience is religiously inspired, but its dogmatism, ruthlessness and self-absorption are entirely secular.

The picture that emerges from this exploration of the second puzzle, that of the relation of conscience to reason, is one of conscience as an aid in practical reasoning. Conscience serves as an authoritative repository of convictions that we draw upon in fulfilment of the commitments, personal and moral, that those convictions embody, and in avoidance of what would distract us from them, be it the genuine claims of competing reasons, or the temptation to exaggerate the attraction of reasons to be something less admirable than we expect ourselves to be and so succumb to irrationality. Conscience thus helps us to live well. Yet the nature of its function is such as to render us vulnerable to moral errors that are peculiarly of its own making. To grasp the full implications of this the functions of conscience will have to be explored in greater detail. Before addressing that problem, however, the issue that remains, and the source of the third puzzle, is the nature of the relationship that conscience places us in with other people and what they may claim of us.

3. Conscience and Dissent

In its most familiar guise, conscience is the voice of dissent, the voice of individual conviction, raised in opposition to what the community has asked of the person whose conscience it is. On this account, a person is compelled to dissent by the moral imperatives that make up the content of his or her conscience. This familiar picture can be called into question from two perspectives. On the one hand, there is reason to believe that conscience also speaks to us in private, reminding us of who we are and what we have committed ourselves to. I have pursued this possibility in the previous section. On the other hand, there is reason to believe that, so understood, conscience is as likely to compel us to conform as to dissent. Indeed, so understood, conscience becomes the voice of dissent only when it is publicly expressed, because it is only the dissenting aspect of conscience that requires public expression in order to be effective. Where conscience prompts a person to conform to a community's moral expectations, its operation is more or less private, indeed may be very largely invisible to other persons. And as in the case of icebergs, the invisible aspect of conscience may be much larger and more significant than the visible. But is it plausible to see conscience in terms of conformity? If so, how far should we see conscience in those terms? If not, what does that tell us about the nature of conscience? These are the questions that I will be pursuing in this section. I will take for granted that dissent is a central, though not necessarily definitive feature of the operation of conscience, and look to see whether that is something that can be reconciled with the conventional understanding of conscience.

In considering the practice of conscientious objection, Joseph Raz reminds us that according to the general understanding of it, conscience is the name we give to a person's beliefs about what is morally required. If and to the extent that is true, however, it would appear to follow that conscience could not do its moral work unless it typically operated to bring people into line with the rational judgment of others. If and to the extent that a person's conscience exists to ensure that he or she does the right thing, it must typically ensure that he or she does what others do. If there is reason to doubt this, then there is reason to doubt the analysis of conscience on which it depends.

If conscience is the name we give to a person's moral beliefs, there seem to be only two alternatives to the conclusion that conscience typically leads to conformity, which I will outline briefly before pursuing in more detail. First, it might be the case that dissent is the product of moral error, on one side or the other, on the part of the community or on the part of the conscientious objector. If that were so, however, it would follow that conscientious objection is exactly as common as conscientious error. Unless such error is typical the exercise of conscience must usually lead to conformity. If that seems implausible, as I think it does, then there is reason to doubt the identification of conscience and moral belief.

On the other hand, it might be the case that dissent is the product of moral pluralism, that is, that it is a product of the fact that the moral world is composed of values that are not only incommensurable but incompatible with one another. Yet moral pluralism does not in itself entail moral dissent, for the simple reason that moral pluralism does not entail the kind of heterogeneous communities within which such dissent is bound to arise. On the contrary, many communities, past and present, have been more or less homogeneous in character despite the fact that they have necessarily drawn their values from a moral world that is fundamentally pluralistic. In fact, moral pluralism generates moral conflict within a particular community only as and when incompatible moral values become vested in the lives of different people within that community. That suggests that it is personal commitment that lies at the root of conscience, and conversely, that conformity and dissent are merely possible consequences of such commitment. What is more, if personal commitment is the root of conscience, and of the dissent that conscience may give rise to, it then becomes necessary to ask the meaning and value of that commitment, and to wonder whether and why it should be confined to moral matters.

Dissent as the Product of Error

The first alternative to the idea that conscience typically leads to conformity can be read in two ways.[12] On the one hand is the suggestion that the conscientious objector is typically mistaken. Communities are on the whole correct in what they

---

[12] There is a third possibility, namely, that what is typical is mistake on one side or the other. In other words, somebody is usually mistaken, but mistake is no more likely on the part of the objector than on the part of his or her community. Yet unless mistake is more likely on one side than on the other each side is as likely to be mistaken as the other, and that seems no more plausible than the idea that one side or the other is typically mistaken.

call for and those who dissent from their expectations are unjustified in doing so. In any particular instance, of course, the objector may indeed be mistaken, and the arguments that Raz develops in support of conscientious objection are designed to take proper account of that fact. Yet it cannot be the case that conscience is typically dissenting because it is typically mistaken. In part this is because it is surely more plausible to regard mistakes as aberrations in the operation of a person's conscience, as I have argued above. Conscientious objection would not enjoy the respect it typically commands if it was typically based on a mistake. What is more significant, perhaps, is the fact that the objector is not the only person with a conscience. The people who create community expectations and the people who endorse those expectations have consciences too. It must be the case, therefore, that the expectations that those people respectively create and endorse are in conformity with the claims of their consciences, and accordingly, that their consciences either have operated to bring them into conformity with the rational judgment of others or have nothing to say on the matter in question. Yet if that is so, then conscience would typically ensure conformity even if conscientious objectors were typically mistaken. It follows that this reading of the first alternative fails to make its case.

The other way of reading the first alternative to the conclusion that conscience typically operates to bring people into conformity with the rational judgment of others is that the conscientious objector is, on the contrary, typically correct in his or her conclusions and that the community is correspondingly mistaken. Once again, there can be no doubt that the conscientious objector is sometimes correct in the substance of his or her objection. Indeed, communities are mistaken in what they call for rather more often than most democrats care to contemplate, and when that is so those who dissent from their expectations are entirely correct to object. But this cannot typically be the case, partly because conscientious objectors are not typically sages, partly because it would then be impossible to draw a rational distinction between the practice of conscientious objection and that of civil disobedience (although admittedly that would not be a concern to those like Raz, who see conscience as no more than a person's moral judgments and so regard the two practices as sharing a common moral foundation), and partly because the operation of conscience very often makes imaginative reference to the judgments of other people as a way of ensuring that the person whose conscience it is acts rationally and does not succumb to the temptations generated by his or her own predicament. This last function is an entirely familiar one, and yet it would be self-defeating if the role of conscience was predicated on the presence of error in the judgments of others. It is true that the reference that conscience makes to the judgments of other people is an imaginary one, but it is also true that the point of the exercise is to bring conscience into line with what are imagined to be the judgments of others. On the face of it, that is an act of conformity, though the distance between what the community is thought to call for and what it actually calls for is a significant one that I will return to later, for it exposes a gap between what conscience commits us to and would otherwise be our beliefs on the matter, however they might have been acquired.

If these stories of error are implausible, as I think they are, then the alternative to them, assuming that conscience is the name we give to a person's beliefs about what is morally required, is that conscience must typically operate to bring people into line with the rational judgment of others. Yet this in turn leads to implausible conclusions about the social role of conscience, and thus calls into question the underlying idea that conscience is morally driven. If it is true that conscience typically brings people into line with the rational judgment of others then the good that conscience does must typically be at the cost of the conscientious person's character. Conscience helps us to avoid mistakes, escape weakness and so find moral resolve by becoming less ourselves. There would be something to regret in this, for all the good that it would give rise to. Many aspects of our character involve the close association of good and bad, so that there is a real loss in avoidance of such qualities or certain dimensions of them. Even if the quality in question is wholly bad, it is often the case that bad qualities of character are part of a package that includes good qualities that cannot be separated from them, so that the loss of a bad quality is sometimes to be regretted because it entails the loss of a package that has worthy elements.

The doubt here, however, is not whether the exercise of conscience gives rise to a loss, but whether the loss that this understanding of conscience would give rise to is a loss of the right kind, a loss that is recognizably the product of conscience. One doubts that conscience produces conformity because one doubts that the exercise of conscience can possibly involve a loss of oneself, at least typically. It is true, of course, that in some cases conscience appears to dictate conformity and so to entail a sacrifice of character and commitment. Yet this appearance may be misleading. Shakespeare famously maintained that conscience makes cowards of us all, because its exercise deprives us of our native resolution, and the idea that conscience is cowardly has been echoed by others since.[13] Yet what Shakespeare seems to have had in mind is not so much the cost of conscience as the cost of rational deliberation, which may or may not be an aspect of conscience. (After all, it is just as possible to imagine conscience without deliberation as it is to imagine deliberation without conscience. If that is the case, then to point out the cost of deliberation is not necessarily to point out the cost of conscience.) And if conscience is to be understood as a name for rational deliberation, then conscience is the name of only one species of reasoning and thus the name of a subset of our moral judgments, for action without deliberation no less expresses the moral beliefs of the actor. The balance of our moral beliefs and consequent actions need not be conforming and thus need not be cowardly as Shakespeare saw it.

Wilde seems to have spoken more accurately when he said, presumably by way of reply and with a broader understanding of conscience in mind, that

---

[13] *Hamlet*, Act III, scene i. See also *Richard III*, Act V, scene iii.

conscience makes egoists of us all.[14] Whatever else it is, conscience seems to be an assertion of oneself. People may disagree as to what is being asserted, but there seems little room to doubt that the exercise of conscience is in some sense an act of self-affirmation. And if that is the case, then there is reason to doubt that conscience is something that would make its typical exercise an act of conformity, and so reason to doubt that conscience is but the name we give to a person's beliefs about what is morally required.

I do not wish to overstate the point being made here. To say that there is reason to doubt that conscience is no more than the name we give to a person's beliefs about what is morally required is not to say that there is reason to doubt the place of morality in the content of a person's conscience. On the contrary, morality seems to be an essential element in the content of what conscience requires, and it follows that conformity is a real and significant consequence of the operation of conscience. What is more, this is a feature of conscience that is almost entirely neglected in the general understanding of conscience, which associates conscience with morality and with dissent. The point of my argument here has been to show that the notorious features of conscience, those that dominate the general understanding of it, do not sit well with one another. We can only make sense of the fact that dissent is a central feature of the operation of conscience, a feature no less central than conformity let us suppose, by recognizing that the place of morality in the content of conscience is dependent on the underlying presence of a characteristic of conscience that generates both conformity and dissent, and of which some aspects of morality are virtually always constitutive. Before turning to that issue, however, it is necessary to consider whether conscientious dissent can be explained in terms of moral pluralism.

Dissent as the Product of Moral Pluralism

The other alternative to the conclusion that conscience typically operates to bring people into conformity with the rational judgment of others relies on the fact that moral reasoning very often yields more than one eligible conclusion. That being the case, it would seem to follow that conscience could call upon a person to dissent from what the community requires of him or her without either falling into error itself or relying upon the premise that the community has fallen into error in what it requires. Dissent arises because the objector and the community are committed to fundamentally different moral beliefs, neither of which is mistaken, and neither of which is better than the other. Freedom of dissent is made necessary by the fact that the alternative to that freedom is suppression of a legitimate moral belief. If the belief is central to a person's life the freedom is essential. If it is marginal to that life, its suppression may be justified. If that is the right way to understand the operation of conscience, it has the additional

---

[14] O Wilde, *The Picture of Dorian Gray* (1891).

attraction of explaining the distinction between conscientious objection and civil disobedience. A person conscientiously objects to what the community requires of him or her because it embodies expectations that, although legitimate, are incompatible with the no less legitimate claims of the objector's conscience. A person goes further and becomes civilly disobedient if and when what the community requires is morally illegitimate.

Plausible as this picture is in many respects it cannot explain the practice of dissent in a way that makes dissent the product of a person's moral beliefs. In part this is because dissent is the product, as I indicated above, not of incompatible moral values, but of incompatible moral commitments, and so arises only when incompatible moral values become vested in the lives of different people, in this case in the lives of the dissenter and the other people who constitute his or her community and thus are the authors and supporters of what the community requires. That suggests, as I have also said, that what lies at the root of conscience is some kind of personal commitment, and conversely, that conformity and dissent are each no more than a possible consequence of such commitment. In other words, moral pluralism is not a sufficient condition of moral conflict. It is not enough that a person correctly believes in something other than that which the community has required. He or she must be committed to that belief, without being rationally required to do so, in a way that makes the belief a part of his or her conscience.

More important, perhaps, moral pluralism is not in itself sufficient warrant for dissent from what a community legitimately requires, because the moral reason that sustains the dissent has no greater claim upon the dissenter than the moral reason that sustains the community's requirement. Both are morally legitimate and neither is morally superior to the other. That is what it means for them to embody moral pluralism. This cuts both ways, of course. In such a case there is no better reason to dissent than there is to conform, or to conform than to dissent. But if dissent rather than conformity is the characteristic outcome of the exercise of conscience, then the content of conscience, and the dissent that it characteristically, or at least very commonly gives rise to, must be informed by more than the presence of values that are incompatible with the values that are embodied in the community requirements that conscience conflicts with. If the claims of conscience are to enjoy priority over the community's requirements, it must be because there is something more to conscience than the moral reasons that compose its substance, something that is itself a reason to give those moral reasons a degree of priority, and so justify dissent. All the indications at this point are that it is some kind of personal commitment that supplies that reason, by virtue of the role that it plays in the life of the person whose conscience it is, and of the value that may be produced thereby.

Once again, I do not wish to overstate the point being made here. There can be no doubt that moral pluralism explains the conflict of morally legitimate commitments that exists when a conscientious objector correctly objects to what a community correctly requires. All that is being proposed here is that the explanation that moral pluralism provides is insufficient to justify conscientious dissent. Something more is required if a moral belief, and the action that it calls for, is to have priority over an incompatible moral belief (and the requirement not to act that the incompatible belief sustains) that is incommensurable with it. If that priority is thought to be supplied by the conscientious person's commitment to the moral belief in question, in making that belief part of the content of his or her conscience, the case for that priority depends on knowing just what role commitment plays in the development and expression of a person's conscience, what value that brings to the life of the conscientious person, and in what circumstances these might be reason enough to justify dissent. That is not to displace or discount the role of moral pluralism. On the contrary it is to explain what gives moral pluralism much of its significance in the lives of different people, for it is to explain one important way in which moral pluralism can become entrenched in the fabric of a life, and so give special significance to that life as a good in its own right, and confer special authority on the values that it serves.

Conscience and Rational Personality

1. Rational Personality and Other Forms of Commitment to Reason

The picture of conscience that emerges from this analysis of the three familiar puzzles that have long attended the consideration of conscientious action, those of its relation to civil disobedience, reason and dissent, is one of conscience as a special kind of rational commitment. I said earlier that we are committed to certain reasons by virtue of our rationality alone, for such reasons are more or less inescapable in any human life. Other reasons, by contrast, are more or less optional for us, either because they are in competition with one another for the limited space in our lives, or because they are incompatible with one another, so that there is room in our life for either, but not for both at once, in the same setting and for the same purpose. In regard to reasons of this kind I said that we had to be doubly committed in order to be committed to their place in our life. Our very rationality commits us to a belief in them as reasons. However our character, our goals in life, our histories, and our previous commitments must be called into play if we are to commit ourselves further to a belief in them as reasons for us.

The commitment that conscience embodies is commitment of a third kind, one that sometimes underpins and sustains commitment of the other two kinds, and sometimes serves as a substitute for them. It is a commitment that makes possible the creation and survival of central elements of what I will call our *rational personality*. Human personality is acquired in various ways, and a great deal of perhaps overly familiar argument has centred on the extent to which personality is something we are born with, something we acquire through the circumstances in which we find ourselves (either of which would make us passive recipients of our personality), or something that we create as a byproduct of decisions we take as to how to live well. For my own part, I am tempted to think that personality is made in all these ways, and further, that the way in which it is made does not matter nearly as much as, or for the reasons that, many people take it to matter. However, that is not the central issue here, although it is part of the background to it. What matters here is that, once acquired by whatever means, human personality can be thought of as divided into pre-rational and rational aspects or functions. Our pre-rational personality includes our psychological and physical characteristics and any circumstances that have become embedded in our lives, such as our homeland, our family, our skills, our fundamental goals in life, and any other aspects of our history that we cannot wholly leave behind. At any given point in our life, this is the material that we have to work with. Age and experience add to it in some ways and detract from it in others. Our rational personality, I want to suggest, is both a kind of complement to this, for it is as much a part of our personality as the pre-rational, and a critic of it, for it enables us to reflect upon our personality as a whole, to find it good or bad in one way or another, to call upon it as an aid in deciding what to do, and to make attempts to amend it where we think amendment is called for. As I see it, our rational personality includes not only our distinctive capacity to appreciate reasons, but our virtues and vices and the demands of our conscience.[15]

2. The Scope of Rational Personality

That is a potentially perilous claim, and before elaborating on it I want to diminish its significance in at least four ways. First, there is no clear division between the pre-rational and the rational. These are not compartments of our personality; they are simply ways of thinking of it. As Aristotle emphasized, virtues are deeply embedded in a person's life, so that they can only be acquired over time, and so that, once acquired, they are capable of shaping action without the need for reflection. Much the same is true of conscience, or at least of its deepest, most central features. In that sense, virtue and conscience are part of our pre-rational personality. Yet that is not to question the distinctive role they play in the rational evaluation of our lives and what those lives are directed to. To

---

[15] I take it that what we describe as the power of reasoning is made up of raw intellectual capacity, intellectual skills, and intellectual virtues and vices, and thus is part of both our pre-rational and our rational personality, in the same way as are the virtues and vices and the claims of our conscience. It follows, however, that insofar as it is personalized the power of reasoning is part of the pre-rational personality (apart from the question of its intellectual virtues). In what follows I will typically refer disjunctively to reason and the rational personality, on the assumption that the claims of reason are not personalized in the way that the rational personality is. If that assumption is mistaken, the mistake is not one that has any bearing on what I have to say about conscience.

notice that virtue and conscience are among the objects of their own evaluation is not to deny them their rational distinctiveness in terms of their scrutinizing and directing functions.

Secondly, then, our virtues and our consciences, if products of our will at all, are certainly not products of our will alone. On the contrary, they are acquired through experience, and thus are rationally inspired just to the extent that experience is rationally driven. Many of our virtues and many aspects of our conscience, are acquired unconsciously, as the residue of experiences that are profound enough to have left their mark on us, whether we like it or not. Once acquired, these aspects of our rational personality are by their nature resistant to amendment, and so are no more liable to be removed by an act of will than to be acquired by will in the first place.

Thirdly, our pre-rational personality is not mere raw material, subject to the scrutiny of reason and a rational personality that are its overlords. Quite apart from the fact that our rational personality is subject to the selfsame scrutiny, albeit at its own hands, our pre-rational personality is suffused with rational implications. Strength of character, to take but one example, is not a rationally empty feature of our personality, waiting to be informed according to the direction of reason and the rational personality. On the contrary, strength of character, like most other aspects of our personality, might be said to suffer from an excess rather than a shortage of rational implications, for it makes a host of things possible, both good and bad. What is more significant, perhaps, those possibilities are built into its very meaning, and it is in that form and for that reason that they become candidates for the scrutiny of the rational personality, and where necessary and possible, to its direction. Secondly, as this description indicates, the pre-rational personality is pre-committed to certain of its implications, whether for good or for ill. Strength of character leads to inflexibility as well as to resolve, and the extent to which it leads to one rather than another in the life of any particular person is part of what we describe when we describe his or her (pre-rational) personality. What principally distinguishes the pre-rational from the rational personality, then, is its inability to scrutinize itself. Strength of character can govern its own use (in ways that might not be susceptible to government by reason and the rational personality) and in that way can help to ensure that it is used well, but it cannot tell us whether it has been used well and why, and so cannot do all the work of ensuring virtue.

Fourthly and finally, not only is our pre-rational personality very often rationally informed, as I have indicated, but our rational personality is very often far from rational in terms of what it calls for. People frequently reason badly, and what is more, over time some of the consequences of their having done so become embedded in their rational personality as vices, and false claims of conscience. Indeed, it is all too often the case that the scrutinizing power of the rational personality is misinformed, so as to call for action that is rationally unwarranted and condemn action that is rationally justified. In doing these things it may well subvert an entirely sound rational implication of our pre-rational personality, so as to divert us from a good action that we would have naturally pursued (or at least, so as to attempt to do so), and direct us to a bad action instead. In short, the rational personality is rational in terms of the role it is called upon to play in our lives, but it is not necessarily rational in terms of the way that role is carried out. Its existence is rational, but its content often is not.

3. Conscience as a Distinctive Aspect of Rational Personality

Deep Commitments

If, as I believe, conscience is part of both the pre-rational and the rational personality, it needs to be distinguished from certain of its companions there, given the similarity of some of its features to theirs. As an embedded aspect of our personality, conscience has much in common with the deep commitments that constitute our goals, our history, and our most basic characteristics. Like those commitments, the claims of conscience can provide reasons for us to pursue one course of action rather than another, for they are capable of directing us to activities and pursuits in which we are likely to flourish, and that will, let us suppose, lend narrative unity to our lives. But unlike those commitments, the claims of conscience are by their nature more or less conclusive. Our goals, our history, and our most basic characteristics are vital elements in our rational universe, but they have no special authority there. They give rise to ordinary reasons, reasons that we are bound to take account of, given their close connection to our lives, but reasons that we take account of by considering them in light of every other reason that has a claim upon us.[16] Our goals, our history, even our most basic characteristics enjoy no special protection, no elevated status. We may be given reasons to have other goals, other histories, other basic characteristics, and if we cannot alter the ones that we already have, our reasons to change will be reasons to regret our inability to do so. The claims of conscience, by contrast, are resistant, though not immune, to the force of such reasons. That, indeed, is the very reason for their existence as claims of conscience. They have, within limits laid down by the meaning and value of conscience, authority over other reasons. As I have noted above, conscience expects us to abide by its claims even when, all things considered and apart from the claims of conscience, there is reason to do otherwise.

The Power of Reasoning

It follows, within the rational personality now, that conscience can be distinguished from our ordinary power of reasoning by the relatively static and

---

[16] For further consideration of the rational claims of character, see T Macklem, 'Choice and Value' 7 Legal Theory 1 (2001), 26–31.

authoritative nature of its function and content. Our ordinary power of reasoning, as I understand it, is simply our capacity to appreciate reasons and to negotiate their significance correctly. In the proper exercise of this power we are bound to attend to every reason that has a claim upon us (including the reasons generated by our conscience), and to give those reasons their due by assessing them in terms of their true force and quality. Our assessment is sometimes deliberative and sometimes instinctive, bearing in mind that we sometimes do better in terms of the reasons that apply to us when we act instinctively than when we deliberate, and vice-versa.[17]

To say these things is to say enough to distinguish our ordinary power of reasoning from the claims of our conscience, to which that ordinary power is bound to attend. Where reasoning is active, conscience is relatively passive; where reasoning is open and attentive, conscience is relatively closed and authoritative. The point of conscience is not to listen and respond, but to speak and determine. There are limits to this, of course. Given that conscience is as much a part of our pre-rational personality as it is a part of our rational personality, it is as much an object of rational scrutiny, assessment, and amendment as it is a source of reasons. If our reasoning is susceptible to the claims of our conscience, our conscience is also susceptible to the reforming power of our reasoning. What matters is that these respective susceptibilities are limited by what is due to reasoning and to conscience as distinctive rational phenomena. Our reasoning attends to the claims of our conscience as reasons, and gives them their due as such. Conscience cannot make claims upon reasoning that would result in irrationality, all things considered and due attention having been given to the value of conscience as a phenomenon distinct from the rational content of its claims. On the other hand, our reasoning is bound to attend to the claims of our conscience as the special kind of reasons that they are, and so is bound to show them the degree of deference appropriate to them, and thereby distinguish them from the claims of other reasons.

Virtues and Vices

Like our conscience, the virtues and vices are deeply embedded in the rational personality. As I have already noted, these are not features of personality that we can either acquire or remove by an act of will. Yet the way in which we acquire virtue and vice, and the way in which we respond to it, differs from the way in which we acquire and respond to the claims of our conscience. Put shortly, the virtues and vices are integrated with our pre-rational personality in ways that most aspects of conscience are not, and that is because it is part of the function of conscience to maintain whatever distance from other aspects of our personality, rational as well as pre-rational, is necessary to preserve its authority over them.

---

[17] For further consideration of reasons and reasoning see J Gardner and T Macklem, 'Reasons', in J Coleman and S Shapiro (eds) *The Oxford Handbook of Jurisprudence and Philosophy of Law* (2001) 440–475.

Some aspects of virtue and vice are both so deeply entwined with aspects of our pre-rational personality, and so distant from the possibility of deliberation, that it makes sense to think that we may have been born with them. At the very least, there is a deep affinity between them and qualities that we cannot imagine ourselves as lacking. Some people seem to be so deeply kind, or generous, or sympathetic, and to have been that way from the very earliest expressions of their personality, that actions in the spirit of those virtues seem not only natural in them but native to them.

The same is not true of conscience, however. Conscience is something that we develop as part of the development of our power of reasoning, because the role of conscience, like that of the power of reasoning, is to scrutinize our beliefs and actions, and that means that it must establish and maintain whatever distance from them is necessary to the success of that scrutiny. The consequent contrast with the virtues and vices is in the particular way that reason informs belief and action. In the case of virtue it is from the inside; in the case of conscience it is from the outside. It follows that we can act virtuously as soon as we can act, or more tentatively, that we can learn to act virtuously as soon as we can learn to act in ways that are capable of manifesting virtue and vice, but we can only act conscientiously once we have acquired the developmentally more sophisticated capacity to reflect on our actions. This in turn means that conscientious action is always self-conscious. Action may be in accordance with one's conscience, of course, without one being aware that it is so, but action can only be in fulfilment of the claims of one's conscience if and when one sets out to make it so. The same is plainly not true of virtue and vice.

4. The Value of Conscience

What need is there for conscience when one has reason and virtue at one's disposal? How could there be anything at stake in Jim's predicament beyond the goodness and badness of the action he is contemplating, and the power of reason and virtue to assist him in knowing where goodness lies and how to live up to its demands? The thought in reply is this. Like character and culture, the commitments embodied in our conscience play a role in our life the value of which is a function, in different degrees in different lives at different times, of certain potentially centrifugal features of the human predicament: the complex, various, and fragmentary nature of the moral world; the fluidity of many of our social forms and practices; the compass of a human life; and the arc of development of certain goods, values, and virtues. Put more specifically, the realization of certain values and virtues in the life of any human being depends upon a degree of personal stability and continuity that, in the absence of an appropriate external guide or authority, may require the scrutiny and direction of conscience. Otherwise those particular values and virtues would be unrealizable by that person. Indeed, and more profoundly, it appears to be the case that certain aspects of our very existence as rational agents depend on the presence of conscience, just as others depend on the presence of virtue and the capacity to reason.

Rational Personality and Rational Agency

Begin, briefly, with the other aspects of the rational personality. We cannot reason other than as autonomous reasoners, for the simple reason that other people cannot reason for us. We may attend to the reasoning of others, and in many cases are bound to do so, but we must then reason for ourselves in order to know how far to accept the reasoning that we have attended to. If we could not reason like this we could not live well. Our personal capacity to reason, in other words, is essential to our capacity to be rational agents, not patients, and our capacity to be rational agents is essential to our living well. By the same token, were the virtues not our virtues, so as to be embedded in our lives, they could not play their proper role in shaping our actions and beliefs. Another person's courage cannot overcome my fear. It can only help me to find courage in myself, as I must do if I am to show courage where courage is called for. In both these ways, then, certain aspects of reasons and reasoning become ours, so as to form part of our rational personality.

But there is more to the story, for the capacity to reason simply brings reasons home to a person, without making them his or her own, and the acquisition of virtues is not necessarily enough to make a person a fully functioning rational agent. While the virtues are by definition resistant to the force of vices, they are not resistant to the rational claims of other virtues, and so are liable to be displaced by other virtues to the extent that they are not indissolubly embedded in the pre-rational personality, that is, to the extent that the virtues of the life that a person has yet to live remain open for negotiation. Without the presence of conscience, therefore, it would be difficult, perhaps impossible, for an agent to establish and negotiate the full implications of his or her particular rational stake in the rational universe.

Conscience enables us to make some part of that universe our own, so as to make reasons that are otherwise more or less optional into reasons for us, and so as to give reasons that are otherwise more or less inescapable particular force and status in our lives. The problem is not the straightforward one, that without conscience we would be overly vulnerable to heterogeneous and multiple rational demands, so that our centres could not hold, to paraphrase Yeats. Rather, the problem is that without conscience we would be liable to react to those demands in the wrong way. Without conscience we would be more vulnerable than we are to the tendency to respond to the centrifugal features of the human predicament by distorting the rational significance of motive and attachment. All too often we fail to look behind the emotional and psychological bonds that connect us to our personal circumstances and condition, so as to discover the values they serve and the reasons they correspondingly give rise to. In doing this we succumb to the temptation to treat the elements of our pre-rational personality as valuable in themselves. Conscience counters this tendency, not by denying the rational significance of motive and attachment, as do some overly detached accounts of reason, but by playing its distinctive role in giving them their proper place. Just how it does this is a function of its content, an issue that I have already touched upon and will take up more fully in the next section.[18] Once conscience has done this, however, in whatever way, motive and attachment then play a more limited, but no less valuable function as the emotional manifestations of our rational personality, the personality that provides us with a rational basis for personal continuity, and of which conscience is a guardian.

Rational Personality, Virtues, and Values

Quite apart from the fundamental role that conscience may play in enabling us to be rational agents, and so establish and negotiate our stake in the rational universe, conscience may play a further role in fostering, within certain lives, the realization of values and virtues that are distinctively dependent upon certain forms and degrees of personal continuity. Beyond the minimum that is necessary to the establishment and maintenance of rational agency, conscience has the capacity to entrench within the rational personality the moral stabilities that are necessary to be a person of a certain kind. Many values in life, and many aspects of virtue, are dependent upon the presence of such stabilities, sometimes as a condition of their very existence, and sometimes as constitutive of their goodness.

The acquisition of virtue is, it need hardly be said, broadly recommended to us by reason, and once acquired, any particular virtue helps to establish the personal stability that ensures its own continuance. That is simply what it means for the virtue to be entrenched as part of our pre-rational personality. Once we have acquired strength of character, for example, that strength of character will help us to remain of strong character, and perhaps grow yet stronger. Yet this process is subject to at least two vulnerabilities. First, reason recommends every virtue to us, and while our particular condition and circumstances may help us to fasten on some virtues rather than others, as the virtues that are particularly relevant to our lives, they cannot fully determine which virtues we should acquire, partly because our condition and circumstances have multiple implications themselves, so as to make a number of incompatible virtues relevant to our lives, and partly because our condition and circumstances are rationally passive, and so do no more than establish the implications of acquiring one virtue rather than another,

---

[18] I will take up there the value of conscience in simply reminding us to be rational, thereby helping to free us, in relation to reasons that are more or less inescapable in any human life, from the tendency of motive and attachment to offer false justification for attempts to escape the morally inescapable. I have neglected that issue at this stage because I am concerned here to identify the distinctive value of conscience. In reminding us to be rational, conscience tells us nothing that reason does not already tell us. That does not mean that the reminder is not valuable, and thus an important element in the content of conscience.

by reminding us of the kind of person we are at any given moment, and of what it would mean for us to change or remain the same. That being the case, they are bound to remit the problem of what person we should be, and which virtues we should acquire, to our power of reason, which is where the problem began. Secondly, therefore, whatever our condition and circumstances may be, there are always reasons to be something other than the kind of people we now are, and so are always reasons to have virtues other than the virtues that are made relevant by our present condition. If the stability of virtue is dependent on the stability of our condition and circumstances, then it is as vulnerable as they are to the claims of competing reasons.

What is true of the virtues that our lives may embody is as true of the values to which they may be committed. We cannot look to our condition and circumstances, or to the values with which our lives are presently engaged, for the continuity that we need in order to pursue certain values. Rather, it is the existence of the requisite degree of continuity that makes possible pursuit of certain values that are only fully realizable over time, or that are only realizable in the setting of other values that themselves are only realizable over time. Many values depend for their full realization on personal commitment to the continuing development of a good, or of the capacity for that good, over a significant period of time. This is because many valuable activities, such as that of being a musician, depend on the kind of knowledge, understanding and skill that can only be acquired with long practice, and so require deep and prolonged commitment from their participants. As I have already suggested, the problem in practice is not normally one of instability, though it is true that in a fluid social environment like the one we live in today such activities are more difficult to pursue, and thus more often abandoned, than they would have been in a more stable environment. One has only to think, by contrast, of past societies such as traditional Japan, that were not only stable in themselves but that consequently fostered the pursuit of activities, such as special forms of art, that required stability not merely across a single life but across generations. In general, however, the problem is less a matter of instability than a matter of finding stability in the wrong quarter, so that people look to what they are in order to know whether what they are doing is good (for them, as it is often put) and whether it should be continued in. In short, absent the intervention of conscience we would be liable to treat our condition and circumstances as having a greater rational authority than they actually possess.

It is important not to claim too much on behalf of the value of conscience. First, the continuity of our rational personality depends not only on conscience but in large part on the contribution made by our condition and circumstances, that is, by our pre-rational personality, guided by reason and informed by virtue. Conscience has a genuine role to play here, but it is a role that is easy to overstate. What conscience can do is to offer a form of continuity that is protected, to some extent at least, against the rational defects that would follow from reliance on the continuities that are suggested by our character and circumstances. The continuities of character are liable to be morally misleading, given that character can be bad, and overly conservative, given that they are necessarily drawn from the person that time and circumstance have made us. This means, on the one hand, that to the extent that conscience is not only part of the rational personality but aspirational and idealizing (as I will try to explain in the next section), its scrutiny can help to protect us from the errors that reliance on our character and circumstances might lead us into. On the other hand, to the extent that conscience is prospective in its outlook and what it calls for, it can help to protect us from undue conservatism, and so can suggest new directions in life, committed to fresh values and displaying fresh virtues.

Yet these are both no more than possibilities, and that is the other reason not to claim too much for conscience. As I have emphasized, conscience is entirely capable of being both wrong-headed and reactionary, for the content of conscience is not only laid down by reason, and thus vulnerable to every rational error that human beings are subject to, but also laid down in ways that are undetermined by reason, given that the value of conscience is dependent on its capacity to offer us forms of guidance that reason cannot provide.[19] That means, of course, that the claims of conscience can be and often are mistaken. We are all too familiar with the dreadful beliefs and actions that people have been committed to by their consciences, and with the dreadful certainties, and imperviousness to reason, that typically attend those beliefs. What is more, the claims of conscience are often conservative, for they call upon people to continue to be the kind of people that they have committed themselves to being, in the face of good reasons to become something better by becoming something different.

The distinctive feature of conscience, then, and the source of its value, is that on the one hand its embeddedness makes it a part of our pre-rational personality, in the same way as our character and our culture, our virtues and our vices. On the other hand, its scrutinizing function places it within our rational personality, in the company of virtue and the power of reasoning. The strengths and weaknesses of conscience are products of these facts, as can be seen by looking more closely at its content.

5. The Content of Conscience

In describing the contours of our personal engagement with reason, and the forms of commitment that it entails, I suggested that conscience is a special kind of rational commitment. It sometimes serves to underpin and sustain and sometimes serves as a substitute for the two standard forms of commitment to reason that characterize our existence as rational agents, and so makes possible the

---

[19] I say undetermined by reason on the basis that determination of what to do in situations of incommensurability or equality becomes a matter of determining which option to pursue. In the former situation the answer is underdetermined while in the latter it is undetermined.

creation and survival of central elements of what I called our rational personality. I also noted that we are committed to certain reasons by virtue of our rationality alone, for such reasons are more or less inescapable in any human life. Other reasons, by contrast, are more or less optional for us, either because they are in competition with one another for the limited space in our lives, or because they are incompatible with one another, so that there is room in our life for either, but not for both at once, in the same setting and for the same purpose. In regard to these reasons, I said that we had to be doubly committed in order to be committed to a belief in them as reasons for us, and thus to a belief in their place in our lives.

Conscience as a Reminder of the Morally Inescapable

The content of any particular conscience tracks the two kinds of rational commitment that conscience may underpin or serve as a substitute for, and so bears a distinctive relation to reasons that are more or less inescapable in any life and to reasons that are more or less optional for us. The first of these relationships is the more familiar. Conscience famously reminds us of what we should think and do at moments when we are motivated to do otherwise. On the brink of committing ourselves to a belief or action we stop to consult our conscience in order to discover whether the commitment in question is indeed permissible, or whether we are merely tempted to think so. In such a circumstance the content of conscience normally takes one of two broad forms, each of which is designed to meet the exigencies of a particular kind of conflict between reason and attachment.

In some respects conscience takes the form of a moral code. It serves as a repository for certain moral conclusions that we have either previously reasoned through for ourselves or have adopted from other people on whom we have reason to rely. In that sense conscience is a kind of codification of our most basic moral commitments. The value of the ability to refer to that codification is twofold. In part it is simply a matter of efficiency, in that it relieves us from having to reason our way to the conclusions that conscience embodies on every occasion to which those conclusions are relevant. With that efficiency uppermost in mind, conscience might be understood as no more than a response to the rational demands of urgent situations, as Dworkin claims. Yet such an interpretation would involve two significant distortions. First, not every intellectually archived rational conclusion is a matter of conscience. Accumulated wisdom only becomes a matter of conscience when we commit ourselves to it personally, so as to make adherence to that wisdom part of our self-understanding as particular rational beings. Secondly, therefore, when conscience reminds us to be moral it is not only for the sake of the reasons that conscience embodies, but for the sake of the self-image and self-respect that adherence to the claims of our conscience gives rise to. Our reference to what conscience has codified, like every reference to conscience, is necessarily self-conscious, and thus is necessarily part of the way we see ourselves as moral beings. This is not to deny that reference to what conscience has codified is valuable because it is efficient. It is simply to say that such value is secondary and contingent.

The more central and characteristic value of the ability to refer to what conscience has codified is a matter of moral resolve, in that it helps to ensure that we do not succumb to the temptation to exaggerate or otherwise distort the very real rational claims that we experience in the form of motive and attachment. The rational peril that we face here is the product of bias rather than haste. Reference to conscience in these circumstances is sometimes reference to a moral code, in the way I have just described, but is more often reference to what might be thought of as a kind of rational jury of our peers. In circumstances of urgency, and where virtue has not already guided us to the correct conclusion, we are bound to refer to conscience as a moral code. However, where deliberation is possible (because time permits), and desirable (because the right answer requires some reflection) we ask ourselves what other people would do in our predicament. In doing this we commit ourselves to the more or less inescapable features of reason and goodness in a way that brings our beliefs and actions into conformity with the beliefs and actions of other people, real or hypothetical. Only in the latter form, however, does the reference to conscience genuinely free us from the distortions of motive and attachment.

When we ask ourselves what other people would do in our predicament the other people we have in mind are sometimes no more than the other members of our community, and what is more, the actions that we anticipate their taking are no more than the actions that we predict they would in fact take. Thus invoked, conscience is indeed a coward, for it asks us to set aside the conclusions that we would reach, not merely under the possibly distorting influence of our motives and attachments, but in the exercise of our own powers of reasoning and our own virtues, in favour of conclusions that are inspired by exactly the same features in other people. So understood, conformity is not merely the consequence of the exercise of conscience in relation to reasons that are more or less inescapable in any human life (as it is bound to be), but the very source of what conscience is said to require. Yet to seek reason by making one's beliefs conform to what other people believe defeats the point of referring to conscience in the first place, which in this setting is to ensure that we do not succumb to the temptation to exaggerate or distort the rational significance of reasons that we experience as motive and attachment. There is no reason to think that the judgments of other people are any less vulnerable to such exaggeration and distortion than are one's own. This is not, I should add, to discount the value of moral expertise, and the need to refer to the judgment of others in order to discover that expertise. Sometimes we do better by deferring to the judgment of people who have special experience and understanding of certain moral matters, but only when such experience is required and the people in question actually have it.

More typically, however, when we ask ourselves what other people would do in our predicament the reference is no more than a heuristic device, one that enables us to see our motives and attachments from a position of relative detachment, so as to appreciate their moral significance from a perspective that is at once fully sensitive to the interests at stake (because it is the perspective of our deliberation) yet entirely indifferent to the question of who is considering those interests (because it is the perspective of our rationality). So understood, conscience functions as a kind of protection against the potentially irrational sirens of motive and attachment. It describes a position that is fully agent-neutral, yet capable of registering the significance of factors that have the weight they do because of the role they play when seen from the perspective of the agent's life.

Conscience as an Arbiter of the Morally Permissible

If some reasons are more or less inescapable in any human life, other reasons, by contrast, are more or less optional for us, so that we must commit ourselves to them, not only by virtue of our very rationality, but by virtue of a belief in the special role that they can play, and should play, in our lives. We thus further commit ourselves to a belief in these reasons as reasons for us. Certain aspects of that commitment, in general those that are backward-looking and conservative, are generated by rational reflection on our condition and our circumstances. We ask ourselves what kind of people we are, and what kind of opportunities and challenges are offered by the circumstances we find ourselves in, and then consider what valuable pursuits people in our position might reasonably commit themselves to. In this way, it might be said, we exercise the discretion that morality offers us in relation to such matters so as to commit ourselves particularly to certain options in life.

Now, as I have already observed, the resources that this kind of enquiry provides us with are backward-looking, and the range of options that it recommends to us in light of those resources is open-ended. Paradoxically, therefore, reflection on our past and present condition and circumstances, as inspirations for our future, provides us with both too little and too much information. On the one hand it suggests options in terms of the kinds of people we now are and the kinds of predicament in which we now find ourselves, and so tells us nothing about the kinds of people we might become and the kinds of worlds that we might move into, other than as extensions and projections of who and what we now are. It thus limits the range of possible lives open to us. In many cases, admittedly, that may be no bad thing, because the options that such an enquiry suggests to us may well be rich enough, and the circumstances that it draws upon may well be stable enough, for us to develop a successful life in terms of them.

However, if we are to enlarge our worlds, as is often desirable and sometimes necessary, we must call upon a resource that will enable us to move beyond what is suggested by our present condition and circumstances, and so must develop an image of ourselves as people other than the people we now are, consider the options that would be accessible to people of that kind, and then direct our energies to becoming the people that we have imagined ourselves to be. This process also works in the opposite direction, of course, so that we contemplate options that strike us as desirable, formulate an image of ourselves as the people for whom such options are accessible, consider the feasibility of becoming people of that kind, and then direct our energies accordingly. Typically, it would seem, the enterprise of imagining our future is likely to work first in one direction, then the other. What matters is that the success of this enterprise depends on the ability to create, maintain and refer to an idealized and prospective image of ourselves, which we then seek to live up to by calling upon as a guide. Part of the role of our conscience is to embody that image.

On the other hand, reflection on our past and present condition and circumstances, as inspirations for our future, also provides us with too much information, for apart from situations of injustice, in which our characters may have become stunted and our circumstances straitened, it normally confronts us with a range of valuable options from among which we must choose one or more to commit ourselves to. Given that the options before us are all valuable, we have as good reason to choose one as to choose another. There is no avoiding the fact that in such a situation we must simply decide. Neither reason nor circumstance can make the decision for us. Nor indeed can our conscience do so, for the content of our conscience is normally a product of such a decision, not its source. Even in those cases where conscience is the source of such a decision, it is only because conscience has been already invested with a particular content, and that investment, when not determined by reason and circumstance, must itself be arbitrary.

Yet there is reason to stick with a choice among options once we have made it, lest we suffer from vacillation and second-guessing. Sometimes the reason to stick with a choice can be discovered by thinking back a stage in one's original enquiry. If I decide to pursue a certain career, at a point when other no less valuable careers are open to me, I may find a reason to continue in that career thereafter in my underlying reason to look for a career in the first place, the reason that made several career paths eligible options for me then.[20] That reason will protect me against the temptation to abandon the career I have chosen and pursue another career instead simply on the basis that the other career was and remains no less eligible than the one that I have chosen. That reason may be reinforced by the reasons generated by my history and circumstances once I have spent some time in the career that I have chosen, so that it has become a part of me, if that is what has happened. But if and to the extent that the career is a new one, or the underlying reason is not there (because, let us suppose, I was never that committed to the idea of a career in the first place) I will need some other rational recourse to protect me from vacillation and second-guessing. Once again, part of the role of conscience is to supply that recourse, by embodying an image of ourselves as the people we have committed

---

[20] See T Macklem, 'Choice and Value', above n 16, 31.

ourselves to becoming. That commitment may have been under-determined by reason in the first place, and thus to that extent arbitrary, but its embodiment in idealized form as a commitment of conscience makes continuance in it just as rational as is the realization of the value that the presence of conscience in our lives makes possible.

Once conscience begins to function in this way it becomes capable of acquiring additional implications, some of which I have examined above. Once we have formed a picture of ourselves as people characterized by certain ongoing commitments to what would otherwise be no more than morally permissible in our lives, we may extend the character of those commitments so as to include other objects. In this way we commit ourselves to doing more than morality calls upon us to do, and so commit ourselves to treating certain aspects of the supererogatory as duties, or to setting standards for ourselves in the conduct of our professional and domestic lives that are higher than success in either of those ways of life demands. In much the same spirit we may commit ourselves to continuing in a particular way of life, professional or domestic, just in order to live up to the image of ourselves that has been embodied in our conscience, as a person who is characterized by commitment of that kind, and so is not susceptible to the claims of rival commitments, not only when those claims represent unjustified and thus irrational temptations, but even when they represent options that are more reasonable than the one we have committed ourselves to.

Sometimes this is a good thing and sometimes it is not. Doing more than morality calls upon us to do is clearly a good thing, as long as it does not entail neglect of some other duty. Setting exceptionally high standards for ourselves in the conduct of our professional or domestic lives may sometimes be a good thing, though it may also undermine our success in other aspects of our lives, and perhaps even in the aspects in question. Being a perfectionist in one's work, for example, may lead not only to neglect of one's family, but to inefficiency and neglect of other aspects of one's job. What is more, it may involve fidelity to standards that make one unable to complete the work in question, or to be dissatisfied with it when one does. It may even involve fidelity to standards that are misguided, or at least that, if not misguided, do not contribute to the values supposed to be realized by those for whom the work was intended. These mistakes are peculiarly the product of conscience, because the point of the work has become not the work itself and the audience for whom it was intended, but the need to live up to the demands of an image of oneself that conscience has created and embodied.

Once again I should emphasize that this is not to suggest that conscience and commitment can be identified. Our commitments to our spouses, our jobs, our families, our friends are not in themselves matters of conscience. We are committed to these things simply because and to the extent that we have reason to be so, because of the kind of people we are, the kind of lives we have led, the kinds of undertakings to others that we have made, and the goodness that a person in our position is able to realize by making and living up to the commitments in question. We call upon conscience only in special cases of moral permission, where we seek to imagine the future without much guidance from the past, and further, seek to structure and be true to the demands of that future, and make our choice among options as to its direction and course, by reference to an image of ourselves as the person we have thereby committed ourselves to becoming.

Ironically, perhaps, in doing this we may render ourselves more susceptible than we would otherwise be to the very defects of motivation and attachment that conscience in its other branch also serves to help us avoid. Conscience here calls upon us to attend to our attachments as a matter of duty, when there may be good reason to do otherwise. By attending to the claims of conscience in such a situation we may honour our self-image at the expense of our obligations to others, trivially so when we tell people things they would be better off not knowing in order to preserve an image of ourselves as truth-tellers, fatally so if, like Jim perhaps, we allow people to die whom we might have saved, in order to keep our hands free of their blood.

6. The Function of Conscience

I have suggested throughout, and particularly in considering the relationship of conscience to reason, that conscience has a kind of authority over other reasons. The claims that our conscience makes upon us do not simply add to the repertoire of reasons before us. Rather, they are mandatory reasons, which tell us to follow their direction, and correspondingly exclude consideration of the other reasons that are relevant to the decision before us and that would otherwise determine its outcome. Obedience to the claims of conscience (and thus respect for their mandatory character) is justified when we do better, in terms of the issue before us, by following them than by setting them aside. We know this, not by considering the issue before us either without regard to the claims of our conscience, or by regarding those claims as if they were ordinary reasons for action, but by considering whether the mandatory character of conscience indeed helps us to do better in this situation than we would do without regard to our conscience, by successfully meeting the concern that it is the special function of conscience to address there.[21]

Begin with a mundane example that does not raise the problem of our obligations to others. Suppose that my conscience calls upon me to finish marking essays, or to wash the dishes, before going to bed. This rule may serve a number of values. It may help to preserve me from a certain species of self-indulgence. It may foster in me a sense of attentiveness to my duties in general. If and to the extent that compliance with the rule achieves those ends,

[21] On mandatory and exclusionary reasons in general see, of course, J Raz, *Practical Reason and Norms* (2nd edn, 1990).

I have reason to attend to my conscience and so to set aside what remain good reasons to go to bed with the essays unmarked, the dishes unwashed. But suppose that my reasons for going to bed have nothing to do with self-indulgence, and that I have a highly developed sense of attentiveness to my duties in general that is unlikely to be threatened by breach of the duty that my conscience seeks to impose here. In that case I should recognize that the claims of my conscience are not absolute, but limited by their tendency to serve the values that conscience exists to serve in any particular setting, and I should accordingly decide whether, all things considered, it would be better for me to go to bed now and complete my tasks in the morning.

Much the same pattern holds when what is at stake is not only more serious but involves obligations to others. Whether we should obey the claims of our conscience, or set them aside and allow our behaviour to be regulated by the ordinary reasons that otherwise apply to it, depends on whether complying with our conscience in any particular setting serves the values that conscience, or at least this aspect of it, is supposed to further there. So if conscience becomes a source of bias rather than an escape from it; if it sets empty standards rather than elevated ones; if it begins merely to burnish and so to serve as an end an image of oneself the value of which is primarily as a vehicle for the realization of other goods, then the claims of conscience should be set aside.

A relatively clear example of this can be found by returning to the distinction I drew earlier between reasons that are more or less inescapable in any human life and reasons that are more or less optional. Conscience has a contrasting, even antithetical role to play in relation to reasons of these two kinds, simply because conscience serves contrasting, even antithetical values in each case. Where reasons are more or less inescapable, in the sense that we are bound to be committed to their claims, conscience serves to remind us of those claims, and so helps to protect us from the irrationalities we might otherwise be led into by the emotional force of our motives and attachments. Where, on the other hand, reasons are more or less optional for us, in the sense that we become fully committed to their claims only as a consequence of our character, our goals in life, our histories and our previous commitments, conscience plays a role in committing us to a belief in those reasons as reasons for us, by providing an idealized and prospective image of ourselves, which we then seek to live up to by calling upon as a guide. In the former case, conscience distances us from our attachments; in the latter case it helps to give those attachments their proper rational force.

In asking ourselves whether we ought to abide by the claims of our conscience, therefore, we must ascertain the character of the action before us, ask ourselves what role conscience properly plays in relation to actions of that character, and then decide whether compliance with our conscience in that setting would meet the concern that it is the special function of conscience to address there. Where the action that we are called upon to undertake is an action dictated by a reason that is not optional for us, but inescapable in any human life, the role of our conscience must be to suppress the claims of our motives and attachments, as unwarranted in that setting. It follows that in that setting it would be wrong for us to give effect to those other aspects of our conscience that serve to foster a legitimate role for motive and attachment, for that role is legitimate in relation only to reasons that are optional for us. Given that the reasons before us are not optional, we are not justified in giving effect to motives and attachments that are in conflict with them, and thus are not justified in giving effect to those aspects of our conscience that would have that consequence.

It follows that a person in Jim's predicament is at risk of making a category error if he declines to kill (assuming that killing is required of a person in his predicament) in order to preserve an image of himself as a person whose hands are free of the blood of others. His only options are to deny that the reason to kill is a valid reason; to argue that while the reason to kill is valid and morally inescapable it is only more or less so and that his case falls within a special exception to the rule (perhaps he is incapable of carrying out the killing through no fault of his own); or to do the killing. What he cannot do is to claim that the integrity of his conscience offers him a moral basis for resisting a reason the nature and force of which attaches it to the life of every human being. That would be to invoke an aspect of conscience that applies to one kind of reason only (because its value depends on the service it offers to reasons of that kind) as an answer to the claims of an entirely different kind of reason, in regard to which conscience has a very different, antithetical role to play.

It is important to be careful here. Reasons that are more or less morally inescapable in our lives are reasons that every person is committed to by virtue of his or her very rationality, and in that sense it is true to say that we are attached to such reasons, and that one of the functions of conscience is to remind us of that attachment, in reminding us to be rational. Yet this attachment is an attachment that we have in common with every other rational being, so that in successfully reminding us of this attachment our conscience simply brings our conduct into line with the conduct of every other rational human being, whose conscience, if not mistaken, is offering him or her exactly the same reminder. That being the case, conscience is no basis for dissent in this setting, unless the dissent is based on an allegation of error on the part of the authors of what is being dissented from. Put another way, the claims of conscience in a situation like this do not allow the conscientious objector to be anything other than a civil disobedient (although of course it might be the case that in such a setting civil disobedience calls for no action other than conscientious objection). It does not allow Jim or anybody else to decide that it would be wrong for him or her to carry out a killing that it would not be wrong for some other person to undertake.

Where on the other hand the reason before us is one that is more or less optional in the life of human beings, yet one that we have committed ourselves to in particular, either as a consequence of our existing character and commitments, or as the result of a bare decision as to the direction in which to take our lives when confronted by more than one morally eligible option, and where we have accordingly embodied that commitment in our conscience as part of our self-image, arguments of conscience must be based on the moral significance of autonomy and investment. We are initially attached to reasons of that kind as the result of decisions that we have undertaken in the exercise of our autonomy, so that respect for our attachment is a consequence of respect for our autonomy in creating it. We are entitled to preserve such attachments, therefore, at a minimum, on the same basis as we are entitled to create them. Any such entitlement is then strengthened by the depth of investment we have made in those attachments. If the attachment is relatively fresh, and other rationally eligible options remain both available and accessible without great cost of change, it is not asking too much of us to ask us to pursue another option, as long as doing so is itself consistent with our autonomy. The more that we have invested in the attachment, however, and the more identified our lives have become with it, the more unreasonable it will be to ask us to change it, and the more our commitment to it, as a matter of conscience or otherwise, is entitled to respect.

None of this is to deny what Joseph Raz has to say on the subject of conscientious objection and autonomy, which has to do, not with when we are right, or with what it would take for us to be right, but when we are wrong, and how far our error in that regard is entitled to respect.

7. The Consequences of Conscience

There is not much to add here to what I have said earlier in considering the third puzzle that attends the question of conscientious action, that of its relationship to dissent. Conscience is most familiar to us in the aspect of dissent, because that is where its demands are necessarily externalized and so made public, and moreover, where the vindication of those claims requires identification of conscience as their warrant. Yet as I have been at pains to emphasize, the claims of conscience are as likely to bring us into conformity with what others expect as to dissent from it, and that is because one of the central functions of conscience is to preserve us from the unfounded claims of motive and attachment. It follows not only that we should not think of conscience through the prism of dissent, for that would be to limit our understanding of conscience, but that in thinking of the consequences of conscience, and their implications for freedom, we need to remember conformity.

Freedom of Conscience

Most academic consideration of the question of freedom of conscience has been focused on the practice of conscientious objection, and for good reason. It is conscientious objection that brings a person's conscience into the open, and so raises the problem of the scope to be given to the claim of conscience to legitimize dissent from what would otherwise be the legitimate expectations of others. The issue of conscientious objection has been thoroughly and ably canvassed in the literature, and while there is undoubtedly more to be said about it, particularly given the view of conscience I have outlined here, I would instead like to say something relatively brief and suggestive about those aspects of conscience that may have been obscured in the familiar accounts of conscience, as a result of the focus of those accounts on the public face of conscience, and so may have been neglected in the consideration of freedom of conscience.

There are two aspects to this neglect, one having to do with the domain of the private and the other having to do with freedom. To begin with the former, if it is the case, as I have suggested, that much of the operation of conscience is private and inward-looking, then much of the support for conscience, and of the freedom on which it depends, must be directed to that private operation. This means that it is not enough for a public regime to ensure proper respect for the practice of conscientious objection. True freedom of conscience depends on the development of an intellectual and cultural environment that is sympathetic to the exercise of conscience in all its aspects, namely, an environment in which people are free to develop within themselves an idealized and aspirational image of themselves as rational beings, reminding themselves of what rationality requires, committing themselves to some portion of what rationality permits, and then conforming to or dissenting from the expectations of others as reason requires in their case. Given that the internal operations of conscience are very largely invisible, and that the proper outcome of those operations may well be the alignment of certain aspects of the agent's beliefs and conduct with the expectations of others, the liberty that is required will typically be positive liberty, and moreover, is likely to be best fostered by the fostering, not so much of freedom of conscience itself, which is not particularly amenable to external encouragement, as of other, related freedoms, such as freedom of expression and privacy, on which freedom of conscience depends for its flourishing.

The other aspect of what may have been neglected in those accounts of freedom of conscience that have focused on the practice of conscientious objection is that of the conditions of freedom itself, in this case the conditions of freedom of conscience. Many have emphasized that freedom is not something that is entirely native to us, in our bones, so to speak. Rather, it is something we have a capacity for, so that our capacity for freedom, like our other capacities, depends for its realization and for its flourishing on suitable conditions for development. It follows that it is part of the role of a liberal state, in fulfilling its obligation to secure the freedom (in certain fundamental respects, at least) of those for whom it is responsible, to secure the conditions within which the capacity for freedom can reasonably be expected to develop. Yet beyond the question of the obligations of the state, and of the degrees of negative and positive liberty that they entail, is the question of the extent to which the state's role in the development and realization of personal freedom is necessary but insufficient. Freedom is not something that the state can fully assure us, either by removing state impediments to its development or by providing proper support for its realization and flourishing. To do these things is to do no more than to establish some of the essential circumstances of freedom. It is then down to each of us, in the individual and collective dimensions of our lives, to make ourselves free, in the successful cultivation of our roles as part authors of our lives.

This may seem too painfully obvious to be worth remarking upon. Yet it is no more obvious than it is inevitable. All too often it is the case that the possibilities for freedom that the state has properly respected are left unrealized by their beneficiaries. There is nothing, to be sure, that the state can or should do about this. To suggest otherwise would be to suggest that it is both possible and necessary for the state to make us free. That would quite clearly be a violation of our freedom, for one of the things that freedom leaves us free to do is to leave our freedom more or less undeveloped. Yet that does not alter the fact that we have a moral responsibility to make ourselves free, for much the same reasons that the state has a moral responsibility to aid us in that endeavour. All too often we fail to do this. In many cases, indeed, we impose upon ourselves or our neighbours personal or cultural versions of the very limitations and confinements that the state would have imposed upon us but for its commitment to freedom. Sometimes this stems from want of courage. Sometimes it stems from a psychological need for structure. No matter. Too often it indicates a kind of passivity, a failure to live up to the responsibilities of being a rational agent. In the particular setting of freedom of conscience, this amounts to a failure to develop a true sense of conscience, and the rational personality of which that is a part.

As ever, one needs to be careful here. People are not under any obligation to maximize the freedom in their lives. Nor is there any ideal way for them to balance freedom and self-constraint in a manner appropriate to those lives. Lives may legitimately be more or less committed to freedom, and may as legitimately be committed to freedom in any of a host of ways. Yet it remains the case that each of us has a responsibility in relation to our freedom that is correlative to and no less important than the state's responsibility in that regard, and further, that our conscience is both a vehicle for, and an embodiment of, that responsibility. We enjoy freedom of conscience as and when we develop our conscience in such a way as to make the exercise of freedom distinctively our own, and that imposes as heavy a burden on each of us as it does on the state.

4

Reason and Religion

Whether secured by law, by tradition or both, the basic political freedoms, such as freedom of religion, matter to us for reasons, reasons that have to do with the value that the exercise of those freedoms is thought to contribute to the lives of those who enjoy them, and indeed, to the community at large. To put it simply, we insist upon those freedoms because we believe that their continued existence is essential to our ability to pursue worthy lives. At the same time, however, we have very different understandings of what it is that makes a life worthy. By this I do not simply mean that we have different goals in life and so have different projects to pursue, different beliefs to maintain. Rather, I mean that we have different understandings of the nature of value itself, different notions of how to assess what makes a life worth living, and so have different perceptions of the role that the basic political freedoms, such as freedom of religion, might possibly play in the construction and pursuit of a worthy life.

These differences in perception are of more than theoretical concern; they have real practical significance. Since our different understandings of the nature of value offer different reasons to secure freedom of religion, they lead to rather different descriptions of the beliefs and practices that should be entitled to the protection of freedom of religion. It follows that the success of a claim to freedom of religion may well turn on the answer to a dispute not only about the particular values that are said to justify the freedom, but also about the way in which those values are to be understood. When we disagree with one another, as we frequently do, over such questions as whether pacifism is a religious belief, and if so whether conscientious objection to military service is entitled to the protection of freedom of religion, our disagreements often, perhaps typically, stem from deeper disagreements about the nature of value. In other words, our practical disagreements here have their roots in theoretical disagreements about value and how to understand it.

In what follows I would like to explore the implications of disagreements about value in this setting by examining two of the most prominent justifications for freedom of religion, justifications that suggest rather different reasons for securing the freedom and so offer rather different accounts of its scope. In my view both of these justifications exhibit serious weaknesses, weaknesses that can be traced to weaknesses in the understandings of value on which they are based.

I want to do more than merely criticize, however, and so I will conclude by offering what seems to me a better justification for freedom of religion, one that is based on a better understanding of the nature of value.

Conventional Approaches to Freedom of Religion

Conventional accounts of freedom of religion, particularly those developed in the context of the First Amendment to the United States Constitution, have tended to address themselves to the question of the proper meaning of the term religion. When claims to religious freedom have been advanced by bodies not traditionally recognized as religious, such as Scientologists,[1] or in support of the exercise of personal convictions not necessarily regarded as religious, such as a conscientious objection to armed conflict,[2] or in support of activities that have not conventionally formed part of religious ceremony, such as the use of moose meat for a funeral potlatch,[3] those claims have been assessed by drawing analogies between the social practices underlying the claims and the practices of well recognized religions, so as to determine whether the beliefs and rituals for which freedom is claimed have parallels in religions to which freedom is clearly due.[4] For example, Kent Greenawalt begins his analysis of religion as a concept in constitutional law by observing, with approval: '. . . no-one doubts that Roman Catholicism, Greek Orthodoxy, Lutheranism, Methodism, and Orthodox Judaism are religions. Our society identifies what is indubitably religious largely by reference to their beliefs, practices, and organizations.'[5]

There is an obvious ambiguity in such accounts of freedom of religion, an ambiguity that arises from the fact that they offer a semantic response to what is apparently a moral question. We are concerned here, not to know how the term religion *is* used, whether in the world at large or in the legal community, but to know how the term religion *should* be used, in the interpretation, the application and the justification of a fundamental freedom. That is to all intents and purposes a moral question. It follows that if a semantic answer is given to that apparently moral question, then either the answer must be taken at face value, in which case it is to be understood as implying that the question is, despite appearances, a

---

[1] *Founding Church of Scientology v United States*, 409 F2d 1146 (DC Cir. 1969)

[2] See *United States v Seeger*, 380 US 163, 166 (1965): interpretation of a statute requiring belief in relation to a Supreme Being was held to include a belief that occupies 'a place in the life of its possessor parallel to that filled by the orthodox belief in God of one who clearly qualifies for the exemption'.

[3] See *Frank v State*, 604 P2d 1068 (Alaska 1979)

[4] For a prominent and relatively liberal version of this approach see JH Choper, 'Defining "Religion" in the First Amendment' [1982] Univ of Ill L Rev 579.

[5] K Greenawalt, 'Religions as a Concept in Constitutional Law' 72 Cal L Rev 753, at 767 (1984). For an argument along similar lines see GC Freeman III, 'The Misguided Search for the Constitutional Definition of "Religion"' 71 Geo L Jo 1519 (1983).

semantic one, or it must be treated as a moral answer to a moral question, albeit in semantic disguise. Otherwise the answer would be simply incoherent. In fact, I believe that the answer must be treated as a moral answer in semantic disguise, for in my view the question of the meaning of religion here cannot be understood other than as a moral question. Let me explain by exploring the alternative.

Semantic accounts of freedom of religion do not tell us, other than in semantic terms, why one understanding of religion should be preferred to another in the application of a fundamental freedom. Yet our reason for wanting to know which understanding should be preferred is not semantic but moral, not descriptive but normative. Our concern is not with linguistics but with justice. In the setting of a fundamental freedom what matters is not how the word religion is correctly used, whether generally or as a term of art, but how it should be used in order to arrive at a just outcome in balancing the requirements of personal autonomy against those of the public good.[6] It follows that a semantic approach to freedom of religion is necessarily dependent upon some prior moral justification which, if not explicitly stated on the face of a given account of freedom of religion, must be treated as implicit in it. In short, the meaning of religion in this setting is necessarily a moral, not a semantic question, and so requires a moral, not a semantic answer. Are there any circumstances, however, in which a semantic answer to that question could imply the moral justification that is needed to save the answer from incoherence?

There is one obvious setting in which that kind of implicit justification might be thought to be available. A number of countries, of which the United States is the most prominent example, have made freedom of religion part of their law, by entrenching that freedom in a written constitution. Accounts of freedom of religion that take such countries as their frame of reference might be understood as implying that the proper justification for the freedom is the fact that its entrenchment was the product of a democratic decision (or some other authoritative pronouncement), whether of a constitutional convention or some other body. In other words, according to such accounts freedom of religion is implicitly taken to be justified by the just character of its source. Whatever reasons may support the exercise of democratic authority necessarily support actions taken by that authority. Having settled the problem of justification in this way, conventional accounts of freedom of religion can then plausibly address the proper application of the freedom by interpreting the concept of religion in exclusively linguistic terms. That is to say, they are able to take the view that in order to understand the concept of freedom of religion and its proper application we should simply ask ourselves what the word religion means, for that is the

---

[6] I am not suggesting here that there is any inherent conflict between the requirements of personal autonomy and those of the public good: see J Raz, *The Morality of Freedom* (1986) at 213ff. I am assuming, however, that incidental conflicts between the claims of autonomy and the public good clearly do arise, and that the proper interpretation and application of a fundamental freedom involves the resolution of such conflicts.

word that the democratic authority used when entrenching the freedom. Once we have discovered the proper answer to that question we will be able to apply the concept in a manner that is justified.

There are ready objections, however, to a reference to democratic antecedents as an answer to the problem of determining the legitimate scope of freedom of religion. Notice, for a start, the conditions that would have to be met before such a line of reasoning could be even entertained. First, and as I have already indicated, freedom of religion would have to be understood as a purely legal right, the moral justification for which lies in the justice of the procedure by which it was enacted into law. Secondly, the application of that legal right would have to be governed by a recognized, presumably democratically authorized rule of interpretation, one that required the right to be understood in semantic terms. In other words, there would have to be a double authorization by some democratic body, an authorization not merely of the guarantee but of its interpretive principle, an authorization that granted one understanding of the word religion (be it a dictionary definition, or the reading said to be intended by the framers of the constitution) the authority of law. Finally, the application of that authorized rule of interpretation to the legal right would have to exhaust the judicial obligation to secure freedom of religion. For that to be true there would have to be a recognized, presumably democratically authorized theory of the judicial role, one that required the judiciary to do no more than apply the authorized rule of interpretation to the legal right, even when to do so would be to fail their moral obligation to give effect to the freedom. That might be the case, for example, if certain practices that would be protected by a moral principle justifying freedom of religion would not be protected by the application of the authorized rule of interpretation to the legal right.

It goes without saying that nowhere are all three of these conditions met. In many, perhaps most parts of the world, freedom of religion has yet to be guaranteed in law. Where it is guaranteed in law, the proper approach to its interpretation remains a matter of great dispute. That dispute is a product of the fact that no democratically authorized rule of interpretation of freedom of religion (or any other freedom) exists, let alone a rule requiring the freedom to be understood in semantic terms. Finally, even where freedom of religion has been guaranteed in law, and even where an approach to its interpretation might at least be alleged to have been agreed upon, it is simply not the case that there is any democratically authorized account of the judicial role that would regard a judge's moral obligation to secure that freedom as exhausted by his or her interpretation of the legal right to it.

What is more to the point here, even if all those conditions were or could be met the problem of justification would be merely postponed, not resolved, for the simple reason that there is a difference between justifying a certain form of authority and justifying what that authority has done. It is right, and so justifiable, that most political decisions, including a decision to secure freedom of religion, be taken by a democratic body, but it does not follow from this that any of the decisions taken by that body are themselves justifiable, other than in procedural terms. Just procedures do not necessarily produce just outcomes, not that is, all things considered and having taken the justice of those procedures into account. Yet, and as I have already indicated, a just outcome in balancing the requirements of personal autonomy against those of the public good is precisely what is sought here.[7]

It follows that if conventional accounts of freedom of religion are to be understood as offering a semantic response to what is inherently a moral question, those accounts must be regarded as inadequate. But surely, for that very reason, this cannot be the best way to understand them. It seems quite implausible to me that the considerations that I have just drawn attention to could have escaped the notice of the proponents of conventional accounts of freedom of religion. If I am right in this then it must be unwise to understand those accounts in semantic terms, whatever their appearance. Surely the better interpretation of them must be that they offer a moral answer to what they recognize to be a moral question, albeit a moral answer that is in semantic disguise. On that interpretation, conventional accounts of freedom of religion offer protection to those systems of belief that have features in common with traditional religions because they take traditional religions to be morally superior to their rivals. It would follow that the apparently semantically based comparison of features between well recognized religions and beliefs not traditionally recognized as religious implicitly recognizes value in, and so offers protection to, those features of belief that can be matched to features of belief that have long been acknowledged to be a source of value.[8]

Once again, there are two ways to understand such a claim, one of which is rather more plausible than the other. First, the claim might be understood

---

[7] This is a matter that deserves greater consideration than I have space to give it in the text. I must admit at once that the rather summary expression of it here runs two points together. However, since I believe that both points are true, their conflation should not serve to undermine the argument that I am trying to make. The first point is that a semantic inquiry into the meaning of religion cannot yield a single right answer without the assistance of moral argument, for a concept such as religion has many meanings and can be put to many purposes, each of which may make a different meaning central to the concept. It follows that a semantic inquiry into the meaning of religion in a guarantee of freedom of religion, even if democratically authorized, would simply beg much of the moral question of what religion should mean there. The second point is that even if and to the extent that such an inquiry could be said to yield a definitive answer, that answer would only give rise to a prima facie obligation on the part of those who are bound to respect a guarantee of freedom of religion to treat that answer as definitive of the guarantee and thus of their obligation. It would not be possible for them to know whether that answer was morally conclusive without further, moral inquiry into the proper scope of the freedom.

[8] I should note here, lest I give the appearance of being unfair, that conventional accounts of freedom of religion typically refer to well recognized religions rather than to traditional religions. However it seems right to equate the two descriptions, since by well recognized the proponents of conventional accounts appear to mean well recognized in their particular cultural tradition. That would explain why, in the passage quoted above, Kent Greenawalt describes what he calls the indubitably religious in exclusively Judaeo-Christian terms.

as a claim that the only valuable religious beliefs are those beliefs that share the features of traditional religions. It would follow, however, that traditional religious beliefs are the exclusive sources of value in this setting and that all other religious beliefs are entirely without value. Not only is this untrue; it is very unlikely that the proponents of conventional accounts of freedom of religion believe it. It would require, for example, that Buddhism be regarded as being without value, since Buddhism is not well recognized in the Western traditions to which conventional accounts of freedom of religion refer.

The second and more plausible way of understanding such a claim, then, is as a claim that traditional religious beliefs, and those beliefs that share their features, are more valuable than other religious beliefs. On this reading, traditional religious beliefs are the pre-eminent, albeit not the exclusive, sources of value in this setting, and it is their eminence that warrants the extension to them of a degree of protection that is denied to other beliefs. In other words, the claim here is that while many religious beliefs are valuable, only a few religious beliefs, well recognized by all of us, have such a capacity to generate value that their continued existence in our culture is essential to our capacity to pursue worthy lives. It will be noticed that underlying such a claim is a particular understanding of the nature of value, commonly described as value monism, coupled with a belief that human well-being consists in maximizing the presence of value in human lives.[9] By value monism I mean an account of value that treats the various sources of value in life as no more than means to the realization of a single, more profound value, such as happiness perhaps, or dignity, or honour, or redemption, a value to which any successful human life must be dedicated and to which all other values can be reduced.

Now, of course, value monism need not be conventional in its account of the sources of value. There is no necessary connection between a monistic approach to value and the view that traditional sources of value, in this case traditional religions, are the exclusive or even the pre-eminent source of value in human life. On the contrary, part of the point of value monism is that it is capable of recognizing and assimilating any number of different sources of value. Nor does value monism need to be coupled with a commitment to the maximization of value. On the contrary, it is entirely possible to believe that there is ultimately only one value to which any successful human life must be dedicated and yet also to believe that that value is not most fully realized by being maximized. In practice, however, and as its application to the question of religious freedom confirms, value monism tends to be both maximizing and conventional, for the following reasons.

First, while it is possible for proponents of value monism to distance themselves from a commitment to the maximization of value, it is only natural to be interested in degrees of value once one has rejected the significance of kind. After all, if

---

[9] The claim must be monistic, for traditional religious beliefs cannot be more valuable than other beliefs except in terms of a common standard of value.

there is only one value to which any successful human life must be dedicated, and yet if in practice human beings commit themselves to the pursuit of values of many different kinds, as they do, the variety of human pursuits, if not simply the product of moral ignorance, is most naturally explained by a desire to accumulate the value, be it happiness or some other, to which all human beings are and must be committed. In other words, the reason that human beings pursue a variety of values that do not ultimately differ from one another is that human beings are engaged in a search for those sources of value that have the greatest capacity to generate the ultimate value that makes life worth living, a value that they hope to maximize in their own lives.[10] If, then, human beings commit themselves to a variety of religious beliefs, it is because they are engaged in a search for the belief or beliefs with the greatest capacity to promote human happiness, or to secure human salvation, or whatever it is that they take to be the ultimate good.

Secondly, as I have just suggested, on a monistic account of value, sources of value differ from one another, not in their capacity to generate different kinds of value, but in their capacity to generate the same value for the same or different kinds of people. While some sources of value, by which I mean some sources of the ultimate value to which all successful human lives must be dedicated, may be equal in their capacity to generate value, other sources of value are clearly superior in that respect. If human beings are committed to the maximization of value in their lives, for the reasons just given, they must be correspondingly committed to the preservation and promotion of those sources of value that have the greatest capacity to generate value. While such sources of value might in theory be found anywhere, they rather naturally tend to be looked for in those sources of value that have been shown over time to yield the most value for the most people, namely, traditional or conventional sources of value, or in this setting, traditional or conventional religious beliefs.

Of course, it might be the case that a society has failed to recognize that certain sources of value possess a high capacity to generate the value to which all human

---

[10] It is commonly assumed that human beings seek sources of value that suit them. The question must be what this means. First, it must mean that the ultimate good is affected by suitability, as it would not be, for example, if it consisted of preserving honour or integrity. Secondly, suitability must mean something more than aptness. Certain activities are not sources of value for anyone. No-one seeks them, though many find them. Other activities are sources of value for some but not others, for they are such as to yield their value only to those with the appropriate capacity. Since people differ from one another, and since they are bound to seek value in activities that will yield value to them as they are, it is possible to explain a certain range in the sources of value pursued by human beings as a product of the differences between those human beings. Yet people pursue a wider range of values than this, for they pursue a number of apparently different values at once, or at least, over a period of their lives in which there is no change in the character of their aptness for value. Why do they do this? It cannot be because their well-being depends on the pursuit of different values, for on a monistic account values are not ultimately different. Two other explanations seem possible, both of which involve the maximization of value. People might be looking for the source of value with the highest yield or they might be confronting a problem of diminishing returns in one source of value and be seeking alternatives to it.

beings must be committed. It might also be the case that a society has failed to recognize that certain sources of value, that have a weak capacity to generate value for most people, have a great capacity to generate value for a few. If and to the extent that this can be proven, novel or marginal sources of value may be fostered and protected in the same way as traditional or conventional sources of value. Indeed, novel or marginal religious beliefs are sometimes granted the benefit of freedom of religion on this basis. However, and again rather naturally, the most widely recognized method of securing the benefit of freedom of religion is to show that the features of a novel or marginal religious belief correspond to the features of traditional or conventional religious belief, and so can be assumed to have a corresponding capacity to generate value. More commonly, however, novel or marginal sources of value are regarded as having a relatively weak capacity to generate value, so that commitments to them, while not prohibited, are not especially protected, for to do so would be to foster and promote commitments that diminish rather than enhance the prospects for the realization of value in human life. In this way the conventional bias of value monism remains intact.

When understood in moral rather than semantic terms, then, conventional accounts of freedom of religion exhibit an overly restrictive view of the kinds of belief that may underpin or at least nourish the pursuit of a successful human life, a view that is a product of the monistic understanding of value that informs those accounts. Such accounts fail to recognize that sources of value, here religious faiths, differ from one another not so much in their capacity to generate the same value for the same or different kinds of people, but in their capacity to generate different kinds of value for the same or different kinds of people. In other words, an unconventional source of value may indeed generate less of the value that the conventionalist notices, but it does so because it is primarily directed to the generation of a different value, one that has a different but no less important role to play in the pursuit of a successful life, at least for all those people who for reasons of character or choice have committed themselves to life projects that depend upon that source of value for some portion of their worth.[11]

Psychological Approaches to Freedom of Religion

For the purpose of exploring religion as a psychological phenomenon, in his 'The Varieties of Religious Experience: A Study in Human Nature',[12] William James adopted what he described as an arbitrary definition of religion, as 'the feelings, acts and experiences of individual men in their solitude, so far as they apprehend

---

[11] I expand upon this in the opening paragraphs of the section entitled 'Faith as a Basis for Freedom of Religion'.

[12] W James, '*Writings 1902–1910*' (1987). 'The Varieties of Religious Experience' was originally delivered as a series of lectures at the University of Edinburgh in 1901–02.

themselves to stand in relation to whatever they may consider the divine',[13] where experience of the divine is understood to mean a personal emotional experience centred upon happy acceptance of the universe and what it requires of each of us.[14] James intended this definition to be flexible enough to include those spiritual beliefs, such as transcendentalism, that involve an acceptance of 'the spiritual structure of the universe' but do not refer to a particular deity.[15] According to James, 'from the experiential point of view' beliefs of that kind are as much religions as are Christianity or Buddhism (itself without a deity, after all).[16]

This distinctive focus on the internal attitude of religious believers has made James's psychological understanding of religion, and others like it that have followed in its wake, appealing to those courts and commentators who have been reluctant to interpret freedom of religion by reference to the external features of religious belief, lest by doing so they enshrine religious orthodoxy. A psychological understanding of religion appears to offer an answer to the concerns about conventionalism and value monism set out above, for it appears to offer the degree of flexibility necessary to permit the recognition and protection of the very different beliefs that people may reasonably commit themselves to in the course of developing and pursuing a worthy life.

According to the most highly developed and most influential psychological account of freedom of religion, every person has a religion, and that religion is composed of that person's deepest commitments or ultimate concerns.[17] However secular those commitments or concerns might seem to others, they nevertheless merit protection as a religion, 'for autonomy of belief can be safeguarded only if the believer is entrusted with the task of articulating and ranking his own concerns'.[18] In other words, the test of what constitutes a religion here is purely subjective.[19] Society can require that a belief or activity be a matter of ultimate concern in order to obtain the protection of freedom of religion, but only the individual can determine what is of ultimate concern to him or her.

It must be said that there are some startling consequences to this point of view. To take the most obvious, this account of religion makes it impossible for anyone to lead a secular life, unless of course his or her life is utterly shallow and inconstant, devoid of anything that he or she could regard as an ultimate concern. Just as surprisingly perhaps, this account of religion makes it impossible to lead a religious life, and to claim the freedom to do so, unless religion is at

---

[13] ibid at 36.   [14] ibid at 36, 42, 44, 50.   [15] ibid at 36.   [16] ibid at 38.

[17] Note, 'Towards a Constitutional Definition of Religion' 91 Harv L Rev (1978) 1056.

[18] ibid. at 1076.

[19] The claim that religion is equivalent to ultimate concern, while giving the appearance of objectivity, is in truth no more than another way of expressing the view that the meaning of religion is a subjective question, for the function of the claim is to transform an objective inquiry into the meaning of religion into an objective inquiry into the content of an individual's ultimate concern, where what is ultimately of concern is whatever the subject takes it to be.

least part of one's ultimate concern.[20] A Catholic, for example, could not obtain the protection of freedom of religion in support of the practice of some tenet of the Catholic religion unless Catholicism in general and that tenet in particular formed part of his or her ultimate concern, and this no matter what view the doctrines of the Catholic religion itself might take on the proper role of religion in individual life.

Of course, to say that consequences are startling is not to say that they are morally unjustified. Is there a way, then, to make moral sense of the claim that freedom of religion should protect what each person takes to be his or her ultimate concern? As I have said, the protection of ultimate concerns appears to offer freedom of religion an attractive degree of flexibility, the very flexibility that is denied by conventional accounts of the freedom's scope. Does the protection of ultimate concerns, in the very act of doing this, rob freedom of religion of its moral authority? In order to address that question it is necessary to be somewhat more precise about what is meant by the protection of ultimate concerns.

There are two possible ways to understand the claim that religion should be equated with ultimate concern, one of which is rather more plausible than the other. First, the claim might be understood as a claim that individual people are in the best position to know what is good for them, and so are in the best position to decide whether a set of beliefs to which they have committed themselves or would like to commit themselves is capable of sustaining their well-being, either comprehensively or in some critical respect. So understood, the claim would be a claim about knowledge of the good, rather than a claim about the content of the good. Some support for this reading can be found in the language in which the claim has been justified. As indicated above, the leading exponent of the identification of freedom of religion with the protection of ultimate concerns has contended that 'autonomy of belief can be safeguarded only if the believer is entrusted with the task of articulating and ranking his own concerns'.[21] To articulate and rank one's own concerns might mean to know one's own concerns and consequently commit oneself to some portion of that which is otherwise recognized to be good, that is, to that which is good other than by virtue of one's commitment to it. To be entrusted with that task is to be entrusted with the the the task of identifying and selecting the beliefs and practices that one's life is to be committed to.

Understood in that way the protection of ultimate concerns is of course perfectly sensible, although it would seem to have more to do with liberty than with religion. People are often, perhaps typically, in the best position to know what is good for them, in this case to know whether a religious belief is capable

---

[20] Moreover, ultimate concern is said to be 'an act of the total personality, not a movement of a special and discrete part of the total being'. It follows that to qualify as an ultimate concern a commitment must be 'unconditional, made without qualification or reservation': ibid at 1076, n 110.

[21] Above, n 14.

of sustaining their well-being. They may be mistaken in their assessment of this but they are less likely to be mistaken than are others. What is more, their opportunity to exploit their knowledge of what is good for them, by acting on their best sense of what is good for them, is a fundamental part of what it means for them to be authors of their own lives, a role that I take to be central to the well-being of every person. This is so even when they are mistaken in their assessment of what is good for them, as they often are.

It seems to me, however, that in fact it is not possible to understand the claim that freedom of religion should be identified with the protection of ultimate concerns as a claim that individual people are in the best position to know what is good for them, for to read the claim in that way would not begin to explain its scope. The fact that a believer is in the best position to know what is good for him or her would suggest that any belief must be freely chosen if it is to warrant the protection of freedom of religion, but it would not and could not be taken to suggest that any belief that is freely chosen should be protected as a religion. Yet that is precisely what the protection of ultimate concerns would require.

The second and more plausible way to understand the claim, then, is as a claim that people must determine for themselves what is good and what is not, and so must determine for themselves whether a set of beliefs is worthy of the kind of fundamental commitment that can be called religious because, like traditional religious commitment, it is a matter of ultimate concern for them. So understood, the claim is a claim, about the content of the good, rather than a claim about knowledge of the good. On this reading, (fundamental) personal commitment is the exclusive source of (fundamental) value in the life of any human being. A belief or practice becomes valuable and so worthy of being protected as religious just because one is committed to it. In other words, the claim here is that any belief is capable of being valued, so that a belief becomes valuable for any particular person when it becomes the object of the appropriate kind of commitment on the part of that person, the kind of commitment that treats that belief as valuable. It will be noticed that underlying such a claim is a particular understanding of the nature of value, commonly described as subjectivism. By subjectivism I mean an account of value that treats value, not as a property of the object that is valued, but as a property of the person who finds that object valuable. Such accounts by their very definition deny the possibility of objective value. They deny that value is a property that is possessed by an object, an object such as a religious belief or a religious practice, and insist instead that beliefs and practices are only valuable if and to the extent that somebody finds them so.

Subjective accounts of value raise concerns of two kinds, one of them entirely familiar, the other perhaps less so. The first concern is that they offer people other than the subject no reason to regard an object, in this case a belief or practice, as valuable and so worthy of respect. If freedom of religion embraces whatever is of ultimate concern to any person, then it must embrace beliefs and practices of all kinds, or at least of all kinds that any person is ultimately concerned with. People are in fact ultimately concerned with beliefs and practices that range from feminism to girl power, from Jesus to Elvis, from loving one's neighbour to participating in key parties. Some of those beliefs and practices can be recognized as valuable, although it might be difficult to recognize them as religions. Others, however, are mere obsessions, devoid of value as far as anyone but those committed to them can tell. The bare fact that a belief or practice is of ultimate concern to someone is no reason for any other person to regard that belief or practice as valuable, and more pertinently, no reason for any other person to respect it. That being the case, the protection of ultimate concerns cannot be the basis for freedom of religion if the foundation for that freedom lies, as it must, in the respect that is owed to it by all members of the community.

The second concern is that subjective accounts of value are incapable of offering subjects themselves any reason to regard an object, in this case a belief or practice, as valuable and so worthy of respect. It is surely significant that subjective accounts of value always maintain an objective aspect, in that they always describe value as an attribute of an object. We say, in apparent subjective mode, and of one person's appreciation of another, that she is beautiful for him, or that he thinks she is beautiful, or that he finds her beautiful. When we do so, however, we preserve a link between beauty and its object. According to subjective accounts of value, of course, this degree of objectivity is merely nominal, for the logic of those accounts is to locate value wholly within the subject, to insist that in the descriptions of beauty just given, beauty flows entirely from the perception of the beholder, so that the beauty there identified is not a property of the woman who is said to be beautiful, but of the man who says she is so. Yet, in fact, it is the objective aspect of such descriptions, the allegedly nominal link that they preserve between beauty and its object, that is entirely responsible for the persuasiveness of those descriptions as accounts of value. Without that aspect they could not be said to identify value, even in the life of the beholder. Rather, what they would identify is a fixation, be that fixation obsessive, so as to amount to an ultimate concern, or be it merely tentative.

When we say of one person's appreciation of another that she is beautiful for him we imply privacy and what it may reveal; when we say that he thinks she is beautiful we imply lack of knowledge and what it may conceal; when we say that he finds her beautiful we imply discovery and what it may yield.[22] Each of those implications is an implication of objective value. Without them, or without some similar attribution of objective value, there would be no beauty to behold. On the contrary, descriptions of beauty would have to be understood as no more than descriptions of the beholder and his idiosyncrasies, and their externality

---

[22] Of course, we also imply the perspective of a third party, but that is another matter, the subject of the first concern. The issue that I am seeking to explore here is the second concern, namely, the capacity of subjectivism to explain value as it is experienced by the valuer.

would have to be recognized as the product of a projection, upon the mirror of the world, of a beauty that the beholder finds only in himself. Yet, in fact, the reason people interact with the world, quite apart from the difficulty of doing anything else, is that there is value in doing so, a value that is not simply the projection of something that those people already possess. In other words, the progress of a life is not merely narcissistic; it is a matter of realizing, in the most creative sense of that word, the beauty that life has to offer. Subjective accounts of value suppress this fact, or refer to it in ways that they set aside as nominal, and in doing so offer no reason for the subject, himself or herself, to find value in the world, or in the context that concerns us here, to regard anything outside themselves as a matter of ultimate concern.

When understood in subjective terms, then, and in my view that is the only way to understand them, psychological approaches to freedom of religion offer an undernourished account of the value of religious freedom, one that cannot explain the hold of that freedom upon society at large or even upon the life of the believer. Psychological approaches to freedom of religion obtain their flexibility at the cost of their substance, develop their attraction at the cost of their meaning. The task, therefore, must be to arrive at an account of freedom of religion that is simultaneously flexible and substantial.

Faith as a Basis for Freedom of Religion

If the nature of value is neither singular nor subjective, as these accounts of the weaknesses in conventional and psychological justifications of freedom of religion would tend to suggest, then the logical conclusion must be that value is both plural and objective. By plural here I mean an understanding of value that regards many, perhaps most sources of value in life as irreducible to any one, more profound source of value. By objective I mean an understanding of value that regards value as a property of the object that is valued, rather than as a property of the person who finds that object valuable. Is it possible to develop a persuasive account of freedom of religion on the basis of value pluralism? If so, then the persuasiveness of that account might reinforce the persuasiveness of value pluralism, and vice versa.

What in religion might a value pluralist value? Assume for the moment that the term religion refers to *collective participation in institutions and practices that manifest a set of beliefs that is not based on reason alone but is held at least in part on the basis of faith*. The key elements in this definition are a set of beliefs, of whatever kind, and the manner in which they are subscribed to, namely as a matter of faith. The definition deliberately (and for the time being) eschews any reference to the content of religious doctrine, for in my view it follows from the rejection of conventional accounts of freedom of religion that the justification for the freedom cannot be found in religious doctrine.

1. Religious and Secular Justifications

I have noted above that conventional accounts of freedom of religion see in the doctrines of traditional religions, and in the institutions and practices that those doctrines inspire, a capacity to generate value that is sufficiently special to warrant fundamental protection. I have argued that in doing so conventional accounts exhibit an overly restrictive view of the kinds of religious belief that may underpin, or at least nourish, the pursuit of a successful human life, for they fail to recognize that sources of value differ in kind as well as in degree. My claim here is that even an inclusive view of religious doctrine cannot serve as the basis for freedom of religion. Let me explain that claim by expanding briefly upon my previous objection to conventional accounts of freedom of religion.

What needs to be shown in order to supply a moral reason for restricting freedom of religion to conventional religious beliefs, say to the Catholic, the Buddhist, or the Puritan, is that the beneficiaries of the restriction make a contribution to human well-being that is not merely different from the contribution made by the victims of the restriction, but different in what makes it worthy of fundamental protection. In other words, it must be shown *both* that some beliefs, and the conduct that they inspire, deserve protection and others do not, and that the distinction between the deserving and the undeserving is the distinction between the religious and the secular, or more narrowly, between conventional religious beliefs and other beliefs.

In my view, the first of these propositions is true and the second is false. Not every religious belief deserves fundamental protection, but those beliefs that deserve protection are not exclusively conventional while those beliefs that do not deserve protection are not exclusively unconventional. Conventional religious beliefs, and the institutions and practices that they inspire and sustain, are not inherently more valuable than unconventional beliefs, nor more vulnerable. There is no moral reason, therefore, to restrict the benefit of freedom of religion on the basis of a doctrinal distinction between what has conventionally been regarded as religious and what has not.

There is a deeper point here, however, and that is that any reliance upon religious doctrine, conventional or unconventional, as the source of the justification of religious freedom is misguided, for religious doctrine cannot be made to yield a commitment to religious freedom that is at once recognizable and acceptable as the basis for a fundamental political guarantee. The reason is a value pluralist one. The account of morality that is embodied in religious doctrine is necessarily partial and incomplete, rather than plural and comprehensive, for even the most tolerant of religions does not and cannot take other accounts of morality to be as true as its own. In itself, of course, there is nothing wrong with this. On the contrary, much individual and group morality displays this form of partiality and is not necessarily wrong to do so, for the account of morality that each of us gives, whether as an individual or as a group, need only be as comprehensive as is required to accommodate the well-being of those to whom we are responsible.[23] But it follows that a partial and incomplete account of morality is inappropriate for adoption by the state, whose policies and institutions must reflect a comprehensive, value-pluralist account of morality if they are not to exclude the recognition of values upon which the well-being of certain human beings depends, human beings who necessarily fall within the ambit of the state's responsibility. It follows further that the freedom of religion whose guarantee lies at the foundation of the state must be based upon, and assessed against, a view of morality that is capable of embracing all those for whom the state is responsible. Religious morality, which is accountable only to those who have freely embraced its tenets, does not and cannot meet this requirement.

What this reveals, then, is that the morality justifying freedom of religion must be secular, not religious. It follows that religious doctrine cannot serve as the moral inspiration for a guarantee of freedom of religion, and that doctrinal accounts of that guarantee, those accounts that assess the meaning and scope of freedom by reference to the content of religious doctrine, are simply misguided. This is not to assume one's conclusions, to say that the morality justifying a fundamental freedom must be secular because the morality justifying any fundamental freedom must be secular. Rather, it is to say that only a secular morality is capable of providing the connection to human well-being that is necessary to justify a fundamental freedom.

2. The Meaning of Faith

If reference to doctrine is to be ruled out, at least initially, the possibility remains that faith itself provides the moral basis for freedom of religion. In order to explore that possibility, it is necessary to explore the meaning and value of faith. At its most basic level, the concept of faith describes the manner in which a particular belief or set of beliefs may be subscribed to by human beings. In that sense of the word, faith exists as a form of rival to reason. When we say that we believe in something as a matter of faith, or to put it the other way round, when we say that we have faith in certain beliefs, we express a commitment to that which cannot be established by reason, or to that which can be established by reason, but not for that reason. The rivalry between the two concepts is real, but not complete, therefore. Faith and reason are modes of belief with different sources and different characters, but not necessarily different consequences. The particular consequences of faith may defy reason, as when faith prompts us to believe or do what we would otherwise have no reason to believe or do, but they may also be consistent with reason, as when faith prompts us to believe or do

---

[23] Partial and incomplete accounts of morality are, of course, inaccurate. My point is simply that they are not necessarily harmful.

what we otherwise have reason to believe or do. Christian faith, for example, asks us to believe in the possibility of a life beyond material existence, with all that that implies, a possibility that rational thought would regard as not merely unverifiable but unknowable, perhaps unintelligible, given the intimate connection between the nature of life and the fact of death, between the evanescence of the human spirit and the materiality of the human body. Yet Christian faith also asks us to believe in the redemptive power of love, a power that rational thought might well endorse. What is important is that in either case faith treats itself as a reason to believe, and to act in accordance with belief, without submitting to the conditions of reason.

3. Faith and Trust

The most obvious rival to the meaning of faith that I have just sketched, and will explore more fully below, is the meaning of faith as a species of trust. As is well known, for some people, patriotic Americans in particular, faith is equivalent to trust, so that it becomes sensible for such people to maintain that they trust in God rather than that they have faith in Him. Just as the concept of trust may be used in the place of faith in this way, so the concept of faith can be used in the place of trust. According to this meaning of faith, it makes sense to say that one has faith in one's doctor, or in one's bank manager, or in one's husband or wife, for the same reasons that it would make sense to say that one had trust in those people.

Yet it seems clear, however, without calling the validity of such usages into question, that a distinction between faith and trust can and should be drawn, for while the two concepts may in some respects overlap one another they are not synonymous. One notices at once, as a matter of ordinary speech, that people tend to trust in the concrete and have faith in the abstract, so that it is common to say that one trusts people or institutions but has faith in certain values.[24] For example, part of the point of maintaining that in God we trust is that to do so makes the presence of God a concrete rather than an abstract fact in the life of a society. Admittedly, this contrast between faith and trust is not perfect, for as I have already suggested, it is clear that it is entirely sensible to say that one has faith in people (the concrete) as well as in values (the abstract), although perhaps it is slightly less sensible to say that one has trust in values as well as in people.[25] Nevertheless the contrast, however imperfect, suggests an implicit recognition in linguistic usage of a significant difference between the two concepts, namely, the very difference set out above between faith and reason as modes of belief.

---

[24] Normally one simply believes in a value, without reference to either faith or trust. One has faith in certain values when one believes in those values in the absence of one's awareness of a reason to believe in them.

[25] One can, of course, trust particular understandings of value, such as social mores or doctrines, because and to the extent that one has reason to rely on the connection between those understandings and true value.

In contrast to faith, one has trust in oneself, or another, or in the safety of the bridge that one is about to step upon, *for reasons*. It would be simply unintelligible to claim that one trusted the safety of a bridge and yet simultaneously to acknowledge that there was no reason to do so. Trust demands the presence of reasons and without their foundation it cannot be justified. Faith, on the other hand, is subject to no such requirement. It may be unreasonable to claim that one has faith in the resurrection of the flesh and life everlasting, but it is not unintelligible. If faith and trust are to be understood as distinct concepts, therefore, it is faith rather than trust that depends upon non-rational belief.[26] One may have faith in oneself, in friends, in certain practices, customs, expectations or beliefs, including religious beliefs, as long as one commits oneself to those people or beliefs independently of any reason to do so.[27] It follows that the concept of faith, when understood as equivalent to trust, is incapable of providing the moral basis for a guarantee of freedom of religion, for faith so understood would be equivalent to reasoned belief. As a general matter, reasoned beliefs are protected by freedom of belief and to offer the same beliefs the same protection in the name of freedom of religion would be simply superfluous. By the same token, to offer reasoned beliefs, or some subset of them, additional protection in the name of freedom of religion would be unjustifiable in the absence of some additional feature of those beliefs, such as the fact that they are held on the basis of faith, now understood as a mode of belief distinct from reason.

4. The Value of Faith

Overcoming Ignorance and Doubt

The most obvious role that might be thought to be played by faith in the conduct of human life is the same role played by trust, namely, to function as a device that will serve to forestall the need of individuals to undertake a reasoned examination and assessment of every significant issue confronting them on every occasion that

---

[26] If faith and trust are regarded as no more than different names for the same concept, as they might seem to be regarded by those who use the phrase 'in God we trust', then the concept in question must surely be rational belief, as the phrase implies, for the idea of trust surely implies rational belief. In that case a third word would have to be found to describe non-rational belief of the kind that commonly characterizes religious commitment. For my own part, I do not regard this as a plausible interpretation of the words faith and trust, since it strikes me as patently correct to say that the word faith is at least *capable* of referring to non-rational belief. If I am wrong in this, however, then another word would have to replace the word faith in the balance of my argument. On the other hand, if the words faith and trust both refer to non-rational belief, then the understanding of the word faith as equivalent to the word trust is no different from the understanding of faith as a mode of belief distinct from reason, the understanding that I have taken to underlie a guarantee of freedom of religion.

[27] According to this account, then, it would seem to be the case that the reason people tend to trust in the concrete and have faith in the abstract, as a matter of ordinary speech, is that people find it easier to perceive reasons to commit themselves to the concrete than to perceive reasons to commit themselves to the abstract.

such an issue may arise. When we have faith in certain values, or have trust in certain people, we are able to rely on those values and on those people as a matter of course, without having to ask ourselves constantly whether that reliance is justified. From this point of view, then, it might be thought that the role of faith, like the role of trust, is to stand in for the knowledge upon which rational judgment must depend. On this account, the presence of both trust and faith in our lives means that there is no need for us to be doubting Thomases, at least in the colloquial sense of that phrase. We do not need to conduct spot checks on the fidelity and integrity of our friends, or our partners, in order to depend on them; we do not need to subject moral doctrine to rigorous and regular examination in order to be guided by it. In this sense faith, like trust, might be said to have a practical, functional aspect, in that it enables us to make commitments of a certain kind, and to act upon those commitments, in the absence of full reason to do so, and thus facilitates the realization of whatever value those commitments are capable of yielding. It follows, according to this account, that the presence of faith and trust in our lives promotes human well-being by enhancing our capacity to pursue certain values successfully.

But is this the true value of faith, or is it the value of faith only if one equates the concepts of faith and trust, as I have already suggested one should not? If the realization of value in these settings depends on the presence of general reasons to believe, reasons that enable us to overcome moments of ignorance and doubt, then that value plainly cannot be realized on the basis of faith as I have defined it, as a mode of belief distinct from reason. In that case one would have to look elsewhere for the true value of faith in the promotion of human well-being.

The doubting-Thomas image, taken literally, offers some sense of the difference between the value of trust and the value of faith and some indication of a more fruitful direction in which to look for the value of faith, for a decision not to place one's finger in the wound, the decision that faith requires, is not simply a decision that forestalls the need to engage in a reasoned examination of the possibility of bodily resurrection, but rather is a decision to believe in the Resurrection despite the absence of any possibility of reasons to believe, or more troublingly perhaps, despite the presence of good reasons not to believe. It is in this sort of setting, in my view, that faith and trust necessarily part company, and that the distinctive value of faith becomes apparent.

It follows from the meaning of faith that the value of faith is something that can only be realized in situations where one believes without regard to reason to believe. The value of trust, on the other hand, can only be realized in situations where one believes because there is general reason to believe, a reason that enables one to overcome one's ignorance and doubt in a particular setting, and thus enables one to overcome the absence of any specific reason to believe, and to act in accordance with belief, that ignorance and doubt give rise to in that setting. Both faith and trust, therefore, enable one to believe and to act in the absence of full reason to do so, but trust depends upon the presence of prior, albeit incomplete reasons, while faith does not depend upon reason at all. Given the difference in their characters, it cannot be assumed that faith and trust are necessarily valuable in the same settings. In which settings then is the exercise of faith justified, and so capable of yielding value, and in which settings is trust the proper response? Or to put it another way, which sorts of ignorance and doubt are profitably overcome by faith and which are the necessary province of trust?

As I have just said, one trusts for reasons, general authorizing reasons that justify one's neglect to seek specific reasons in specific settings. One trusts one's bank, for example, for general reasons, and it is those general reasons that justify one's neglect to seek specific reasons to rely on the bank's probity whenever one makes a deposit. Trust thus makes it possible to benefit from the bank's probity without having to confirm that probity in every step of one's dealings with the bank. It is also possible to have faith in one's bank, but it would clearly be unwise to do so, for in the absence of reasons to believe in the bank's probity, faith in that probity cannot be regarded as valuable, and indeed may well be harmful.

If the point of facilitating action in the face of ignorance and doubt is to facilitate the realization of certain benefits, as this account assumes, then the value of trust and faith in that setting is entirely dependent on there being some benefit to realize. Where there is no reason to expect that benefit, there is no reason to regard the enterprise as valuable. Since there is no reason to have faith in a particular consequence, there is no reason to expect that the exercise of faith will facilitate the realization of beneficial consequences, and thus no reason to regard the exercise of faith as valuable in terms of those consequences. To have faith in one's bank despite the absence of any reason to do so is simply foolish, for belief in one's bank is justifiable and so valuable only where there is reason to believe that the bank will behave honestly, and that reason is something that faith cannot offer. Trust is what is called for in such a setting.

It follows that it is trust, not faith, that enables us to bridge the unknown, overcoming ignorance and doubt where there is some deeper, underlying reason to do so. Where there is reason to believe, one should trust, not have faith; where there is reason not to believe, both faith and trust are misplaced.

Leaps into the Dark

This gives rise to an obvious problem. The assessment of value, and thus the assessment of devices such as fundamental freedoms that are designed to yield value, is necessarily rational. Yet faith is not based on reasons. How can an irrational attachment be rationally determined to be valuable? Are we driven to the conclusion that faith is incapable of yielding value other than accidentally, as when it calls upon us to endorse what we have independent reason to endorse? The answer is negative in form. One of the things that we have to deal with in life, and one of the things that can affect our well-being, is the unavailability of reasons. The quest for reasons in life is sometimes troublesome and difficult, but at other times impossible. Where the quest for reasons is impossible, but commitment is potentially valuable, faith can come into play. It follows that there is reason to seek, and value in finding, a way to come to terms with the unknowable where to do so is necessary to human well-being.

It is often the case in life that one cannot know in advance that something is worth doing, because it is in the nature of the project or activity that one can only know whether it is worth doing by doing it. This is not simply a matter of lack of information. Rather, it is a question of activities the value of which derives in part from the very fact of commitment to that activity, so that the value of the activity is unknowable in advance of commitment to the activity. When we decide to move from one city to another, or to exchange one job for another, or to start living as the partner of one person rather than another, we necessarily commit ourselves, to a neighbourhood, to a workplace, to a man or woman, without full reasons to do so, for one can only know fully whether a neighbourhood is worth living in by living in it, whether a place is worth working in by working in it, whether someone is worth living with by living with them. In each of these settings an act of commitment has to be made in advance of the existence of the value that might justify the commitment, and that act of commitment cannot be based upon reason, therefore, but must be based on faith.

All ventures into the unknowable, then, all leaps into the dark, depend on faith. Or to put it somewhat differently, faith is required in order to make any commitment that involves a projection into the future where one's ability to realize the value that arises from the commitment is incompatible with the existence of sufficient reasons for making the commitment in the first place. It follows that faith is facilitative of those activities that depend on the connection between oneself and others, or between oneself and certain sets of circumstances, when a search for reasons to commit oneself to those activities would be inconclusive. Activities of that kind often constitute valuable options in life. In such settings faith provides a basis for action in the absence of any possibility of adequate reasons for action.

This does not mean that all ways of coming to terms with the unknowable are valuable. It may well be that some questions that confront us should simply be left unanswered, that some commitments that are offered to us should be left ungrasped, that we should be prepared to acknowledge the mysteries of life and to accept the limits of our condition. It is certainly the case that some purported responses to such questions and commitments are dangerous or worse. It follows that the role of faith in enabling us to make leaps into the dark is a necessary but not a sufficient condition for regarding the exercise of faith as valuable, and hence for protecting the institutions and practices that make faith possible.

5. Religion and its Value

Faith as I have so far considered it involves commitments that there can be no prior adequate reason to make, because the nature of the commitment is such that the value of the commitment is unknowable until the commitment is made. Religious faith, however, is typically attached to beliefs in and commitments to matters which, from the perspective of rational believers, are far from unknowable and which there may well be reason to make or not to make. Assume that the elements of religion are as I described them above but with a doctrinal qualification. Religious doctrine, it seems fair to say, has been traditionally and typically based upon a set of beliefs first, about the nature and purpose of human life, and in particular, about the possibility of a life other than material existence, and second, about the nature of the good, and in particular, about the possibility of moral grounds that lie beyond human life and beyond human reason. The question is whether faith in such matters is justified, and if so, when and under what circumstances it is justified.

Are the topics of religious belief truly unknowable, and if so, must they be addressed on the basis of faith in order to enable human beings to make commitments that are essential to their well-being? From a full rational point of view, the view that most human beings adopt, the answer must be no. A commitment to life itself, and to the various projects that constitute the particular life of any person, does not involve a venture into the unknowable, and indeed could not be thought to do so unless one regarded life as being so bound up with death as to make the fact of life as unknowable as the fact of death sometimes appears to be. Even from that point of view, however, life could not be said to amount to a venture into the unknowable, for from a rational perspective death is no mystery, however upsetting it may be.

By the same token, a commitment to the good and all that it requires of us does not involve a venture into the unknowable either, for moral grounds do not lie beyond human life and are not inaccessible to human beings on the basis of reason. On the contrary, it is a necessary feature of morality that any account of it must be fit for human beings and the lives that they are bound to lead,[28] and it is one of the principal functions of human reason, a function that reason has long and successfully discharged, to offer us a rich and complex account of the content of that morality. It follows that human well-being, which clearly depends upon a complete commitment to life and a full understanding of morality, is not necessarily dependent upon an act of religious faith.

But is this true for all human beings? Is it the case that we are all capable of adopting a fully rational point of view in response to all issues that confront us, or should be? If what is required here is an approach to well-being that is capable of accommodating the character and commitments of very different people, and if the guarantee of certain rights and freedoms is one way of ensuring that the well-being of every person, however idiosyncratic, is capable of being realized, is it not essential that the guarantee take into account the fact that for some people the nature of life and the content of morality are unknowable on the basis

---

[28] See J Raz, 'A Morality Fit For Humans' 91 Mich L Rev (1993) 1297.

of reason alone? For such people faith in the beliefs that form the content of religious doctrine is critical to the achievement of well-being, for their character is such that their well-being requires them to commit themselves to what, again for them, is and must remain unknowable. The question is whether they are to be condemned for this, or whether our account of morality and the institutions and practices that serve to implement that morality must be such as to serve them as they are. The answer clearly depends on the nature of the beliefs to which they have committed themselves.

There is an important difference between religious faith and the individual and local acts of faith that are often involved in commitments to new neighbourhoods, new jobs, or new relationships, and the difference is that religious faith is not faith in the value of a particular commitment, but faith in the value of a belief that is designed to sustain all or at least most of one's commitments in life. Following the line of argument sketched earlier, faith is valuable where the inability to make the commitments that faith makes possible would have a negative impact on well-being, both because the commitments in question are potentially valuable and because failure to make them would be harmful. The challenge of religious faith, then, is that it does not merely function as the trigger for the making of a commitment, like faith in a new neighbourhood, a new job, or a new partner, but, just because it is faith in a certain set of beliefs, governs the character of any consequent commitment and so governs the value of that commitment. It follows that religious faith serves the well-being of religious believers if and to the extent that religious beliefs have the capacity to inspire commitments that are capable of contributing to well-being. In such circumstances religion may be critical to well-being and so worthy of fundamental protection. Otherwise there is simply no value in religious faith.

6. The Price of Faith

As a general matter, then, the value of faith, be it religious or secular, is not merely facilitative, in the sense of making easier what could otherwise be done through reliance on reason. Rather, the abdication of rational assessment that faith requires creates conditions of confidence that are essential to the pursuit of certain valuable activities and relationships. In the most literal sense of the phrase faith means that one does not have to be a doubting Thomas: one does not need to have placed one's finger in the wound to believe in the resurrection of the body.

And yet that example also suggests the price of faith. The difficulty with faith, secular or religious, is that it often serves as a substitute for knowledge and reason in settings where those are not only available but constitute a sounder basis for action and belief. New relationships, for example, may require an act of faith, as I have argued above, but the scope of that faith must be carefully circumscribed, for new relationships must also be consistent with reason. This is not simply to say that faith is a necessary but not a sufficient condition of any new relationship.

Rather, it is to say that faith is a necessary condition of a new relationship in certain dimensions of that relationship only, namely, those dimensions the value of which cannot be determined until one has committed oneself to the relationship. Other dimensions of the relationship must be rationally founded if the relationship overall is to contribute to the well-being of both parties. Relationships that are founded on faith and faith alone are valuable only by chance (in terms of the fundamental compatibility of the parties) and as the result of ongoing acts of concern, commitment and good management, acts that are themselves rationally based (in terms of the capacity of the parties to develop and pursue their relationship successfully).

It follows that faith, which can be vital to the achievement of well-being in some dimensions of life, those dimensions where reasons are unavailable, will undermine well-being if and when it is invoked in dimensions where reasons are both available and constitute a sounder basis for action and belief. As far as religious faith is concerned, this means not only that religious beliefs must be capable of furthering well-being but that the endorsement of religious belief must be confined to those people whose well-being depends on it, as described above, and further, must be restricted to those dimensions of their lives where their well-being depends on it. Faith is inappropriate as a wider guide either to the individual pursuit of well-being or to the collective exercise of responsibility for the design of institutions to further that pursuit.

The Place of Religion in Public Life

1. Freedom of Religion

If freedom of religion, properly understood, is founded upon the value that faith in certain beliefs, beliefs in matters that are for some people inaccessible on the basis of reason, is capable of bringing to the lives of those people, then the essence of the freedom must be to offer protection to the institutions and practices that foster and express the beliefs in question. As far as freedom of religion is concerned, therefore, religion refers to *collective participation in institutions and practices that manifest a freely given personal commitment to a particular set of beliefs, commitment to which is capable of enhancing human well-being; beliefs that are not based on reason alone but are held, at least in part, on the basis of faith.*

I must stress that this definition is a term of art, designed to meet the purposes of a fundamental political guarantee. It does not pretend to be acceptable to, or to capture the full value of, any or all of the institutions and practices that have traditionally been regarded as religions. Such is not and could not be its purpose, for the role of the definition is, as I have said, to describe the scope of freedom of religion as a fundamental political guarantee in a secular constitution, not to describe the scope of religion itself.

It will be clear at once that this definition of religion is based upon the preliminary definition that I offered above, now modified to recognize that religious faith is not valuable except when attached to a set of beliefs that are capable of enhancing human well-being. This modification does not mean that the value of a particular religious belief is dependent upon the existence of a necessary connection between endorsement of that belief and the achievement of well-being, for no commitment, whether to a person, to a course of action or to a set of beliefs, can ever be expected to guarantee well-being. Nor does it mean that the value of a religious belief is a function of the degree to which that belief sustains human well-being, for commitments are not susceptible to that kind of evaluation. Rather, it means what it says, that religious belief must possess the capacity to enhance the well-being of those who commit themselves to it. Whether it ultimately does so will depend upon them, upon others and upon chance.

It is important to emphasize, however, that apart from the requirement that there be a connection between belief and well-being, this definition of religion is entirely silent, and hence entirely open-minded, as to the content of religious doctrine. Any belief that both is and must be held on the basis of faith, in the sense described above, whether or not it bears any similarity to conventional religious beliefs, is entitled to fundamental protection under the rubric of freedom of religion if it is capable of enhancing human well-being. It follows, as will be explained more fully below, that the distinction between protected and unprotected beliefs should no longer turn on comparisons between the content of traditional and non-traditional religious doctrines, but should be determined by a frank examination of the contribution that any doctrine held on the basis of faith, be it traditional or non-traditional, is capable of making to well-being. If what are commonly known as cults, for example, are to be denied the protection of freedom of religion it must be because and to the extent that commitment to those cults diminishes human well-being, not because of the success or failure of a comparison between the doctrines espoused by those cults and conventional religious belief.[29]

The Relationship between Religion and Well-Being

Yet to describe the scope of freedom of religion in such expansive terms is a trifle misleading, for I have already indicated that the range of religious belief that is entitled to the protection of a fundamental guarantee is not in fact unlimited, but is necessarily constrained by the contingent nature of the capacity of faith to enhance well-being. In other words, the requirement of a connection between

---

[29] This is to ignore for the moment the very real possibility that cults should be denied the protection of freedom of religion because commitment to them is normally not freely given, as the above definition of religion requires, but rather is obtained and maintained by a form of psychological manipulation that is inconsistent with free will.

faith and well-being places significant constraints upon freedom of religion, albeit not the same constraints as have been recognized in conventional analyses of that freedom.

I have argued above that faith, which can be vital to the achievement of well-being in certain dimensions of life, those dimensions where reasons are unavailable, will undermine well-being if and when it is invoked in regard to dimensions of life where reasons are both available and constitute a sounder basis for action and belief. It follows that religious belief is only capable of enhancing well-being if and to the extent that it calls for faith in regard to dimensions of life where reasons are inaccessible to the believer. Conversely, religious belief will undermine well-being if and to the extent that it calls for faith in regard to dimensions of life where reasons are accessible to the believer. In short, religious faith must be confined to realms where reason is inaccessible and yet belief is necessary to well-being. Outside those realms religious faith diminishes well-being, not so much because its consequences may not coincide with the consequences of rational belief, but because the exercise of rational thought in relation to the selection and pursuit of goals in life, to the extent that it is accessible, is a necessary element in the achievement of human well-being. It follows that any definition of religion that is designed to serve the purposes of a fundamental guarantee by linking religious faith to human well-being must successfully distinguish those two realms.

In my view this can only be done by imposing two requirements upon any belief that presents itself as a candidate for the protection of freedom of religion, first that the belief in question be freely endorsed, and second, that the content of that belief be confined to those dimensions of a believer's life in regard to which his or her well-being depends upon faith. The first of these requirements is entirely familiar, the second less so. Yet each is a necessary, albeit not a sufficient condition of the link between faith and well-being.

Free endorsement of belief is not only central to religious tradition (cults aside) but is a long-standing feature of freedom of religion, and for good reason. The fact that a religious belief has been freely endorsed is the surest evidence of the believer's own conviction that his or her well-being depends upon faith in the substance of that belief. But that in itself is not enough to establish a link between faith and well-being, for believers may be and indeed often are mistaken as to the value of their beliefs. To put it from the opposite perspective, if a belief is genuinely capable of serving well-being, the fact that it has been freely endorsed is the best evidence available that it serves the well-being of the particular believer in question. However, the fact that a belief has been freely endorsed is not in itself evidence that the belief is genuinely capable of serving well-being, for the act of endorsement has neither the power to make a belief serve well-being nor the capacity to determine whether or not that belief is actually capable of serving the well-being of the believers in question. In short, beliefs do not serve well-being just because they are freely endorsed.

How otherwise, however, are we to determine that the content of religious doctrine is restricted to those dimensions of the believer's life in regard to which his or her well-being depends on faith in that doctrine? The answer is in some respects familiar. Freedom of religion has always recognized restrictions on the content of religious doctrine, namely, the semantic restrictions that have been relied upon to determine whether a set of beliefs qualifies as a religion or not. I have argued above that supporters of those restrictions have mistakenly taken the features of traditional religions to be definitive of the scope of freedom of religion. Yet while the features of traditional religions can no longer be regarded as providing a template for access to freedom of religion, they remain reasonably sound illustrations of faith-based beliefs that have been formulated in such a way as to ensure that their adherents are offered access to religious faith in order to deal with issues that they find unknowable, while leaving those adherents free to rely upon reason in all other aspects of their lives. It follows that there may be good reason to protect the exercise of traditional religious beliefs, not out of an unwarranted attachment to history or habit, but because of the connection between adherence to those beliefs and the achievement of well-being, a connection whose existence we have always assumed but never tested. It further follows that any exploration of the scope of freedom of religion, and of the link between religious faith and human well-being upon which that freedom depends, requires that we both test the assumption that adherence to traditional religious beliefs serves well-being and examine the possibility that adherence to other faith-based beliefs also does so.

I suggested above that religious doctrine has been traditionally and typically based upon a set of beliefs first, about the nature and purpose of human life, and in particular, about the possibility of a life other than material existence, and secondly, about the nature of the good, and in particular, about the possibility of moral grounds that lie beyond human life and beyond human reason. It is clear that for some, indeed perhaps for many human beings, a rational approach to such matters is either intellectually inaccessible or psychologically unendurable. Yet the ability to come to terms with those matters is frequently, perhaps normally, essential to the achievement of well-being, and where reason cannot provide that ability, faith must step in. It follows that the value of traditional religious faith lies in its capacity to enable certain people to make commitments, to the project of a life and to the moral values that sustain that project, commitments that are essential to the achievement of their well-being, despite the inaccessibility to them of any reason to do so.

That much I have emphasized already. What is important for present purposes is that this predicament and the response to it is one that human beings who do not share in it can recognize and respect without themselves either endorsing or seeing reason to endorse. It is often the case in life that one can recognize the legitimacy of doubts and uncertainties that one does not share and sees no reason to share. This is because there is a zone of perception beyond the known and the unknown, a zone of understanding beyond the reasonable and the unreasonable, 'when the only truth ascertainable is that nothing can be known',[30] a zone where issues are widely recognized to be in some sense mysterious or unknowable. There are things that we do not know and there are things that we cannot know. The precise scope of the latter zone is in dispute, so that certain issues fall into it for some people and not for others. Moreover, the ability to deal with issues that fall into this zone is essential to the achievement of the well-being of some people but not others.

It is in regard to issues that fall into this zone that religious faith may be essential to well-being, and correspondingly, it is upon such issues that religious doctrine must be focused if it is to attract the protection of freedom of religion. If a body of people claims that Jesus lives and that they depend upon faith in that fact for their sense of purpose in life, it is possible for us to recognize and respect that claim without either endorsing it or seeing any reason to endorse it, for faith in the Resurrection and its implications is one way of coming to terms with death, an issue that we can all recognize to be in some sense genuinely mysterious.[31] But if a body of people claims that Elvis lives and that they depend upon faith in that fact in order to carry on in life we would be forced to conclude that they needed professional help, for belief that Elvis is still alive and eating cheeseburgers is not a way of coming to terms with death or any other mystery in life but is simply an unfortunate and damaging consequence of the cult of celebrity.

On the other hand, and as I have already observed, beliefs about the nature of the good, beliefs that are central to most doctrines that are conventionally recognized as religious, are clearly far from unknowable, for the requirements of morality do not lie beyond human life and are not inaccessible to human beings on the basis of reason. On the contrary, morality is by its nature fit for humans, as it must be in order to offer us guidance as to how to live well. However, what is indeed a mystery to some people, and can be recognized as such by others who do not themselves see any mystery in it, is the metaphysical foundation of morality. For many people, morality simply has no credible basis apart from that provided by the authority of a deity who is believed to have laid its requirements down. For such people it is impossible to believe in true goodness without believing in God. That being the case, faith in God provides a foundation for and so fosters the practice of goodness in their lives.

---

[30] JS Mill, *Three Essays on Religion* (1874), in JM Robson (ed), *Collected Works of John Stuart Mill* (1969) vol X, 405.

[31] I suggested above that death is no mystery, but I recognize that this is a controversial claim as to which reasonable people disagree. At its best, the promise of the hereafter that religion sometimes offers its adherents enables people to cope with the fear of death, which might otherwise be sufficiently incapacitating to undermine critical aspects of their well-being. At its worst, however, this promise makes life of little value, and death to be welcomed. This is as true of many species of Christianity, past and present, as it is of other faiths, most notoriously today, certain alleged species of Islam.

Yet it is essential to notice that the warrant for religion here is the warrant offered by the mysteries of metaphysics, not of morality. We have reason to respect religious beliefs that are prompted, to some extent at least, by the rational mystery (to the religious believer) of certain aspects of metaphysics, and so have reason to respect belief in a deity as the source of morality. Yet we have no like reason to respect the substance of the morality that belief in a deity gives rise to, for the substance of morality is not in any sense mysterious, given its essential role as a guide to human beings in leading their lives. It follows that we are bound to respect the content of religious beliefs only to the extent that we have reason to respect what they call for.

The topics of traditional religious doctrine are of course not the only mysteries that people find it impossible to deal with or to live with, nor is traditional religious doctrine the only way to address the topics that it focuses upon. Yet it remains the case that those topics are paradigmatic examples of matters that for many people are unknowable and yet essential to the achievement of well-being. It follows that in assessing whether commitment to a faith-based belief is capable of enhancing well-being the question will be, not whether the belief in issue has doctrinal features in common with traditional religions, but whether like them it enables people to address and overcome matters that we can all recognize if not accept as being in some sense profoundly mysterious and so inaccessible on the basis of reason, and yet respect as central to the achievement of the well-being of at least some people, those who freely endorse a faith-based response to them.

Religiously Inspired Conduct

There is a further, related point to be made here about the role of religious institutions and practices. The presence of such institutions and practices is essential to the survival and development of faith in religious beliefs, the existence and nourishment of which depends first, upon contact with the sources of revelation, second, upon the guidance of clerics (for want of a better word), and third, upon the commitment of other believers. In this respect faith-based beliefs differ somewhat from rational beliefs, and it is that difference that is the source of the requirement that freedom of religion extend to the protection of religiously inspired conduct, despite the fact that conduct based upon other beliefs is entitled to no such protection.

It is true that rational beliefs also depend first, upon sources (in the form of a history of reasoning), second, upon the guidance of scholars, and third, upon contact with other thinkers, and so might be said to be parallel to religious beliefs in those respects. One might be tempted to conclude that as a matter of consistency protection ought to be accorded to the institutions and practices that sustain both types of belief, rational and non-rational, or neither. It is also true, however, that these features of a culture of rational belief are separately guaranteed by other rights and freedoms, whether formally expressed in a constitution or not, such as freedom of expression, freedom of association, and the right to a decent education. By contrast, the institutions and practices that foster and sustain faith in religious beliefs are and must be a direct reflection of the distinctive, non-rational character of the belief in question and so must be protected as such. In other words, those institutions and practices cannot be independently guaranteed but must be treated as necessary implications of the guarantee of freedom of religion, for they cannot be fully described other than by reference to the content of a particular religious belief and what the protection of that belief entails.

In short, the guarantee of freedom of religion extends to religiously inspired conduct because a religion is not a set of ideas like any other, but rather is a faith-based institution and set of practices, the character and consequences of which are from a rational point of view idiosyncratic and consequently must be protected idiosyncratically.

2. Non-Establishment of Religion

There is one final point to be made about the place of religion in public life. I have already suggested that freedom of religion does not require a rule against the establishment of religion, although in practice, of course, freedom of religion has been closely associated with that rule as the result of their conjunction in the First Amendment to the United States Constitution. Yet in support of my suggestion and in opposition to the lessons of American constitutional practice stands the fact that in certain countries where freedom of religion is apparently enjoyed, such as England, there is an established church, and in other countries where there is a written constitution with a guarantee of freedom of religion, such as Canada, there is no constitutional rule against the establishment of religion.[32] Of course, it might be the case that the people of England do not now enjoy freedom of religion to the extent that they are affected by the presence of an established church, and similarly it might be the case that the people of Canada do not now enjoy freedom of religion to the extent that the failure to entrench a rule against the establishment of religion has permitted one or another religion to be established, officially or unofficially, as Catholicism might once have been thought to have been established in Quebec.

In fact, I do not believe that this is so. Indeed, notwithstanding the lessons of American constitutional law I find it in some ways difficult to see how a rule against the establishment of religion could possibly be regarded as an aspect of freedom of religion, given that any account of freedom of religion implicitly or explicitly assumes that the primary purpose of that freedom is to promote the well-being of religious believers; that establishment is on balance a benefit to those believers, a benefit that may be critical to the well-being of at least some

---

[32] Although certain aspects of the rule against establishment, as expounded in United States law, have been held to be implicit in a guarantee of freedom of religion. See *R v Big M Drug Mart Ltd* [1985] 1 SCR 295, 339–41.

of them; and that the rule against establishment prohibits any establishment of religion, however ecumenical, however tolerant, and so denies religious believers the very real benefit of the presence of religion in public life. In other words, the purpose of freedom of religion is to secure to religious believers a benefit to their well-being, namely the value that adherence to religious faith is capable of giving rise to, the very benefit that the rule against establishment at least partly denies to them.[33]

It is true, of course, that the rule against establishment has the effect of guaranteeing a form of equality to different religions, by ensuring that no religion enjoys precedence over any other by reason of its having been granted a privileged place in public life. Yet this is not a form of equality that can be said to make any contribution to the well-being of religious believers,[34] for it secures its egalitarian goal by ensuring that no religion enjoys the benefit of establishment, thus eliminating the contribution that establishment makes to the well-being of religious believers, rather than by ensuring that all religions enjoy whatever benefit is enjoyed by any one religion, thus securing equal access to any established practice.[35] In fact, the effect of the rule against establishment is to protect the interests of those who do not believe at the expense of those who do, and therein, in my opinion, lies its justification.

In the debates surrounding the entrenchment of what has become known as the Bill of Rights, namely, the first ten amendments to the United States Constitution, different views were taken of the establishment clause and its justification. Some thought that a rule against establishment was a corollary of freedom of religion. Others, most famously Thomas Jefferson, believed that a rule against establishment was necessary for the protection of the public realm against the influence of religious belief. Yet others, such as James Madison, took a compromise position.[36] It will be clear from the course of my argument, and

---

[33] I am assuming that freedom of religion offers no protection to those who lack religious faith. For more on this point, see the next section.

[34] Unless, of course, this privatization of religion ultimately contributes to the well-being of the adherents of what would otherwise have been the established religion.

[35] I should also note that the egalitarian argument for a rule against any establishment of religion does not merely fail to serve human well-being but implicitly assumes that an ecumenical establishment of religion is impossible, as is surely not the case. It is true that one cannot invoke an ecumenical understanding of the meaning of religion as part of the justification for a semantic approach to the interpretation of freedom of religion, for one can only be ecumenical in one's approach to religion once one has decided what religion means, or ought to mean. Nevertheless, it follows that once one has decided what religion ought to mean, there is no logical reason why one could not then grant the benefit of the establishment of religion to all those practices that meet that definition. There is moral reason not to do so, however, and it is this that in my view constitutes the justification for the rule against any establishment of religion.

[36] For a summary account of these different views, see L Tribe, *American Constitutional Law* (2nd edn, 1988) 1158ff. These were actually views as to the overall place of religion in public life, a place ultimately secured by both clauses of the First Amendment, rather than views about the establishment clause alone, but of course the fact that these views apply to the free exercise clause does nothing to diminish their application to the establishment clause.

particularly from my earlier discussion of the necessity for a secular basis for freedom of religion, that I am broadly of Jefferson's view.

Given that religious beliefs are adhered to, not on the basis of reason alone, but at least in part on the basis of faith, and given that the impact of faith, as a mode of belief distinct from reason, is to impart to beliefs that are held on the basis of it a character that is singular, stable and partial, as opposed to plural, comprehensive and evolving, it follows that the requirement of non-establishment is simply a reflection of the moral limitations of religious belief, limitations that do not detract from the value that religious belief is capable of contributing to the lives of those who freely endorse it, but limitations nevertheless that make that belief unacceptable as a basis for the design of state institutions and state practices, even when expressed ecumenically. In other words, the rule against establishment insulates state institutions and practices from the straitening effect upon morality of religious belief, thereby ensuring that those institutions and practices are capable of fostering valuable ways of life that religion does not recognize and may even forbid (even when ecumenically understood), ways of life that are critical to the well-being of at least some of those to whom the state is responsible, namely, those non-believers whose way of life is inconsistent with the requirements of one or more religious beliefs. One does not have to look far for instances of such non-believers. Homosexuality, for example, is condemned by certain religious beliefs, yet the ability to pursue a homosexual way of life free from public censure is clearly essential to the well-being of some, indeed many people.[37]

In short, the moral character of religious belief places it in conflict with value pluralism and so leads to the common requirement of liberal political cultures that there be no establishment of religion. This is a corollary of freedom of religion only in the sense that like that freedom, and indeed like any other right or freedom, the rule against establishment reflects and respects the basic moral requirements that govern the just design of state institutions and state practices.[38]

3. Application

As one moves from the problem of defining freedom of religion to the problem of applying the freedom that has been so defined one is forced to face the question of what difference, if any, a shift in the justification of the freedom and a consequent modification of its definition makes or should make to the present beneficiaries and non-beneficiaries of that freedom. Would the approach to

[37] This chapter is concerned with the general principles underlying freedom of religion, so I cannot address here the specific implications for that freedom of what is also true, namely, that for many people the ability to combine religious commitment with a homosexual life is critical to the pursuit of well-being, with the consequence that well-being is denied to them when their religion is homophobic, as it often is.

[38] It follows that the presence of an established church in countries such as England does not violate freedom of religion but does violate the equally necessary rule against any establishment of religion.

freedom of religion that I have advanced here, if adopted, have the consequence of denying fundamental protection to certain faith-based beliefs that we have traditionally recognized as religions, while extending that protection to other faith-based beliefs that we have traditionally refused to recognize as religions?

I have already suggested that traditional religious beliefs should continue to be protected under the approach that I have recommended, provided that it can be demonstrated that what we have always assumed to be true is in fact true, namely, that belief in the doctrines of those religions, when freely endorsed on the basis of faith, is capable of enhancing human well-being in the manner indicated above. Indeed, were this not so, and were most traditional religious beliefs not protected under this approach, the approach would have to be judged a failure, for the semantic constraints upon any explanation and justification of freedom of religion are such that an approach to freedom of religion that excluded a significant number of traditional religious beliefs from the scope of the freedom could not be regarded as an acceptable account of freedom of religion, although it might of course serve as an acceptable account of some other freedom.

The question remains, however, to what extent the approach to freedom of religion that I have advanced would offer protection for the first time to faith-based beliefs that we have heretofore refused to recognize as religions; would offer a different form of protection to faith-based beliefs that we have heretofore recognized as religions; or would deny protection to what we have previously protected as religion. While I clearly cannot offer answers to every sort of hypothetical question that might possibly be raised as to the scope of freedom of religion, or perhaps even to all the questions that I have just sketched, a few examples may help to give a sense of what this approach to freedom of religion that I have advanced might entail in practice.

The first example is the example of marginal, unconventional religious beliefs. Two questions arise here, first, whether such beliefs are entitled to fundamental protection under the rubric of freedom of religion, and second, if they are so entitled, what degree and scope of protection they are entitled to. As to the first question, I have already indicated that under the approach that I have advanced here a decision whether to extend protection to the institutions and practices that express and sustain belief in what is alleged to be a religion should be based, not on a comparison between the doctrines of the alleged religion and the doctrines of traditional religions, but on a frank examination of the contribution that faith in the doctrine of the alleged religion is capable of making to human well-being. The result of such an examination would not necessarily confirm conventional conclusions as to the non-religious character of what are commonly described as cults, for example.

On the one hand it is indisputable that faith in the doctrines of self-destructive, or suicidal cults, such as those led by Jim Jones or David Koresh, is incapable of enhancing human well-being. On the other hand, it is less clear whether faith in the doctrines of quasi-religions such as Scientology is incapable of enhancing well-being. It is true that there seems to be reason to question whether the doctrines of Scientology are at all times freely endorsed by their adherents. If they are not, then they cannot be said to enhance human well-being, for the reasons given above. If they are, however, then the further question must be whether the content of the doctrines of Scientology is such that faith in that content is capable of enhancing human well-being, by enabling the adherents of Scientology to address and to deal with matters that are for them unknowable and yet central to the achievement of their well-being, matters that can from the rational point of view be recognized to be in some sense genuinely mysterious or unknowable, albeit not necessarily so. This is a question that I cannot pretend to answer myself. I can note, however, that conventional approaches to the question of whether Scientology is a religion deserving of fundamental protection have not addressed this question at all, but have instead contented themselves with a comparison between the doctrines of Scientology and the doctrines of traditional religions, a comparison that for the reasons given above is in my view an illegitimate means of determining the scope of freedom of religion. It follows that while I would be privately surprised if the institutions and practice of Scientology merit the protection of freedom of religion, I recognize that it is only possible to know that this is so by asking straightforwardly whether Scientology is capable of enhancing human well-being, in the ways and under the conditions that I have described.

Other marginal, unconventional religious beliefs raise somewhat different questions about the scope of freedom of religion. In particular, under the approach that I have advanced here a belief is only entitled to the protection of freedom of religion if and to the extent that it is held on the basis of faith. A set of beliefs that is endorsed entirely on the basis of reason is not a religion, at least not for these purposes, and is not entitled to be protected as such. This may be what the United States Supreme Court had in mind when it observed in *Wisconsin v Yoder*:

> . . . if the Amish asserted their claims because of their subjective evaluation and rejection of the contemporary secular values accepted by the majority, much as Thoreau rejected the social values of his time and isolated himself at Walden Pond, their claims would not rest on a religious basis. Thoreau's choice was philosophical and personal rather than religious, and such belief does not rise to the demands of the Religion Clauses.[39]

It is not clear from this passage whether the Supreme Court's objection to the idea that Thoreau's beliefs were religious was based on the view that those beliefs were merely subjective or were philosophical. Indeed, the Court seems to have equated the two. Nor is it clear whether, as a matter of fact, the Court was correct in its characterization of Thoreau's beliefs. But if the Court meant to say

[39] *Wisconsin v Yoder*, 406 US 205, (1972) 216.

that Thoreau believed what he did because he had arrived at a reasoned rejection of the prevailing values of his time, then in my view it correctly concluded that Thoreau's beliefs did not constitute a religion. According to the account that I have given, religion must be based on faith, not reason, for it is the presence of faith that gives religion its distinctive capacity to enhance human well-being.

What, then, of atheists and agnostics? In my view the answer is clear and follows from what I have just said. Atheism and agnosticism are rational positions, the essence of which is either to deny or to remain non-committal as to the legitimacy of religious faith. That being the case atheism and agnosticism plainly do not warrant the protection of freedom of religion, although in practice the related requirement of non-establishment of religion is likely to yield them a similar degree of protection.

Other categories of belief may be less easy to characterize as rational or non-rational. Political beliefs are typically based on reasons, but from time to time commitment to them may change its character, either temporarily or permanently. We are all familiar with political commitments that it is only possible to explain in terms of faith. Does it follow that such commitments are entitled to the protection of freedom of religion? The answer, in my view, is that there is no categorical bar to the protection of a political faith on the basis that it has become a religion, but that in practice such protection is unlikely to be accorded, for when political beliefs come to be matters of faith it is generally because it has come to be recognized that the connection between the realization of those beliefs and the achievement of human well-being is, from any rational point of view, extremely dubious.

The final question of application, as I have already indicated, is what degree and scope of protection faith-based beliefs are entitled to once it has been shown that they are entitled to the protection of freedom of religion. To some extent, there can be no general answer to this question. Freedom of religion protects the institutions and practices that express and foster faith in the doctrines of a particular religion. The character of those institutions and practices is as varied as the character of the doctrines that they foster and give expression to. Beyond that, the limits to the freedom can only be determined as they are now determined, by asking to what extent an alleged exercise of freedom of religion fulfils the purposes for which that freedom has been fundamentally guaranteed, and by weighing the answer to that question against the purposes for the sake of which, it is alleged, that freedom is presently being infringed. Since I have given an explanation of the purposes for which freedom of religion has been fundamentally guaranteed that differs from the conventional explanation of that guarantee, I must expect that this weighing process and its consequences will correspondingly differ from the present process and its consequences. Yet I cannot say exactly what that difference will be without going through the weighing process myself on a case by case basis, something that I clearly cannot do. What I can say, however, is that the focus of the first branch of the inquiry must be on the question of religious faith and the extent to which an alleged exercise of religion can be said to express that faith in a way that fosters human well-being. In other words, those who wish to claim religious freedom for their conduct must be able to show that the conduct in question is central to the possibility and the practice of their faith, and further, that their faith is central to their well-being. This is something quite different from what they have traditionally been expected to show.

This shift in focus might well give rise to somewhat unfamiliar conclusions concerning the freedom that is owed to the doctrines and practices of traditional religions. The approach that I have advanced here is likely to offer those religions protection of a rather different character than the protection they have traditionally enjoyed; in exceptional cases, it may even deny them protection altogether. I have already suggested that in principle traditional religions can expect that the bulk of their doctrines and practices will continue to be protected under the approach that I have advanced here; indeed, I have even suggested that the approach would be a failure were traditional religions not so protected by it. It does not follow, however, that traditional religions can expect to be protected in precisely the same way that they are now protected, for there is no particular reason to believe that the present approach to the scope of freedom of religion has yielded conclusions that correspond precisely to the conclusions that would be yielded by a faith-based approach to the freedom. If, as I have argued, traditional religions should continue to receive fundamental protection because, and only because, they constitute paradigmatic examples of beliefs that offer their adherents the possibility of faith in relation to dimensions of life that those adherents reasonably regard as inaccessible other than on the basis of faith, dimensions of life that are critical to their well-being, then traditional religions should be denied protection to the extent that they have misidentified those dimensions of life, so as to embrace matters in regard to which reason is not only accessible but constitutes a sounder guide to the achievement of human well-being. Since this is not the test that traditional religions have had to meet in the past it is almost inevitable that if asked to meet it now they would receive a different, perhaps lesser protection.

There should be nothing particularly surprising or disturbing in this, however. On the contrary, it simply confirms and continues an accepted historical trend in the modern era. The story of the modern era has in part been the story of the ascendancy of reason in relation to matters that were once regarded as inherently matters of faith, and thus as matters falling within the exclusive preserve of religion, matters such as the exercise of moral conscience, the expression of moral and political belief, and the investigation of our place in the world and beyond. The ascendancy of reason in relation to these matters has not displaced the role of faith, as the continuing existence of religious conviction confirms, but it has limited the authority of faith in what has become a secular society. Faith in such matters remains permissible, indeed is guaranteed freedom by the state for the reasons that I have advanced in this chapter, yet that freedom is now limited by the requirement that the pursuit of faith involve no harm to others and require no endorsement by the state.[40] To put it from the opposite perspective, faith in such matters may be denied the protection of freedom of religion, and indeed often has been, in settings where reason is not only accessible, but constitutes a sound and necessary basis for the achievement of human well-being. We do not, for example, permit parents to insist that the state provide their children with a form of education that reflects their particular faith, nor do we permit parents who wish to opt out of the system of public education to insulate their children entirely from the requirements of that system, such as its basic syllabus, even where those requirements are incompatible with the parents' faith. There is no reason to assume that this ongoing process of secularization has now come to an end. The approach to freedom of religion that I have advanced here neither furthers nor curtails the process; it merely makes its reflection in freedom of religion explicit, as it surely should be.

My purpose in this chapter has simply been to describe the contours of a value-pluralist account of religion, and to suggest that unlike the conventional and psychological approaches to freedom of religion, a faith-based approach to the freedom, like value pluralism itself, is at once sufficiently flexible to accommodate the well-being of every human being and what that requires, and sufficiently substantial to offer other human beings reason to respect and to sustain the quest for well-being on the part of each of their fellows.

---

[40] See the discussion above of the rule against any establishment of religion.

5

Entrenching Bills of Rights: Judicial Power and Political Freedom

Much talk of human rights, and of the legal instruments used to secure them, is deeply unrealistic. Admirers claim that the legal entrenchment of human rights will transform society for the better, providing us with a fresh set of values for a godless age.[1] Critics claim that entrenchment will transform society for the worse, diminishing our democratic institutions by reference to a reactionary set of values from a less enlightened age.[2] The difference between these two positions masks the extent to which they display a common understanding of the institutional significance of bills of rights. Bills of rights, admirers and critics agree, transfer power from legislatures to courts, and this matters a great deal, enough to transform society. Whether it is a good or a bad thing depends on one's view of the character and possibilities of the two institutions. If one is sceptical of the judiciary one is bound to be sceptical of bills of rights, and to place one's faith in Parliament instead. If one is sceptical of Parliament one is bound, for lack of an alternative, to support bills of rights and place one's faith in the courts that sustain them. Yet none of this can quite be true, at least not as so expressed.

Broadly speaking, there are two possible responses to claims of this kind, one simple and the other more refined, each containing a measure of truth, each revealing what the other obscures. The simple response is to take the claims at face value, and simply deny what has been simply put. Despite appearances, bills of rights do not transfer power from legislatures to the courts.[3] The next section will assess this response, what it illuminates, and what it distorts. The more refined

---

[1] See, for example, F Klug, *Values For a Godless Age: The Story of the United Kingdom's New Bill of Rights* (2000).

[2] See, for example, K Ewing, 'The Unbalanced Constitution' in T Campbell, K Ewing and A Tomkins (eds), *Sceptical Essays on Human Rights* (2001) 103. In singling out these pieces by Ewing and Klug I do not mean to suggest that they bear any distinctive responsibility for the prevailing view that bills of rights transfer power from legislatures to courts. On the contrary, this is a widely accepted view, and Ewing and Klug are but two of the most recent and most prominent of its exponents.

[3] I do not wish to mislead in any way. I should say immediately, therefore, that I speak here and for the time being of bills of rights as they are conventionally understood. In newer and slightly less familiar settings bills of rights may be more likely to transfer to the courts what could reasonably be regarded, at least for practical purposes, as tantamount to legislative power, as explained in the third

response is to probe the claims, by distinguishing among the kinds of powers that might be thought to have been transferred, legislative and constitutional, and the kind of duties that such powers may give rise to, positive and negative. Clearly the courts have acquired a novel power, and just as clearly their exercise of that power has diminished the power of the legislature. Yet it remains a question what kind of power they have acquired, to what extent it has been acquired from the legislature, so as to make it sensible to regard the power as having been transferred from one institution to the other, and to what extent any such transfer is politically significant.[4] Consideration of this response will occupy the third and fourth sections.

In order to make the presentation of the issues clear, particularly in the first two sections, where possible I have relieved the text of the burden of certain marginal questions by transferring consideration of them to the notes, which as a result amplify and support the argument without being essential to it.

The Power of Review

The simple response plainly requires immediate qualification, to save it from denying the obvious. It is unquestionably the case that bills of rights confer new and important powers upon the courts. If and to the extent that rights and freedoms are given fundamental or constitutional status, so as to impose legal obligations on the legislature, it falls to the courts, as the body whose duty it is to determine authoritatively the existence and content of legal obligations, to decide what the requirements of the constitution are and whether they have been complied with. Constitutional courts must decide, for example, whether the legislature has unreasonably infringed freedom of expression. In so deciding they undoubtedly set limits to the power of the legislature, limits that are not discoverable in the broad language of the bill of rights itself and that would not exist apart from that bill. There can be no denying that this is an important limit on the power of the legislature and possibly on democracy; a limit described by an inherently unrepresentative body; a limit that is new to the United Kingdom and one that there is reason both to celebrate and to regret.[5]

---

and fourth sections. See n 5 and the cross-references there for consideration of the very real transfer to the courts of the power to establish a constitutional agenda.

[4] I should emphasize that it is normative power I have in mind here, not effective power. For discussion of the distinction see HLA Hart, 'Legal Powers', *Essays on Bentham* (1982). It is a common assumption that normative power implies effective power, so that if Parliament is normatively supreme it must be all-powerful. Yet one needs only to think of historical examples of weak and strong kings with identical normative powers to realize that this is untrue. Typically, government is ineffective not because it is incompetent, as many on the right believe, but because social and other realities make its goals unattainable by anybody, or by anybody's intentional action. In what follows I say nothing about effective power, although analogical and consequential points could be made.

[5] In referring to a bill of rights in the context of the United Kingdom I am referring to the combined impact of the Human Rights Act 1998 and the European Convention on Human Rights.

Yet the power that the courts thus acquire, important as it is, is not the same power that Parliament lost. What Parliament has lost is the power, for example, to regulate expression in ways that the bill of rights, as interpreted by the courts, would regard as unreasonable. This power of regulation has not in any sense passed to the courts. No bill of rights gives the judiciary the power to regulate expression or otherwise restrict the fundamental rights and freedoms set out in it, let alone the power to do so unreasonably. On the contrary, bills of rights merely empower courts to make declarations of incompatibility, declarations that have different implications in different jurisdictions. If a legislature seeks to censor speech, a constitutional court may declare the censorship incompatible with the bill of rights, but it cannot then supply a different scheme of censorship itself. Courts have no power to enact legislation or even to repeal it, and bills of rights do nothing to change that fact.[6] Indeed, certain bills of rights go further, and make the courts as subject to their requirements as the legislature, so constraining both.

The extent to which the Act on its own limits the power of Parliament is a matter of debate, but the extent to which the European Convention ultimately does so is not. Similarly, in referring to the role played by constitutional courts I am referring, in the United Kingdom context, to the combined role played by courts in this country and at Strasbourg.

It should also be emphasized, because it is a common source of confusion, that a transfer of the power to establish a constitutional agenda (a power that might otherwise be the property of the legislature or some other, presumably democratic institution) has significant legislative implications, both negative and positive, and for that reason is easy to mistake for a transfer of legislative power. To the extent that a constitutional agenda is concrete and explicit, the transfer of the power to establish that agenda is to the entrenching body, whose decisions in that regard bind subsequent legislatures. To the extent that a constitutional agenda falls to be established by interpretation, as is the case with most provisions of a bill of rights, the transfer of the power to establish that agenda is to the judiciary, whose decisions similarly bind the legislature. Judicial decisions as to the scope of a constitution's requirements thus have the necessary effect of invalidating or compelling legislation, actual or proposed, and that effect may be what matters most to all involved. Yet it must be remembered that judicial decisions do these things only in response to legislative action or inaction, never at the courts' own initiative, and more important, only as a byproduct of the power that a bill of rights genuinely transfers to the courts, namely, the power to shape the content of the bill's provisions. To conflate the two powers, constitutional and legislative, one transferred to the courts and the other not, tempting though it might be in light of the undoubted legislative ambition underlying certain constitutional decisions, is a mistake which generates misguided and frequently counterproductive responses, in particular the attempt to address and remedy as legislative concerns what are in fact constitutional concerns, notwithstanding their legislative implications. To take but one example, the qualities that best fit a body to exercise legislative power are not necessarily the qualities that best fit it to exercise constitutional power, making it misguided and very probably counterproductive to endow a constitutional body with the qualities that would fit it for the exercise of legislative power, as one would naturally seek to do if one believed that legislative power was what the constitutional body exercised. See below for consideration of the implications of constitutional power. See n 18 for consideration of the value of representativeness in the judiciary.

[6] When a constitutional court declares that legislation is incompatible with a guaranteed right or freedom it does no more than establish the attitude of the courts to that legislation. Despite appearances, a court that strikes down legislation, or reads legislation in a way that goes beyond interpretation (sometimes called reading down and reading in), does not repeal or amend the legislation. Only the legislature can do that. The legislation remains on the statute books unaltered, until the legislature decides to remove or amend it, although the courts will no longer endorse it as written.

   The point can be illuminated by drawing an analogy to another sort of constitutional requirement, which the courts are also responsible for authoritatively determining. In a federal state, the constitution allocates certain powers to the national government and other powers to regional governments. Let us suppose that the national government has the power to regulate national and international transportation while regional governments have the power to regulate regional transportation in their jurisdiction. It then becomes the responsibility of the courts to determine the scope of the subject matter allocated to each level of government; to characterize any form of transportation that either level of government seeks to regulate; and to declare invalid any regulation that exceeds the limits of the power granted to the enacting government by the constitution. These issues are rarely easily resolved. When does regional transportation become national? What of the regional railway a subordinate line of which runs into another region? What of the local coach company a minority of whose journeys cross into another country? What of international agreements on transportation safety, implementation of which significantly affects the operation of local enterprises? And so on.

   The power to determine these issues is an important one, and provides reason to regret as well as to celebrate a federal system. Many forms of regulation, whose complexity defies easy classification as national or regional, are vulnerable to challenge on the ground that they trespass on the powers of the other level of government. The limits to the powers of government, national or regional, are for the courts to define, and the uncertainty of those limits, and their categorical character, mean that they are in practice limits on the power not only of each level of government, but of all government. It follows that where a court is assigned (or assumes) the responsibility of upholding the requirements of a federal constitution, it acquires the authority not only to determine the balance of power in the federation, preferring either the region or the nation as it sees fit, but also and indirectly, to set limits to the overall power of the people as a democratic community.[7]

   It is true that in doing these things courts make law, whether by their treatment of the legislation, or by defining the scope of a right or freedom in ways not dictated by the text of the bill of rights itself. It is also true that certain scholars, most notably HLA Hart, have described this process of law-making as legislation: *The Concept of Law* (2nd edn, 1994) at 134–35. I do not wish to deny this function of the courts, although I think the term legislation is a misleading description of what they do when they make law. My point is simply that in describing and upholding the requirements of a bill of rights the courts do not exercise the power to legislate that they thereby deny to Parliament. For further consideration of 'judicial legislation' see J Gardner, 'Legal Positivism: 5½ Myths' 46 Am J of Juris (2001) 199, at 214–18.

   [7] This suggests that those who deplore the entrenchment of a bill of rights on the ground that it diminishes the powers of the people as a democratic community should deplore the entrenchment not only of the bill of rights, but of federal and quasi-federal structures, such as those involved in the devolution of powers to regional governments in Scotland and Wales and in the granting of powers to supra-national institutions such as the European Community. As the text points out, the powers of the people as a democratic community are diminished by federalism whether the institutions

What the courts plainly cannot do under a federal constitution, however, is legislate on transportation themselves. On the contrary, the legislative power their decisions withdraw from one level of government is correspondingly recognized in the other level of government. Otherwise the power falls into abeyance. Typically, if the national government cannot regulate a form of transportation, the regional government can. Whether this is a good or a bad thing depends on the view one takes of the appropriate balance between local sensitivity and national purpose in the regulation of transportation. Sometimes, however, the power denied to one level of government is not correspondingly recognized in the other. It may be the case that a form of transportation can only be regulated effectively by the sort of collaboration between levels of government that a federal constitution makes difficult or even impossible. If so, this is simply the price of federalism. It is a price determined by the courts and paid by the community as a whole in return for the other benefits that federalism brings, or is thought to bring. But whether the effect of the courts' decisions is to transfer power from one level of government to another, or to deny it to government altogether, it is never to transfer power to the courts themselves. The policing of the exercise of legislative power, important as it is, is not the exercise of legislative power itself.

The same holds true, though perhaps less obviously so, where the constitution is concerned with the allocation of rights and freedoms rather than with the allocation of legislative powers. Where rights and freedoms are fundamentally entrenched, the power to legislate is constrained by the courts' power to prevent legislation. Where the courts uphold the requirements of a bill of rights they withdraw power from Parliament but they do not correspondingly acquire power themselves. In securing rights and freedoms they do not assume the guardianship of those matters that Parliament once enjoyed. Constitutional courts cannot decide which forms of speech should be tolerated and which should not; they can only determine whether and to what extent Parliament may decide such matters itself. If the courts determine that Parliament may not decide such matters, then the power of decision falls not to the courts but to the bearers of the right or freedom in question.

I have used freedom of expression as an illustration, but the analysis can be readily extended to other freedoms. When the United States Supreme Court decided, in *Roe v Wade*,[8] that the states could not regulate access to abortion in the first trimester of pregnancy, it gave the power of decision on that issue not to the courts, but to pregnant women. Nor is the analysis confined to the case of fundamental freedoms, as these examples might suggest, though just how far it extends to the positive as well as the negative duties of government, and how far those correlate with rights and freedoms, are matters I will postpone to the third section.

---

to which powers are ceded are themselves democratic or not. The division of powers between two levels of democratic government inevitably diminishes the power of government, of whatever kind, in that territory.

[8] 410 US 113 (1973).

Privatizing the Public Good

The simple position requires more than qualification, however. To be fully accurate it will need to be significantly refined. Yet to do so will involve discarding its simplicity, together with the insights that simplification yields, the simplicity that makes it possible to speak, without distortion, of bills of rights as transferring (or not transferring) legislative power to the courts, for better or worse. It will be necessary to distinguish among the forms of normative power that might be thought to be possessed by a legislature in the absence of a bill of rights, positive and negative (section 3), legislative and constitutional (section 4); to determine which of those powers, if any, have been transferred; and finally, to decide what the implications of such transfers might be. But before leaving the simple position it is worth considering what, in its unrefined condition, it can actually tell us.

If the argument in the previous section is correct, the significance of bills of rights does not lie in the fact that power over their content is placed in the custody of the courts, for that is simply not the case. Typically, and still speaking simply, whatever power is denied to Parliament by bills of rights, as they are interpreted by the courts, is correspondingly recognized in the bearers of those rights, namely the people, individually and collectively.[9] Otherwise it falls into abeyance. If the courts decide, for example, that Parliament may not regulate a certain aspect of expression, the power to permit or restrain that aspect of expression is transferred primarily to those in whom the courts have correspondingly recognized a freedom.[10] Where self-restraint is impossible or unlikely in the absence of an external authority, as it may be if self-restraint by one person depends on a degree of reciprocity that is undermined by presence of freedom in another, the power to regulate expression ends.

This is one reason for the general popularity of bills of rights. The wisdom of their entrenchment does not turn on whether we should be governed in these

---

[9] Simplification here conceals the fact that to the extent that the people, so described, acquire normative rather than merely practical power as the result of the entrenchment of a bill of rights, it is not, strictly speaking, the same normative power denied to Parliament, since the people have no capacity to establish norms by legislation, other than through Parliament or some other legislative body, all of which are subject to the terms of the bill of rights. For the most part, therefore, the normative power once exercised by Parliament (or other legislature) falls into abeyance in the presence of a bill of rights. See the text and n 10.

[10] More precisely, the power to regulate is transferred in the first instance to the holder of the freedom, here the speaker, in whose hands it becomes a species of self-restraint, and in the second instance to all those who are not themselves bound by the terms of the bill of rights, here the other members of the speaker's community, separately and together, in whose hands it may become a species of enforced conformity. I should emphasize that this discussion of privatization is focused on rights to freedom, such as the right to freedom of expression. Rights to freedom ground immunities. Whether and to what extent those immunities permit, or even inspire, private normative power is an open question: see n 12 for further consideration. The implications of rights as positive duties are considered in the next section.

respects by the legislature or by the courts. It turns on whether we should be so governed by the legislature or by ourselves.[11] The recognition of a constitutional right or freedom is recognition of the capacity of rights-holders to decide these matters for themselves. It displays respect for each person's capacity for self-government. But it also suggests that bills of rights are part of a broader contemporary disenchantment with the ability of public institutions to secure the public good. They are one more step in the progress of what is loosely described as privatization, perhaps a more radical step than that involved in the sale of public assets and the commercialization of public services.[12]

[11] In this regard it is worth noting that many critics of bills of rights have misinterpreted the significance of entrenchment and so have misunderstood the nature of their intellectual opposition. Critics believe that bills of rights require the people to be governed by the courts rather than by the legislature with respect to all matters that rights and freedoms refer to and so protect. It follows that bills of rights are to be condemned by true democrats, for they transfer power from the representatives of the people to the courts, which are taken to be representatives of an élite. In fact, however, bills of rights require the people to govern themselves in these respects, rather than be governed by their elected representatives. It follows that the intellectual basis for bills of rights, to which their critics are opposed, is anarchistic (or more precisely, autarchist) rather than élitist. (On autarchy and anarchy, see S Benn, *A Theory of Freedom* (1988)). Put another way, critics of bills of rights need to show the value of government and the authority it exercises, to which bills of rights are genuinely opposed, rather than the value of self-government, which bills of rights can reasonably claim to secure.

Admirers of bills of rights also misinterpret the significance of entrenchment when they seek a more representative judiciary on the basis that the courts now exercise powers once exercised by Parliament and over which it is desirable to maintain some degree of democratic control. In fact, bills of rights call upon courts to exercise familiar powers, for they expect the courts to police the exercise of jurisdiction to ensure that it is not ultra vires, albeit on new and rather vague, or at least broadly framed, grounds. It follows that while there may be reasons to make the courts more representative of the population at large than they now are (see n 18), those reasons do not include the fact that the courts have acquired powers once possessed by Parliament, for that is simply not the case. Indeed the task of describing reasonable limits to the legislature's capacity to infringe rights and freedoms is not only familiar but might be thought to call for a set of narrowly technical skills quite distinct from the function of representation.

[12] The term privatization embraces a number of rather different transfers of power from public to private hands, making it important not to assume that the features of one form of privatization are necessarily true of another. When a government privatizes an institution or activity it abandons certain realms of normative and effective power. Just which realms of each form of power are abandoned and which are retained varies with the institution or activity being privatized, the kind of power exercised through it in government hands, and the kind of power exercised through it in private hands. So while on the face of it the privatization of state corporations simply transfers commercial power into private hands, in doing so it deprives the state of the ability to exploit that power for normative ends. That normative power may fall into abeyance, but it may survive, albeit in altered or truncated form. The operation of a privatized airline or railway, for example, may be shaped and disciplined by a scheme of state regulation, by corporate response to pressure from the state, the public, campaign groups or the media, or even by self-inspired self-regulation. Privatization here reduces the scope of the state's normative power, and correspondingly increases the scope of private normative power, by transferring the ability to exploit commercial power for normative ends from state to private hands. Similar consequences attend the privatization of state activities, though what the state yields there is the development and implementation of administrative policy rather than the exercise of commercial power.

By contrast, what I have described as the privatization of a legislative role, through the entrenchment of a bill of rights, differs in its implications from other forms of privatization in

This connection between bills of rights and privatization becomes both explicit and familiar when rights are recognized in the hands of corporations. When corporations are recognized as persons to be protected against unreasonable search and seizure by the state, and so are secured against government inspection, or when corporations are recognized as persons entitled to freedom of expression, and so are secured against government regulation of their advertising, both courts and commentators are openly concerned about privatization. The argument I have offered suggests they are wrong to think that the extension of rights and freedoms to corporations is what makes privatization an issue here, though they are right to ask whether the privatization is warranted in corporate hands, albeit that the question may lack the significance they take it to have.[13]

Whether the entrenchment of fundamental rights and freedoms is a good or a bad thing, therefore, depends on the view one takes of the values served by privatization in this domain. Why might it be thought better for people to govern themselves in these matters without the intervention of the state? It should be emphasized that the question here is not the question of the value of freedom. It is the question of whether the value of freedom is better secured by preserving a zone of private action through a judicially administered bill of rights, or by preserving a zone of public space through Parliamentary decision, a zone which constitutes the conditions of freedom.[14]

There are several possible answers to the question. At a popular level justification for a bill of rights is commonly based on moral scepticism. People should be able to decide such matters for themselves, it is thought, because the right answer in such matters is entirely a matter of taste, and so depends entirely on who one is. Were that the only justification for a bill of rights it would be both

---

that entrenchment specifically forbids the kind of state regulation that may continue to be applied to privatized institutions or activities. That being the case, it is tempting to regard the normative dimensions of the former legislative role as having been ended by entrenchment rather than privatized. Yet in fact the entrenchment of a right to freedom is as compatible with the subsequent exercise of normative power over that freedom by rights-holders, individually or collectively, under pressure or at their own initiative, and in many of the same ways, as is the privatization of state institutions and activities. Indeed, there is evidence to suggest that the creation of immunities through the exclusion of state regulation in a certain domain not only permits but may even inspire the exercise of private normative power over the same domain. In short, public immunities do not always entail private immunities, though such immunities may sometimes follow. See note 15 and accompanying text, and the final section.

[13] Freedom of expression, for example, inevitably secures the expression of business proprietorships and partnerships against government regulation, either of which would then be entitled to exercise that freedom to advertise the wares of corporations, national and multinational, however offensive those wares might be. Nor could recourse to corporate freedom by proxy be countered by focusing on the commercial character of such advertising, since most expression has a commercial aspect, with the possible exception of academic and charitable activities.

[14] I speak here of rights to freedom. Bills of rights also contain rights that do not imply private freedom, such as the right to a fair trial. From the practical point of view, power over these matters would appear either to be transferred to the courts or to fall into abeyance, but the practical point of view is too blunt to be strictly accurate here. On rights as positive duties, see the next section; on what exactly is transferred, see the section entitled The Politics of Entrenchment.

confused and self-defeating, for it would offer no ground for respect from others, including the judiciary.

More promisingly, it is often thought that people should be able to decide such matters for themselves because they are in the best position to know what kind of people they are and what is good for them in these respects. This claim can be extended beyond the realm of special knowledge. If and to the extent that freedom in a particular respect is greatest when one is left to one's own devices, freedom is best secured by an instrument which ensures that is the case, such as a bill of rights. If and to the extent, however, that freedom depends on the support of the state, so that one is most free when the resources necessary to one's freedom are most fully ensured by government, freedom is best secured by a combination of private and public endeavour, a combination that a bill of rights prevents. The entrenchment of a bill of rights thus resembles recent forms of economic privatization, such as the sale of public assets and the commercialization of public services, in its commitment both to the idea that the public good is secured through private freedom, and to the further idea that private freedom is achieved without the intervention or support of the state.

These two distinct commitments suggest two distinct reasons to be concerned at the cost of a bill of rights. For those who doubt the value of private freedom in securing the public good, there is reason to count the cost of a bill of rights in terms of the collective endeavours that it makes difficult or even impossible. This is the familiar complaint of socialists and traditional conservatives. But even those who accept the value of private freedom in securing the public good may well believe that the full achievement of private freedom requires the support of the state. They may reject the idea that it is merely a matter of being left alone by the state, as a bill of rights assumes. This is a complaint for liberals to make.

Being left alone by the state, it should be noted, is not the same thing as being left alone. Where freedom of expression is constitutionally entrenched the censorship not practised by the state may well be practised by one's neighbours. Indeed, given the strength of the human impulse to censor what one does not approve of, the removal of one censor is very likely to shift the tendency to another censor. One notices in this regard that personal eccentricity, and private tolerance of it, is often widespread in societies where a doctrine of conformity is publicly insisted on, by church or state, while personal conformity and private intolerance are as often widespread in societies where a doctrine of freedom is publicly insisted upon, by a bill of rights or otherwise.[15]

---

[15] It is important to be careful here, and not to assume that personal freedom is to be equated with the presence of its constitutional guarantee. A commitment to personal freedom can be publicly insisted upon in a number of ways, so that societies without a bill of rights may be as committed to that freedom, and may consequently exhibit as much personal conformity and private intolerance, as societies with a bill of rights. See the final section of this chapter. It is also important to notice that private censorship of expression is not the only form of conformity that may be engendered by public freedom. On the relationship between freedom and conformity, once again see the final section.

Rights as Positive Duties

Refinement begins with modification, and more particularly, with what on the face of it looks like a significant concession, so significant indeed that if read back into the previous argument would appear to cast doubt on the soundness of the simple response. Yet, paradoxically, the perception that makes the refinement, and the counter claims it sustains, both sensible and persuasive ultimately gives rise to a dimension of understanding that supports the insights of the simple response, albeit in a refined and qualified form. Bills of rights do not normally transfer legislative power to the courts, but they can, and sometimes do.

As the discussion in the previous section may have suggested, the story I have told so far is plainly over-simplified and culturally dependent. It assumes that constitutionally entrenched bills of rights impose only negative duties upon a legislature. This may be very largely true in practice but it is certainly not true in principle. To reprise a familiar distinction briefly, rights and freedoms can give rise to negative duties, positive duties, or both. On the one hand they may *prevent* state action, so securing a zone of personal freedom in which one is *allowed* to do what one wants. On the other hand, they may *require* state action, so securing the opportunities and resources necessary to the achievement of freedom, a condition in which one is *able* to do what one wants. Or bills of rights may do both these things, preventing some state actions and requiring others.

Conventional bills of rights, and the familiar civil and political rights and freedoms they contain, are understood to give rise to negative duties in those whom they bind. Freedom of expression, for example, in some ways the most fundamental of our civil and political freedoms, is conventionally understood to forbid censorship by the state, not to require the provision of libraries or other sources of information, necessary as these may be to full freedom of expression. Yet certain more recent bills of rights, and the economic and social rights they contain, are understood to give rise to positive duties in those whom they bind. Indeed, they typically explicitly require the provision of goods such as welfare, or social housing. This is not a necessary consequence of their subject matter. Just as it is possible to understand political rights in positive terms, so it is possible to understand economic rights in negative terms. As constitutional lawyers know all too well, early understandings of economic rights, such as that prevalent in the United States in the *Lochner* era, were purely negative in form, so that freedom of contract was understood to prevent rather than require state limitation of working hours.[16] However the alignment of the two classes of rights and freedoms with the two types of duty has become a recognized convention, albeit one that

---

[16] *Lochner v People of State of New York*, 198 US 45 (1905).

might change over time. Civil and political rights, it is currently accepted, give rise to negative duties, economic and social rights to positive duties.

Now, some who are otherwise opposed to bills of rights would like to see all rights and freedoms entrenched, if any are. They believe that a society that entrenches only the familiar civil and political rights and freedoms commits itself, at the fundamental level of its constitutional structure, to what they regard as a reactionary conception of the duties of government, for it commits itself to securing the implicitly negative, and hence reactionary, civil and political duties of government, while neglecting its implicitly positive, and hence progressive, economic and social duties. If we must be governed by the judiciary, they say, let us ensure that we are governed with an eye to the concerns of the left, not merely those of the right.[17]

In so saying, however, they do more than call for attention to economic and social concerns as well as civil and political concerns. The entrenchment of civil and political rights and freedoms, and the negative duties they are conventionally understood to give rise to, has the effect I have described in the previous two sections, and so involves no transfer of legislative power to the judiciary (at least when simply understood, and so subject to the refinements that I will offer in the next section). However, the entrenchment of economic and social rights, and the positive duties they are conventionally understood to give rise to, appears to have very different consequences, and so to involve a genuine, if indirect transfer of legislative power to the judiciary. In this setting, the power to establish a constitutional agenda appears to be tantamount to the power to establish a legislative agenda, for in determining the content of the legislature's positive duties the courts broadly determine the content of the legislation that is to be enacted in fulfilment of those duties. In this setting, then, it seems only natural to conclude that there has been a transfer of legislative power to the judiciary, in all but formal terms. That conclusion needs to be challenged, and the challenge will lead to refinement, but both will be postponed to the next section, so as to concentrate here on the implications of the conclusion, to the extent that it is true. However, it would be helpful to make clear first what the appearance is, and why bills of rights have made it an issue.

When a court determines the content of a social or economic right, such as a right to welfare, or to social housing, it lays down a scheme for legislative action. That scheme may be precise or it may leave a certain amount of room for the legislature to exercise discretion as to details. Either way, however, there can be no denying the legislative character of the court's determination. It is true that the bare existence of a social or economic right is the product of democratic decision, perhaps by Parliament itself, and it follows that the courts' affirmation

---

[17] See, for example, Ewing, above n 2, at 112–16.

of that bare existence adds nothing to the prior democratic decision and so cannot in itself be described as legislative. Yet courts rarely if ever stop there, and their determinations of the content of a positive duty to enact legislation, those determinations that establish to whom the duty is owed, on what terms and conditions, and with what consequences, are the very stuff of legislation and, but for the existence of the bill of rights, and the presence of positive duties there, would indisputably have been within the normative power of Parliament.

In this respect the positive duties set out in a bill of rights, unlike the negative duties considered in the first section, are to be contrasted with those provisions of a constitution that establish a federal state or union, those provisions that allocate legislative powers between national and regional (or multi-national and national) levels of government. Federal constitutions only very rarely create positive duties. For the most part they assume the existence of a will to govern, and so do no more than seek to constrain the exercise of that will by each level of government. As a result, the obligations they create are almost exclusively negative in form: they tell each level of government what it can and cannot do. To return to the earlier example, one level of government may have the power to regulate local and regional transport, while the other level has the power to regulate national and international transport. If either level of government chooses to regulate transport, the courts will ensure that it does not stray outside the power allocated to it by attempting to regulate a form of transport that may legitimately be regulated only by the other level of government. But if one or the other level of government simply leaves unregulated what it is entitled to regulate, whether by choice or through neglect, the courts have nothing to say. It is bills of rights, therefore, that introduce the possibility of fundamental duties to govern, albeit in limited and specific form. And since bills of rights are relatively novel (outside the United States at least), and since the presence of positive duties in them is more novel still, this raises the question of whether Parliament ever possessed the power to impose positive duties of this kind on subsequent Parliaments, so as to make it accurate to speak of a transfer of the power to create them from Parliament to the courts.

This gives rise to a tempting but ultimately tendentious objection to the picture presented so far, which is to characterize the role played by the courts in the articulation of positive duties as constitutional rather than legislative, and so claim that Parliament's legislative power is unimpaired by the presence of a bill of rights. The objection could be strengthened by the doubts just referred to as to the prior possession by Parliament of those constitutional powers that have been assigned to the courts (explicitly or implicitly) by the bill of rights. Some believe, for example, (though most opinion is against it) that Parliament has the power to bind its successors (in substance as well as form) and so prevent future Parliaments from undoing what it has done. If real and if exercised, that power would give rise to a negative duty: it would set limits on the freedom of action of future Parliaments by telling them what they could not do. On the other hand, however, few if any believe that Parliament has a similar capacity to impose positive duties on its successors, so as to compel them to do what it has not done. Yet even if both beliefs were correct, the objection is tendentious (at least as so framed) because the question before us is not whether the power exercised by the courts is constitutional rather than legislative in form, but whether function here follows form in the way that it is said to. Is the constitutional role played by the courts in this setting really a new and distinctive role, or is it simply the legislative function, now displaced? If the powers now exercised by the courts were not originally possessed by Parliament (and so cannot be said to have been literally transferred) it might be thought that one of the implications of their non-existence has been to preserve for Parliament the freedom of legislative action that the bill of rights has allegedly transferred to the courts.

The challenge to the simple response must therefore be regarded as unimpaired at this point. Those who are otherwise attracted to the simple response are bound to concede that if and to the extent that the courts are assigned the responsibility of articulating a legislature's positive duties, as they are when social and economic rights are fundamentally entrenched, what is tantamount to a transfer of legislative power has indeed taken place. So the entrenchment of social and economic rights would mean that it would be for the judiciary to decide, for example, what level of social welfare government should provide, and what the terms of access to social housing should be. Whether this is a good or a bad thing depends on the view one takes of the degree of economic and social understanding now present among the judiciary, or that could be made present there without turning the courts into the sort of representative institution that it is the purpose of a bill of rights to withdraw power from, thereby defeating the whole exercise.[18] The irony, however, is that the only people calling for a transfer of legislative power to the judiciary are the very people who oppose such a transfer on principle.

Some rights, it should be noted, in particular the right to equality, have uncertain implications in this regard. It is clear that they imply negative duties,

---

[18] There are two ways in which the judiciary might be made representative, only one of which would defeat the purpose of a bill of rights. On the one hand, the judiciary, and indeed the legal profession as a whole, might come to embody the abilities and aspirations of a broad range of people, and so might incorporate the distinctive capacities and perspectives of the socially and economically disadvantaged, of racial and cultural minorities, and of women, instead of focusing its recruitment upon privileged white men, as it now appears to do. This in no sense would defeat the purpose of a bill of rights. It would make the judiciary more representative than it now is, but fundamentally it would make the courts more pluralistic, more flexible, and probably better. On the other hand, the judiciary and the legal profession might be made more representative of the society they serve, so as to reflect, in proportionate degree, what are understood to be the salient features of the population, be those racial, religious, social or sexual. This would defeat the purpose of a bill of rights, at least in the setting of rights as positive duties, for it would return responsibility for the articulation of those duties to the very sort of representative institution that it is the purpose of a bill of rights to withdraw power from, albeit an institution still composed by a different process, namely, appointment rather than election. The first approach is pluralistic without necessarily being representative, the second is representative without necessarily being pluralistic, the reason being that a distinction may be politically salient without reflecting any difference in judicial capacity, and vice versa.

and so prevent the government from discriminating between its citizens on certain grounds, including race, sex, religion, sexual orientation, national or ethnic origin, and mental or physical disability. It is much less clear, but entirely possible, that they also imply positive duties. If and to the extent that they do so, it will be for the judiciary to decide what social and economic policies are necessary to ensure the equality of those people who are protected against the grounds of discrimination set out in the bill of rights. As things stand, equality rights are still sufficiently novel that a conventional understanding of their implications as negative, positive, or both, has yet to develop. What is more, it is not clear what understanding should develop, just what would be a good or a bad thing here. Is the judiciary, or should it be, the sort of progressive institution that could reasonably be expected to grasp the predicament of those whose lives are defined, wholly or partially, in terms of disadvantaged ways of being, and then fashion the policies that government must pursue if it is to play its proper role in relieving that predicament? There is reason not simply to be sceptical of such a project, as critics of bills of rights are, but to regard it as fundamentally misguided.[19]

Of course, none of these things has to follow. Conventions change with time. It is entirely possible that in the future civil and political rights and freedoms will come to be understood in positive terms, or that economic and social rights will come to be understood in negative terms, or some mixture of the two. If so, the implications of the entrenchment of a bill of rights will change, but not necessarily for the better. A different understanding of civil and political rights and freedoms would impose positive duties on the state, duties defined by the courts, and so would effectively transfer the power to govern those matters from Parliament to the courts, rather than to the people, as at present. It would then be for the courts to determine, for example, the obligations of the state in the provision of information, and perhaps even of education. On the other hand, a different understanding of economic and social rights and freedoms would impose negative duties on the state, and so would transfer the power to govern those matters from Parliament to the people, rather than to the courts, as is proposed. It would then be for the people, under the protection of the courts, to practise self-government in economic and social matters, so securing the free market that *Lochner* called

---

[19] It is worth noting that while the entrenchment of negative freedoms involves the privatization of the public good, in the manner described in the text above, the entrenchment of positive freedoms has the opposite effect, of making the private public. This is because negative freedoms restrain government activity, and so make private what would otherwise be public, whereas positive freedoms dictate government activity, and so make public what would otherwise have been private. In fact, of course, the distinction is rather more profound than this, because negative freedoms, whatever their scope in principle might be, are in practice limited to the restraint of actual government activity, or at most perhaps, certain contemplated government activity, and so do not extend to all possible government activity, whereas positive freedoms are by their nature just as extensive in practice as they are in principle, subject only to the restraints imposed by the conditions of a particular culture and by the inclinations of the judiciary there. For further discussion of this issue and of the particular question of whether fundamental equality rights should be regarded as implying positive duties, see T Macklem, 'Making the Private Public' 44 McGill L J 197 (1999).

for. One may doubt whether either of these possibilities is what the advocates of the entrenchment of economic and social rights have in mind.

The Politics of Entrenchment

1. Governance and Non-Governance

However, the concessions granted in the previous section raise concerns rather more significant than I have so far allowed. If the entrenchment of a bill of rights transfers some dimension of normative power from Parliament to the courts, for practical purposes at least, is not the transfer just as real when negative duties are at stake as it is in the case of positive duties, contrary to what I claimed at the outset? The power exercised by the courts to create negative duties may be formally constitutional; it may be a power that Parliament never possessed, so that strictly speaking no transfer of it to the courts has taken place; it may be a power that is not best understood as legislative, so making it better to speak of it (as I will in the balance of this section) as a power (not) to govern rather than a power (not) to legislate. Is it not the case, nevertheless, that the restraint thereby imposed on Parliament by the courts in accordance with the bill of rights is tantamount to the restraint that Parliament would otherwise be entitled to exercise over itself? If that is so, does it not vindicate the conventional understandings, sketched at the beginning of this chapter, that the simple response claimed to deny? In developing an answer to these questions I will begin by clarifying the nature of what is transferred in the case of negative duties, and go on to explore what that transfer tells us about the significance of entrenchment generally, be the duties it gives rise to negative or positive.

One last refinement is necessary, therefore, and it may appear to take the account to a place close to where it began. Let me approach the issue by way of a metaphor. I have relied throughout upon an active conception of government, but government need not be thought of in this way. Imagine an absolute dictator whose project it is to ensure the absence of all government in his or her domain. In order to save the dictator's project from self-contradiction one must imagine further that it is possible to secure the absence of government (in the active sense) by means other than active government itself. Perhaps the dictator, unlike real dictators, is not only gifted at persuasion but is committed, by the terms of his or her anarchic project, to eschew the use of force, or even authority. It seems undeniable that the dictator's regime would be a government, and that the project of not governing (in the active sense) would itself be a form of governance. Nor should there be anything particularly surprising in this. The dictatorship I have imagined is simply a dramatic version of a familiar political phenomenon, in which the objective of governments is to govern as little as possible, in certain respects at least.

To recognize this is to recognize that, notwithstanding what I have said so far, the entrenchment of rights to freedom and other negative duties does indeed involve a transfer of power from Parliament to the courts, for it transfers to the courts a power that, at least arguably, was once Parliament's alone, namely, the power *to ensure* the absence of government (in the active sense) in the domain that the freedom describes.[20] In respects such as these bills of rights trace the contours of non-governance, and in doing so describe a governmental project, a project that they entrust to the courts.[21]

What is more, to recognize that non-governance is itself a form of governance is to reaffirm the very parallels that the previous section sought to undermine, between rights that give rise to negative duties and those that give rise to positive duties. As a matter of logic, it must be the case that if the entrenchment of one form of duty transfers power from the legislature to the courts (as the previous section acknowledged), so must the entrenchment of the other form of duty. Differences in the content of the duties will be mirrored in the powers transferred, so that positive duties become powers of governance and negative duties become powers of non-governance, but those differences cannot qualify or contradict the common fact that power has been transferred, for that follows from the fact of entrenchment itself, and the judicial review that entrenchment implies.

2. Constitutional and Legislative Powers

On the face of it then, the effect of these observations is to reaffirm the truth of the very claim that I set out to challenge, namely, that bills of rights transfer power from Parliament to courts. How far this is the case is a question that I will turn to in a moment. It is worth noting immediately, however, that the affirmation involved is one that proponents of the claim would be reluctant to embrace, for it robs the claim of its political significance and much of its explanatory power. The entrenchment of the civil and political freedoms that are the mainstay of most contemporary bills of rights is the entrenchment of a project of non-governance. The power that it transfers is the power to ensure that nothing is done. From the political point of view there are many reasons to object to such a project, and

---

[20] There is an ambiguity latent in this description. In Parliament's hands the absence of government may be ensured either as part of a legislative project or as part of a constitutional agenda, assuming what is much disputed, that Parliament has the power to limit its successors by establishing a constitutional agenda. In the hands of the judiciary, however, the absence of government can be ensured only by the realization of a constitutional agenda, notwithstanding that the role of the courts in the establishment of that agenda, through their interpretation of the provisions of the constitution, very often has significant legislative implications. For further consideration see the paragraphs following n 23.

[21] It is true that Parliament retains the power not to legislate as the freedom requires, but this is only to say that Parliament has the power not to do what it would be told not to do if it did not get there first. In that sense it is also true that Parliament retains the power to legislate as positive duties require it to legislate, and as it would be told to do if it did not get there first. In fact these are merely corollaries of the point made in n 6, that only a legislature can amend or repeal legislation. They do not alter the fact that there has been a transfer of normative power, negative or positive, from Parliament to the courts.

to object further to its fundamental entrenchment,[22] but they do not include the fact, for example, that it is undemocratic to be not-governed by the courts rather than not-governed by Parliament. This is because democracy is an active good, and so matters to government in the active sense. It is possible to make a democratic decision not to govern, as is normally done when fundamental freedoms are entrenched, by special majority or otherwise, but it is not possible to not-govern democratically. What is true of democracy is true of the other concerns that animate the hopes and objections to the transfer of power from Parliament to the courts. Those concerns are engaged only by the active power of government. Government inaction is incapable of character, so that one cannot mourn or praise the fact that responsibility for it is placed in the hands of one body rather than another.[23] Parliament may be democratic, the courts élitist, but non-government by either looks the same.

Yet it is important to be clear precisely how and why this is the case. As was emphasized above, the entrenchment of fundamental rights and freedoms confers no *legislative* powers on courts, positive or negative. What entrenchment does transfer to the courts, whether from Parliament or some other institution, is the power to establish a constitutional agenda, be the content of that agenda positive, so requiring legislation, or negative, so preventing legislation. To the extent that positive duties are fundamentally guaranteed, for example, it falls to the courts to ensure the existence of legislation; to the extent that negative duties are fundamentally guaranteed it correspondingly falls to the courts to ensure the absence of legislation. In both cases the power that is transferred to the courts is the power to *ensure* legislation or its absence, by establishing a constitutional agenda through the interpretation of the provisions of a bill of rights. In neither case is there any transfer of the power to legislate or not to legislate itself. Indeed, given that each of those powers implies the other, there could no more be a power in the courts not to legislate than there is a power to legislate.

---

[22] In particular and by way of illustration, what entrenchment permits the courts to do is to extend the scope of non-governance to include forms of corporate expression that Parliament has sought to regulate and that the authors and supporters of the bill of rights expected Parliament to be able to regulate. The courts' power to establish significant aspects of a negative constitutional agenda in this way is the power to immunize, interstitially at least, certain speakers and certain forms of speech, and so to ensure non-governance in those domains.

[23] In general, inaction is entirely capable of character. That character depends, however, on whose inaction it is and what it is in the face of. In this setting inaction is always the inaction of the government. Where a bill of rights is entrenched, government inaction is enforced by the courts. This gives rise to questions of effectiveness, considered in the text below, but it does not make the inaction the courts' inaction, and so does not alter its character in that respect. Secondly, the terms of a bill of rights establish just what government inaction is to be in the face of free speech, for example. Given that those terms are typically couched in broad language, it is the responsibility of the courts to articulate them more precisely. In doing so the courts establish, at least marginally, the scope of the project of non-governance. This articulation both has character and is something to be concerned about, but its character is the character of an action, and concern about it is concern about the constitutional project of ensuring non-governance, considered in the text above, not about the way in which that non-governance takes place.

This is not to say that the power that is genuinely transferred to the courts, the power to ensure legislation or its absence, has no legislative implications. On the contrary, both aspects of that power have significant legislative implications, albeit to contrary effect. Where the courts possess the power to determine the scope and content of the positive duties entrenched in a bill of rights they possess the power to determine, more or less, the content of legislation, and so indirectly possess the power to legislate themselves. Where the courts possess the power to determine the scope and content of the negative duties entrenched in a bill of rights they possess the power to determine the scope and beneficiaries of an immunity from the power to legislate, and so indirectly possess the power not to legislate themselves. It follows that if there is a difference to be found between the entrenchment of positive and negative duties, as I have claimed, it must lie in a difference between the implications of ensuring legislation and those of ensuring its absence (thereby indirectly legislating and not legislating), namely the difference between the implications of governance and non-governance considered above.

Yet this analysis shows something more than the significance of the distinction between governance and non-governance, and what it shows is that in the preceding sections of this chapter I have entertained, and provisionally accepted, first, too quick a conflation of the legislative and the constitutional, that is, of constitutional power (which the courts clearly possess) and legislative power or what is tantamount to it (which they may or may not consequently possess), and second, too ready an assumption of the political significance of the exercise of legislative power. As to the first point, in fact these are very different normative powers, even when exercised by the same institution, and the distinction between governance and non-governance is but one instance of the implications of that difference. It is the role of constitutional powers to structure the exercise of legislative powers, but the structure is never so fine-grained as to be capable of fully directing the enactment of legislation. The legislature always retains a measure of discretion in the fulfilment of its constitutional obligations. This gives rise to the second point, namely, that it is the political import of that discretion, which is only contingently related to its scope or depth, that determines the significance of entrenchment. Put shortly, the more significant the legislative freedom left to Parliament, the less significant is the constitutional power bestowed on the courts (whether by transfer or otherwise). And the significance of the freedom left to Parliament turns on rather more than the positive or negative character of the duties that constrain its exercise.

In practice, the normative significance of the distinction between the constitutional and the legislative tends to be obscured by certain obvious real-world consequences for the legislature of judicial determinations of constitutional duties (positive or negative), consequences that appear to suggest a continuity between the two levels of normative power and their significance. It is this appearance of continuity that leads to the widespread conflation of constitutional and legislative norms, whether this is thought to be for the good (according to the admirers of bills of rights) or for bad (according to their critics). In my own analysis, which sought to distinguish negative and positive duties in this respect, it led to the conclusion that negative constitutional duties transfer only the power of non-government (or non-legislation) to the courts (with the implications considered above) while positive constitutional duties transfer a genuine power of government (what is tantamount to legislation). Only the latter transfer of normative power, I suggested, is politically significant; the former is so empty in the hands of its holders as to be tantamount to no transfer at all.[24] There is some truth in this conclusion, and it is that truth that sustains the correctness of what I have called the simple response, but as a general proposition the conclusion is much too quick, for the connection it suggests between the two kinds of norm is much too tight.

The truth in the conclusion can be simply explained. Life being what it is, negative duties tend to imply more options than do positive duties.[25] A negative duty forbids something in particular yet permits everything else. A positive duty, however, compels something in particular, though it may leave, and at the constitutional level, where duties are expressed in very abstract terms, always does leave, room to choose among ways of complying with its requirements. Positive duties thus appear to be more constraining than negative duties just because they appear to imply fewer options. Positive constitutional duties appear to be more constraining on the legislature than negative constitutional duties, just because in the case of positive duties decisions at the constitutional level appear more or less to dictate decisions at the legislative level. And where one level of norms more or less dictates the content of another level of norms it becomes reasonable to regard the two as continuous. Constitutional determinations thus become tantamount to legislative determinations. But even here the appearance is misleading. The significance of freedom, including the democratic freedom of the legislature to enact (and not to enact) what legislation it wishes, is a function of the character and value of that freedom, not its scope. It follows that the significance of entrenchment, and the power it bestows on the courts, is contingent upon the form and content of what is entrenched and the value and character of the legislative power it leaves to Parliament. Positive and negative duties are simply the most prominent illustration of this.

This has a number of implications, which can be roughly aligned with the distinction between positive and negative duties, as the simple response suggested. In terms of that distinction itself, the implications of the entrenchment of fundamental rights are the implications of governance and non-governance as I have described them above. In particular, the creation of negative constitutional

---

[24] This explains why it is difficult to distinguish an insignificant transfer (the true state of affairs) from absence of any transfer. The simple response adopts a practical point of view, treats the two as equivalent and so denies the existence of a transfer.

[25] Jonathan Bennett maintains that this is not merely a tendency; negative and positive duties are distinguishable only in terms of the numbers of options they imply: 'Whatever the Consequences' *Analysis* 26 (1966) 83.

duties involves a genuine transfer of power from Parliament to the courts, but the power transferred is the power of non-governance, a power the implications of which remain the same whether it is in the hands of the legislature or the courts. Or to put it more precisely, the creation of negative duties, first, confers constitutional power on the courts; second, may consequently transfer to the courts what is tantamount to legislative power (to the extent that it is sensible to think of a legislative power not to govern); but third, granted the second step, the transfer is politically insignificant because it is incapable of political character.

3. Political Significance

But this shows something more still, namely, that the power to determine the content of constitutional norms, and thereby determine the content of legislative norms, need not be politically significant, for it may not much matter which institution is doing the determining. That is true of more than negative duties and the non-governance they imply. One obvious instance is where the function of entrenchment is largely symbolic, as it may be whether the duty it gives rise to is negative or positive. Entrenchment is largely symbolic where there is little or no question of the legislature failing to do what the constitutional duty in question requires it to do (or not to do). In contemporary liberal societies, for example, there is little or no question of legislatures attempting to suppress political speech, as they once did through the crime of sedition, and so there is little or no political significance to the entrenchment of a right to freedom of political speech. The same holds true where the duty in question is positive rather than negative, for example, the duty to hold a general election every five years, and to recognize the right of citizens to vote in that election. Here again there is continuity between constitutional and legislative norms, but here too the continuity is politically insignificant, not because it involves non-governance, for positive duties are as open to symbolic entrenchment as are negative duties, but just because the entrenchment is symbolic, so that its political significance is a function of that symbolism, not of the interpretation and application of what has been entrenched.

It is worth noting as an aside, however, that the political insignificance of symbolic entrenchment cuts both ways. It means that the courts should not be looked to as bulwarks for the protection of foundational rights such as that to freedom of political speech, and bills of rights should not be entrenched in that expectation, for the continuity between the constitutional and the legislative in this setting is such that the courts very often find themselves as exposed as the legislature to the kinds of pressure (terrorism, for example) that may unexpectedly call those rights into question. This is not to suggest that courts never make a stand against a determined legislature in protection of a fundamental right, for clearly they sometimes do just that. But it is to notice that their overall record in this regard is not notably less shameful than that of legislatures, and to suggest that at least one reason for this is that the role played by both courts and legislatures in regard to such foundational rights is largely symbolic, so leaving both institutions relatively unpractised in the protection of those rights, and as vulnerable as one another to certain unexpected and strident imperatives of the political community they both must serve.

Otherwise, it seems to me, the political significance of entrenchment, and of the power it confers on the courts and withdraws from the legislature, depends on four factors, all of which must be satisfied to establish significance. It depends, first, on the entrenchment of rights in relatively general and abstract terms that leave the courts plenty of room to manoeuvre. It must be said that nearly all constitutional provisions meet this condition. It depends, secondly, on the significance of what is denied to the legislature. Entrenchment may lack political significance because it is largely symbolic, as explained above, but it may also, and more commonly, lack significance because the determinations left open to the courts by the broad language of the constitutional provision are as one to the legislature, so that there is little or no political import to a court's decision to prefer one to another. A court that makes a constitutional determination of this kind is in much the same position as a common law court (or indeed an administrative tribunal) that makes a determination in the ordinary course of interpreting and applying a statute. The power to make this kind of fine-grained decision has been genuinely transferred (for practical purposes, at least) from the legislature to the courts, but the transfer lacks political import because the legislature has no interest in the particular way the decision is made, indeed, has transferred the power to another institution just because it saw no adequate reason to be so interested.

The significance of entrenchment depends, thirdly, on the active or passive character of the judiciary, something quite different from the politics of the judiciary. It is common to couple images of the radical and the reforming judge, and almost as common perhaps, to couple the illiberal and the immovable. Yet there is no necessary link between judicial progressiveness and judicial activity, or their opposites. Many judges with progressive inclinations quite reasonably believe that their institutional position calls for them to exercise restraint in their decisions, particularly if those decisions involve challenges to legislation. On the other hand, many judges with the opposite political instincts are entirely prepared to change the law, even when that involves overturning legislation, if they think the legislation would be better overturned. But lawyers are familiar with the phenomenon of activist courts, and indeed the activist legal eras they can come to define, and it is that activism that may make the existence of a constitutional power, and the legislative power it practically implies, politically significant.

The significance of entrenchment depends finally, and more familiarly, on the existence of a political difference between the legislature and the courts. Suppose that an activist court fleshes out the abstract terms of a constitutional provision, and in so doing decides between outcomes that are not as one to the legislature. The court's decision then becomes potentially significant politically, but it is only actually so if and to the extent that the court reaches a different conclusion from the one that the legislature would have reached itself. This is less commonly the case than is sometimes assumed. Democrats often complain of the decisions reached by constitutional courts, but it is not always clear that the legislature would have acted differently in the absence of a bill of rights. Sometimes it is politically advantageous for a legislature to be able to hold a court responsible for decisions that it would otherwise have had to take itself.

4. Conclusion

So, and to conclude, the simple view of entrenchment and its significance is that the constitutional power bestowed upon the courts by entrenchment is tantamount to a legislative power, yielded to the courts by the legislature, for better or for worse. The simple response to that view denies this in part. The entrenchment of negative duties confers no legislative power on the courts, or more precisely, the legislative power that it confers upon the courts is empty of political significance. Only the entrenchment of positive duties, a recent and still relatively uncommon phenomenon, transfers what is tantamount to legislative power from Parliament to the courts, and for that reason we should perhaps be slow to entrench positive duties, given that their implications are very different from those of the negative constitutional duties with which we are familiar. From a practical point of view, this simple response has much to tell us, as I have tried to explain in the second and third sections and will explain further in the balance of this section. But the truth of the matter requires a more refined response, one that recognizes the different implications of constitutional and legislative normativity, analyses what is at stake in the entrenchment of particular constitutional duties, and assesses the political significance of entrenchment in terms of the legislative power, and consequent political freedom, that entrenchment of a particular duty leaves to Parliament.

What can be said in general of the claim that bills of rights transfer power from Parliament to the courts is that the claim is partially, albeit indirectly so, but only if the idea of power is understood to embrace two different and contradictory forms of government, both the active government with which we are all familiar, and non-government. As I have suggested, that is plainly not the way the claim is understood by its proponents, for the character of their hopes and concerns at the transfer of power to the judiciary reflects an active conception of the power to govern. It is possible that the presence of ambiguity in their position may serve certain political ends, as is commonly the case with ambiguity in rhetoric. Nevertheless the ambiguity raises real concerns, for while the transfer of both forms of power matters, it matters in very different ways.

A transfer to the courts of the power to govern in the active sense raises just the hopes and concerns that proponents of the claim have articulated; yet by and large no such transfer has taken place, for what conventional bills of rights guarantee, and assign to the courts, is the exercise of the power not to govern. On the other hand, a transfer to the courts of the power not to govern, which is by and large what has taken place, raises no such hopes or concerns, for they are predicated on the supposed implications of the fact that the power to govern is in the hands of one institution rather than another and yet, effectiveness aside, there are no such implications when what is at issue is non-governance.

Any possible political mileage aside, the consequence of ambiguity here is that critics of bills of rights, for example, find themselves objecting where objection is unwarranted (or at least is unwarranted on the ground they offer), while calling for the very regime to which their objections apply. We may object to non-governance, in the form of the entrenchment of civil and political freedoms, but not because of the transfer of legislative power to the judiciary that it supposedly involves; we may seek to guarantee governance, by entrenching economic and social rights, but if we do so we should begin to be concerned at the transfer of legislative power to the judiciary that it effectively implies.

I have made the point with reference to critics of bills of rights, but its logic extends to admirers as well. We may have reasons to look forward to a world in which certain freedoms are fundamentally entrenched if, for example, the exercise of those freedoms is not only a good thing but will be more secure as a result of entrenchment. Yet those reasons cannot include the fact that the courts can be expected do a better job than Parliament of governing (in the active sense) in those respects, for there is no such fact: the non-governance that the entrenchment of rights to freedom secures is not sensitive to the character of the institution responsible for executing it.

So we need to pay attention to the character of what is or may be entrenched, and direct our praise and criticism accordingly. If rights to freedom are what is in issue, then our concern must be with the project of non-governance. That concern should be as acute when non-governance is the responsibility of Parliament (whether functioning constitutionally or legislatively) as when it is the responsibility of the courts. It can only become more acute when one body or the other is more effective at securing non-governance, and then only by reason of that effectiveness, for within any given realm non-governance varies in degree only, not in kind. On the other hand, if positive duties are what is in issue, then our concern must be not only with the content of those duties, but with the character of the institution that is entrusted with their description and enforcement.

The Corrosion of Social Forms

Surely there is more to the story than this, however. If the implications of fundamental freedoms are as relatively straightforward as I have claimed (at least at the simple level), how could it be that both proponents and critics of their entrenchment have failed to grasp them? Is it possible that their views, rather than being simply misguided, represent the displacement of rather deeper hopes and fears? The answer, it seems to me, is to be found in certain implications of the very existence of public freedom, implications that are both more complicated and more obscured in the fabric of our culture than the issues considered so far.

The point goes beyond an immediate concern with the implications of fundamental guarantees. Fundamental guarantees are only one aspect of public freedom, and so cannot rightly be held responsible for all of freedom's implications, be they good or bad. Yet fundamental guarantees have become so central to the culture of public freedom in contemporary Western society that undue responsibility, in the form of credit or blame, tends to be attributed to them for what freedom yields, or is thought to yield. My purpose in what follows is to explore what I take to be some relatively neglected implications of public freedom, implications that may help to explain the impetus underlying what would otherwise seem unwarranted criticism and praise of bills of rights.

One of the interesting, and superficially puzzling, consequences of public freedom is an apparently correlative tendency to private conformity. It has been commonly observed, of course, that countries with a constitutionally entrenched bill of rights, such as the United States, are not obviously more free, in the respects that the bill of rights addresses, than those countries without a bill of rights, such as the United Kingdom before the European Convention on Human Rights and the Human Rights Act 1998. If the observation is correct, then censorship and conformity would seem not to be as vulnerable as one might have hoped to the presence of a bill of rights. Yet, in fact, the evidence only shows, as Joseph Raz has pointed out,[26] that there are different ways to secure public freedom, some of which are more effective than others in certain cultures. In societies where tradition matters, freedom may best be secured by traditions of freedom. Plainly that is not possible in non-traditional societies. However, if non-traditional societies are, either consequently or coincidentally, societies where law particularly matters, then freedom may best be secured there by legal guarantees. So whether a society's commitment to freedom is covert or overt, implicit or explicit, latent or patent, the degree of public freedom may be much the same. That said, it remains the case that in societies where other forms of guarantee are unavailable, and in particular in societies where tradition no longer much matters, public freedom, in the form of relief from censorship, for example, may indeed require and so be promoted by the presence of a bill of rights. A bill of rights will not eliminate censorship or enforced conformity, but it may well be necessary to their reduction.[27]

---

[26] In *The Morality of Freedom* (1986) 258. It is worth noting that different ways of securing freedom have different consequences for different freedoms. Certain freedoms, and certain aspects of freedom, are most effectively secured by certain means, be they political traditions or legal guarantees. Indeed, some freedoms can only be secured by such means. So it is possible, and indeed seems to be the case, that a bill of rights is crucial to the existence of certain freedoms, most obviously those that are unsupported by tradition. On the other hand, much of the culture of public freedom as we know it, including that very respect for the courts on which bills of rights depend for their effectiveness, is not susceptible to articulation in a bill of rights, and so depends on tradition for its survival. This means that even in a culture of fundamental legal rights those committed to public freedom need to show some tenderness to tradition.

[27] Ironically, this suggests that public freedom in the United States, a non-traditional society with a well developed tradition of public freedom, may not require the presence of a bill of rights,

What is less commonly observed is that societies with a culture of public freedom, however secured, often display a powerful tendency to private conformity, one that seems to be more than merely residual. There is as much evidence of this in contemporary Britain, a society with little experience of a bill of rights, as there is in contemporary America. The culture of celebrity, for example, prominent in both societies, is notorious for the so-called 'wannabes' it gives rise to. In the realm of personal style, the freedom to look as one pleases, a freedom that is relatively recent and so might be thought to be appreciated still on the very bases on which it was won, is now commonly exercised with conformity in mind, so that people seek to look as much like celebrities as possible, whether by direct imitation, or by sharing the cachet of brands endorsed by the celebrity.[28] Is there a connection between the two phenomena, of public freedom and private conformity, and if so, is it one of cause and effect? It seems to me that there is such a connection, and that it lies in the potentially, though not inevitably, cancerous relationship between freedom and social forms, and specifically, in the inherent tendency of freedom to destroy the very social forms and practices on which its value depends.

As most of us have learned from experience, we do not invent or construct the worlds within which our lives find meaning and significance. Rather, we obtain access to the values, familiar and unfamiliar, on which the success of our lives depends, through the medium of the social forms and practices available to us.[29] By definition, familiar values come to us embedded in the social forms and practices of our culture, be that culture native or adopted, so that we are bound to participate in those forms and practices, and hence in the culture, in order to gain access to the values. Yet even novel values, and novel settings for familiar values, are rarely produced from whole cloth, in the revolutionary manner, though from to time that may be both true and necessary. More commonly, they are produced incrementally, through the development and extension of familiar social forms and practices, even where the function of the familiar forms and practices is no more than suggestive, inspiring new values and new forms by reason of condemnation rather than admiration of those previously available.

So we pursue the activities, careers, forms of companionship and ways of life that are available to us in the world we happen to inhabit, and so become skiers or surfers, gamekeepers or geologists, serial monogamists by pursuit of our

---

unless, of course, the tradition of public freedom in that society has been developed in light of and so is dependent upon the existence of a bill of rights, as may also be the case.

[28] Such conformity is tempered by the extent to which it is possible to choose which celebrity to emulate (so making it possible to be non-conformist in terms of one's peers) and which aspects of a celebrity to emulate (so making it possible to be original in terms of interpretation if not of innovation).

[29] On the relationship between well-being (that is, the successful pursuit of valuable goals) and social forms see R S Raz, *The Morality of Freedom*, above n 26, 307–13. On the idea of a social role as a cluster of rights and duties with a social function see Downie, *Roles and Values* (1971) 121–45.

own inclinations or lifetime spouses by arrangement of our families, modern liberals or aboriginal conservatives, as circumstances permit. Nor are social forms as broad-grained as this description suggests. It is not simply that we, or more precisely, the athletic and prosperous among us, tend to become skiers rather than surfers in response to the particular geography and climate of our habitat. That commitment made, the time and place of our upbringing will affect whether we are downhill or cross-country skiers; the challenging or sybaritic character of our culture or sub-culture will affect whether we ski off-piste or on; and our age and cultural politics will affect whether we are conventional skiers or snowboarders. And so on. All these things are open to challenge, of course, as I have already indicated, but the challenges themselves constitute social forms that are structured in response to the social forms that would otherwise prevail, so that while dwellers in a cold climate may well choose to surf instead of ski they are bound to do so through the social forms of travel and escape, not to mention those of iconoclasm and élitism.[30]

Yet clearly there is rather more to the story than this. Otherwise we would be very largely trapped in the logic of existing social forms, as some post-structuralists believe we are. One of the more important implications of personal freedom, however, is that it permits us to challenge that logic. As participants in a liberal culture we are familiar with the idea that our freedom is not confined to what is good. On the contrary, it asks others to tolerate the bad in us, not merely the plural character of the good we may pursue. We are perhaps even more familiar with the idea that our freedom is not confined to a choice among existing social forms, or their rivals, but permits us to question and challenge those forms with a view to their reinvention, perhaps expects us to do so. Freedom is as much about innovation as anything else, and for many that is the primary source of its value.

The absence of fixed restraints upon freedom means that nothing is exempt from its dissolving force. It does not follow that freedom is as apt to promote what is bad as what is good, for the point of freedom, as most of its agents and proponents are well aware, is to improve our lives, which it can only do by connecting them more closely to what is good. Our pursuit of freedom is sometimes irrational and often misguided, but on the whole not so much so as to make our lives worse. We do not pursue freedom blindly, but with an eye to the good, and terrible as our mistakes have been, they are not reason to believe that freedom is morally indifferent. What is true of the relationship between freedom and the good, however, is not true of the relationship between freedom and social forms. Freedom is not animated by conservatism in the way that it is animated by concern for the good. On the contrary. The point of freedom is not to preserve existing social forms, but to question and challenge them, not simply for the sake of the good that might be discovered in their alternatives, but for the sake of the

---

[30] A departure that is sufficiently radical, as some departures in modern art have been, becomes difficult to comprehend, as art or as anything else.

challenge itself, and the good that it can give rise to even when its immediate consequences are bad, or at least no better than what freedom has overthrown.

The point should not be overstated. Proponents of freedom are not intellectual adolescents, rebels without a cause. In part this is because the pursuit of freedom is by and large animated by concern for the good, as I have already noted. Were that true of adolescent freedom, adolescence would be a less dangerous condition than we know it to be. But in part it is because questioning and challenge are central to the development and evolution of social forms. Most obviously, the exercise of freedom is not confined to the making of choices between existing options, nor could it be. The world we live in is always changing, and social forms must be regularly adapted to reflect that change. In this way some social forms become historic; others become confined to certain cultures. But there is more, for the adaptation of social forms is not merely reactive. The world we live in changes, in part, because social forms change, and social forms change, in part, because such change has become an end in itself. When we question and challenge the forms and practices of our society, and imagine replacements for them, we test old worlds and discover new ones. In doing so we bring new life to old ways of being and new ways of being to life. The result is not necessarily progress; the new world may be incommensurable with the old or worse than it. But it does mean that the life of freedom is as much about creation as it is about consumption and that, in itself, is a good thing.

Two qualifications are necessary here. First, the exercise of freedom is obviously compatible with a certain respect for social forms. Contemporary liberal societies permit, indeed encourage their members to choose who to marry, for example, and what career to pursue. In doing so they do not destroy the social forms of marriage and career, or rob them of their value, as traditionalists sometimes claim, but simply give them a liberal cast. Liberal societies destroy forms of marriage and career that are dependent upon pre-assignment, but they make possible forms of marriage and career that are dependent upon choice, such as those called for by ideas of romantic love and self-fulfilment. Yet it remains true that the compatibility of freedom and social forms is dependent upon the restraint of freedom, in this case restraint of the freedom to reinvent all aspects of marriage, or of a career. Were we free to reconsider all the terms of marriage, the number and nature of its participants, its objects, and so on, the very idea of the institution would begin to dissolve, because its very meaning would have become a subject of freedom.[31]

Secondly, the consequences of freedom might be thought to be less threatening than I have suggested in settings where there is no general cultural commitment

---

[31] Some readers may find the example of freedom of religion more persuasive. If the content of that freedom is such that any fundamental concern is to be regarded as a religion, as is the case in some settings, then the meaning of religion begins to dissolve. See the chapter entitled 'Reason and Religion'.

to freedom, so that the exercise of freedom is restricted to certain recognized matters, such as those set out in a bill of rights, for example. Yet, in fact, freedom is not so restricted in any liberal society, nor could it be. On the one hand, as I have noted, the legally recognized freedoms of a bill of rights depend upon the existence of a broader culture of freedom for their effectiveness. On the other hand, such broad cultures of freedom are unrestricted in their objects, and are bound to be so if they are to preserve some of the most important aspects of freedom, namely those of thought and expression. Freedom implies the ability to call into question the shape of freedom itself, including that embodied in prevailing liberal assumptions, not because those assumptions are bad ones, or because their very establishment as assumptions is illegitimate (as deconstructionists claim), but because true freedom exempts nothing from exploration, examination, and possible change. After all, every society is committed to at least some freedoms, because every society is bound to leave some room for individual choice and decision. What distinguishes liberal societies is their commitment to freedom itself, and therein lies their value and their danger.

Yet if the connection between freedom and value is more or less assured, as I have suggested it is, why should we be concerned about social forms, given that there is little prospect of them disappearing altogether, leaving us in chaos? True, there is reason to mourn the loss of any worthy social form, as traditionalists emphasize, but against that must be set the reason to welcome its replacement. What does freedom threaten then, other than an attachment to the present and its familiar forms? The answer, it seems to me, is to be found in the nature of the connection between social forms and value.

Admittedly, there is probably little to be said in general about the connection between value and the speed with which social forms disappear and develop. Clearly some forms, including the more complex and sophisticated, are slow to develop; just as clearly others are quick to develop. Were there reason to suspect an inverse relationship between rate of development and value, there might be reason to conserve those social forms with some history of development and some prospects for the future. Yet there is no such reason. Slow developing social forms are not more valuable than those that evolve rapidly, though they may be more sophisticated and more challenging.

Still, there is something persuasive in the idea of such a connection, and that is because there is some truth in it, although it has to do with the recognition of value rather than the development of social forms. Social forms may evolve quickly but an understanding of their value does not. Connections between form and value are rarely self-evident. Nor are they particularly susceptible to assessment in the abstract. On the contrary, connections to value are ultimately experiential, so that the more innovative a social form, and the greater its distance from the social forms of the recent past in which our experience and understanding of value has been set, the less we know of its worth. Its connections to value then need to be tested, and its form revised in consequence, through a long process of trial and error.

This means that the rapid dissolution of existing social forms, a phenomenon that seems to be gathering pace, is the rapid dissolution of well recognized avenues of value and disvalue. However quickly we may replace those forms, their loss leaves us in a state of relative ignorance as to the worth of our activities and pursuits. We must endorse replacement forms either on the basis of faith rather than reason to believe in their value, which we have no reason to do,[32] or on the basis of novelty and origins in freedom, and the value that those are assumed to confer. This may help to explain the contemporary tendency to endorse pursuits on the basis of their status as freely chosen, rather than on the basis of their distinctive value, be that intrinsic or instrumental. Homosexual conduct, for example, is often championed, not because it is good, as it is, but simply because it has been freely chosen by the parties involved, and in the realm of sex at least, anything goes as long as it has been freely chosen. Or so we are asked to believe.

The example can be extended across social forms, sophisticated and unsophisticated. Contemporary popular culture is saturated with social forms that are compatible with comprehensive personal freedom, rapidly forming, rapidly dissolving, arbitrarily established, and endorsed as valuable primarily on the basis of their status as chosen. Celebrity culture and similar social forms flourish because of their success in fulfilling these requirements. They offer roles and role models, much of the appeal of which lies in novelty, fluidity, and substitutability. I do not mean to suggest that these roles and role models necessarily lack true value, or possess it only in limited degree. That would be to endorse what I have denied, namely, that social forms that develop slowly are more valuable than those that develop quickly. I mean only to suggest that we are in no position to know the distinctive value of these roles and role models, which have been developed, one is bound to notice, in implicit recognition of that fact, so as to suggest that such knowledge is unnecessary.

Something rather similar happens in more sophisticated settings. Contemporary intellectual thought is marked in many respects by a commitment to questioning in the broadest possible sense, so as to expose to simultaneous challenge the most basic assumptions of intellectual endeavour, such as the very possibility of reason and of value. Once again, I do not mean to suggest that there is no reason to challenge our assumptions here, or no value in the challenge offered, though it sometimes becomes difficult to comprehend that challenge

---

[32] Even where the relationship to reason is non-deliberative it is necessary to be aware at some level of the value or disvalue in a given social form. Faith is no answer here, for there must always be reason to show faith, and so act in the absence of reasons, and there is no reason to show the sort of comprehensive faith that would be needed to underwrite general participation in the social forms of freedom, nor is there even a candidate for such a reason, other than the values of novelty and origins in freedom, discussed above.

without relying upon at least some of the assumptions it seeks to question. It is certainly possible that our present understandings of reason and value are seriously flawed, and there is no logical difficulty in entertaining that possibility, or seeing value in the questions it gives rise to. But to read contemporary intellectual thought in that way is to constrain the scope and supposed power of its challenge, and so limit its intellectual freedom, in ways that its proponents would not accept. Much contemporary thought seeks to challenge not merely existing understandings of reason and value, but the very idea of reason and value as matters to be understood. Such radical thought is thus more comprehensively committed to freedom, at least in the realm of thought, than the liberalism it seeks to overthrow.

These are settings in which the rapid dissolution and evolution of social forms threatens our ability to recognize the value or disvalue of the forms we are thereby expected to live through and so find value in. This is not true of all social forms, of course, and in particular is not true of those social forms that exist as vehicles for creativity. The relationship between those forms and the values they serve tends to describe a trajectory over time, from an initial, doubtful grappling with their promise of access to value, to a flowering of their valuable possibilities, to exhaustion. Freedom to challenge these forms at any stage of their evolution, and to secure their replacement with new forms and new possibilities, is central to the realization of the value of creativity. Yet even here freedom is the potential enemy of its value. Certain directions in fine art, for example, today those directions that are generally described as conceptual, commonly yield conclusions that are difficult to recognize as artistic, not because they fail to conform to some canonical understanding of what art is, for that is something that any worthy piece of art is liable to challenge, but because the depth of their challenge to existing understandings is such as to sever profoundly their connection with any known aesthetic, and because the social forms that their vision might give rise to, worthy or unworthy, are as yet indecipherable, and are likely to remain so given that they are likely to be soon supplanted by new directions with new and just as profound challenges to offer.

The response to the challenge posed by freedom in these settings is twofold. On the one hand, in certain liberal settings we endorse social forms because we know we need them as our means of access to value (not merely because we are psychologically committed to them). Since the social forms that we have to choose among in these settings all express liberty, and since we have no basis upon which to choose one rather than another in terms of the depth or character of its value, we unsurprisingly treat the social normativity that is built into the very idea of a social form as a substitute for the justified normativity that we are unable to assess, and further, treat the depth and scale of popular commitment to these social forms as a measure of their value. We do simply because others do it, or more profoundly, because the fact of their doing it has become a matter of value for us. Adherence to these social forms thus becomes, ironically, a matter of freely chosen conformity. This tends to be most visible in popular culture, where social normativity is by definition most general, but it is also present in many subcultures, sophisticated and unsophisticated, though it tends to draw less attention to itself there. The most obvious example of the latter is the political correctness movement in its American form, which uses the freedom granted by the Bill of Rights to establish and enforce conformity to a code of thought and expression that American governments are prevented from establishing by the presence of the Bill, a code of correctness that is revealingly called political precisely because it stands in for the code that government would otherwise have provided, or claims to.

The alternative is the frank embrace of chaos. In the political realm this manifests itself in the popularity of certain forms of anarchism and direct action. In the sexual realm, as I have indicated, it manifests itself in the popular belief that anything goes as long as it has been freely chosen. In the intellectual realm, as I have also indicated, it manifests itself in formally subversive movements such as postmodernism. The examples could be multiplied. To call these various tendencies chaotic is not to claim that they lack form. As the examples show, the embrace of chaos in any given setting soon acquires a social form. But the special feature of these social forms is that they are forms whose role it is to hold forms at bay, including their own, if possible, and so prevent questions of value from obtaining purchase. As far as their participants are concerned, that is their value.

So it is freedom, it seems to me, not bills of rights, that is the real issue here. Bills of rights are merely an occasion for concern by those who are concerned by freedom, and then only on the thesis that such bills both enlarge freedom and do so unacceptably. As I have argued, neither aspect of that thesis need be true. Indeed, and unsurprisingly, the entrenchment of a bill of rights rarely enlarges freedom, at least in the short run, for the disposition that leads a government to endorse the entrenchment of a bill of rights is the disposition to endorse the freedoms that the bill enshrines, which, in the absence of the bill, would have been recognized directly and incrementally, by legislation or its repeal, for much the same political reasons that, as it turned out, inspired entrenchment, and in much the same terms. In fact typically, and regrettably, bills of rights are accepted by governments, and litigation under them structured, not so as to enhance personal freedom by privatizing certain matters, but so as to divest responsibility both for the matters privatized and for their privatization, from a government that has become unconfident to the point of despair about its capacity to address those matters, onto others, namely, the entrenching body, the courts, and the people.

It follows that the different responses to the entrenchment of a bill of rights that I drew attention to in introducing this chapter are in the end perhaps best understood as different responses to the enhanced freedom, and corresponding overthrow of existing social forms, that entrenchment is thought to promise, matters about which some people are hopeful and some are pessimistic. The hopeful among us actively look forward to the overthrow of existing social forms, and the established values that those forms give access to. This is what it must mean for them to contemplate a fresh set of values for a godless age, difficult as it may be on the face of it to comprehend a basis on which one could evaluate a new set of values without either anticipating the new, so making the evaluation empty, or preserving the old, so judging the new by its conformity to the old. What is actually at stake here, however, is not a fresh set of values but a fresh set of social forms, which need not imply fresh values, but which it is thought will simply do a better job of assuring human dignity than existing social forms have done. At least that is the promise from the hopeful to the hopeless.

The pessimistic among us, on the other hand, mourn the loss of existing social forms, for a combination of reasons: sometimes because they remember how hard won those forms were; sometimes because they regard social forms, and the order they impose, as legitimate only where the forms are democratically authorized, as the forms of freedom need not be; and sometimes because they are attached to the particular values embodied in those forms, many of which arose in an era a good deal more sympathetic to their beliefs than is the present day, and are correspondingly opposed to the values that the social forms of personal freedom yield, or are thought to yield. Put simply, these are people whose personal and political vision requires a set of social forms that personal freedom cannot be counted on to provide. They are not confined to the conservatives and socialists who, for obvious reasons, make up most of their number. They also include liberals, for the reasons set out above.

These observations may themselves seem pessimistic and conservative. Perhaps they are, but if so it is only because good liberals have as much reason as anyone else not to be unequivocally optimistic about the displacement of existing social forms, indeed more particularly and poignantly so perhaps, not simply because the forms in question today are very often the products of liberal achievement, for achievements that are born of good questions must be prepared to yield to better questions, but because liberal questioning has begun to threaten the value of liberal commitments in a way that matters, given that there is no obvious answer, within the repertoire of liberal resources, as to how the threat might be tamed in a manner consistent with liberalism. There are many possibilities for equilibrium between freedom and social forms, but not everything counts as equilibrium, and while there is little reason to be concerned at the possibility that we will lose equilibrium altogether, there is some reason to be concerned that we have lost, or are in danger of losing, equilibrium in certain critical respects, critical because they make knowledge of value possible, and so offer us some protection from blindness and folly in its pursuit.

Index